Praise for The Truth about Eden

"Those who love the Lord also love His holy house. We sometimes struggle to understand the symbolic representations contained therein. In this unique and enlightening book, Alonzo L. Gaskill helps us understand and appreciate the significance of the story of the Fall of Adam and Eve as it relates to us and our temple worship. For those seeking a better understanding of symbolism, this book is a must read!"

—Ed J. Pinegar
Former president, Manti Temple

"Few things are more fascinating to Bible-believing people than the scenes in the Garden of Eden. We find ourselves wondering what it would be like to have a complete account, what is literal and what is figurative, and just what Adam and Eve knew. In this unusual work, Professor Gaskill gives us insight into these questions. In the process, he masterfully shows us how thoroughly the Adam and Eve story applies to us. This is a book worth reading."

—Robert L. Millet
Professor of ancient scripture, Brigham Young University

THE *Truth* ABOUT EDEN

THE *Truth* ABOUT EDEN

UNDERSTANDING *the* FALL
and OUR TEMPLE EXPERIENCE

ALONZO L. GASKILL

CFI
An imprint of Cedar Fort, Inc.
Springville, Utah

ISBN 13: 978-1-4621-1253-1

Published by CFI, an imprint of Cedar Fort, Inc.
2373 W. 700 S., Springville, UT 84663
Distributed by Cedar Fort, Inc., www.cedarfort.com

LIBRARY OF CONGRESS CATALOGING-IN-PUBLICATION DATA

Gaskill, Alonzo L., author.
The truth about Eden / Alonzo L. Gaskill.
    pages cm
Includes bibliographical references and index.
Summary: Explains how the Fall of Adam and Eve is essential to the plan of salvation.
ISBN 978-1-4621-1253-1
1. Plan of salvation (Mormon theology) 2. Fall of man. 3. Adam (Biblical figure) 4. Eve (Biblical figure) 5. Eden. 6. Church of Jesus Christ of Latter-day Saints--Doctrines. 7. Mormon Church--Doctrines. I. Title.

BX8643.S25G37 2013
233'.14--dc23

                    2013007625

Cover design by Shawnda T. Craig
Cover design © 2013 Lyle Mortimer
Edited and typeset by Emily S. Chambers

Printed in the United States of America

10 9 8 7 6 5 4 3 2

Printed on acid-free paper

Other Books by Alonzo L. Gaskill

Love at Home: Insights from the Lives of Latter-day Prophets

Sacred Symbols: Finding Meaning in Rites, Rituals & Ordinances

The Lost Language of Symbolism—An Essential Guide for Recognizing and Interpreting Symbols of the Gospel

Odds Are You're Going to Be Exalted—Evidence that the Plan of Salvation Works!

Know Your Religions, Volume 1—A Comparative Look at Mormonism and Catholicism

To all those who wish
to better understand
the Holy Temple

Contents

Acknowledgments

FIRST AND FOREMOST I wish to acknowledge the invaluable work of my research assistant, Vance R. Bohman, who spent countless hours working on this manuscript. His research, insights, and suggestions have not only improved the final text but also serve to highlight his great love for, and vast knowledge of, the restored gospel of Jesus Christ. I express my deep appreciation for his contributions, which have been significant and sundry.

I also want to thank those who reviewed this text and offered helpful suggestions: Judson Burton, Matthew B. Christensen, Paul E. Damron, Scott C. Esplin, Juan S. Henderson, Robert L. Millet, and Katheryn West.

In addition, I express my gratitude to the editors and staff at Cedar Fort for their fine work in preparing this manuscript for publication.

Finally, I remind readers that this book is not a publication of The Church of Jesus Christ of Latter-day Saints, nor does it necessarily represent the official position of the Church or the publisher. I bear sole responsibility for the content of this book.

Introduction

THE GOSPEL OF Jesus Christ is incomprehensibly broad, amazingly deep, and unquestionably profound. Its doctrines, restored through the Prophet Joseph and his successors, have the power to satisfy the cravings of the spiritually hungry. They answer the questions that have plagued mankind for millennia. Admittedly, there is an important distinction to be made between doctrine and opinion (or popular belief). Acceptance of the *official* doctrines of the Church, prophetically revealed, is requisite for exaltation in the celestial kingdom of God. However, belief in the numerous appendages to these *true* doctrines—appendages that constitute theories, applications, and opinions of men—is *not* crucial for exaltation. Indeed, those who hope to be saved will likely need the ability to discern between the two.

The doctrine of the Fall serves as a good case study on this principle. One contemporary Latter-day Saint author wrote: "When teaching about the Godhead, the Prophet Joseph Smith said, 'If we start right, it is easy to go right all the time; but if we start wrong, we may go wrong, and it [will] be a hard matter to get right.' The same guideline is important when we teach about the Fall."[1] How true this is. Within the Church are many competing views on what exactly happened in Eden. On tangential, non-salvific issues, even the presiding Brethren have their own personal opinions.[2] Yet, on the actual doctrine, there is *absolute* harmony among the apostles and prophets. They have taught, and we testify, there was a Fall early in this earth's history. It was foreordained to be part of the plan that was instituted before this world was. Without this Fall, each of us

1

would be eternally stranded in the premortal world, hopelessly without prospect of obtaining a physical body. Without this Fall, none of us could gain the mortal experience so necessary to our progression. And without the Fall (and the resulting Atonement), a resurrected, celestial body would have been withheld from each of God's creations. This is the doctrine! Many of the other ideas we traditionally share or contemplate regarding the Fall are interesting, but in the end, theoretical—and must be understood as such.

What follows on the pages of this book is but one approach to the Fall. This treatment is not presented as the official doctrine of the Church—although there is much doctrine in this text. Rather, what is presented here is one author's view on the subject. Sadly, there was no way (in a book of this length) to present *every* popular approach to this significant subject. Thus, only one side of the coin is provided here—the one that this author believes to be the most convincing. The reader will quickly notice the plethora of sources provided in support of the ideas contained in this text. Beyond their ability to aid the reader's further study, the voluminous number of references has been provided for primarily one purpose: to establish the fact that this is an approach with substantial support.

In Doctrine and Covenants 91, the Lord speaks to the Prophet Joseph regarding the Apocrypha—a collection of ancient religious texts held by Latter-day Saints to be extracanonical. Among other things, the Lord says of these nonscriptural religious texts: "There are many things contained therein that are true. . . . Therefore, whoso readeth [them], let him understand, for the Spirit manifesteth truth; And whoso is enlightened by the Spirit shall obtain benefit therefrom" (Doctrine and Covenants 91:1, 4–5). In the spirit of that inspired counsel, this book occasionally draws from ancient and modern non-LDS religious texts. Of course, we do not use these to formulate doctrine. That comes *only* from the Lord through His authorized servants—the divinely called and appointed prophets and apostles. However—as is borne out by the LDS fascination with C. S. Lewis—some non-LDS sources seem to see the gospel through lenses quite similar to our own. Where one of the early Church fathers or a contemporary non-LDS theologian has offered an insight or application of a verse that is harmonious with the position of The

Church of Jesus Christ of Latter-day Saints, we have felt comfortable quoting them. A brief appendix has been provided to help broaden the reader's understanding of these less familiar sources.

Finally, it may be worth noting that *technically* the content of this book is not new—although to many the ideas will seem new. Certainly the concepts contained in this book have been taught by prophets—ancient and modern. Nevertheless, some readers will be unfamiliar with the ideas contained herein, and a few will even be bothered by the words of prophets, divinely given but infrequently quoted. As the Prophet Joseph noted, even the Saints do not do well when taught something that is unfamiliar to them, or that goes contrary to what they have always believed.[3] What follows is simply proposed as food for thought. It is a small offering advanced in the hopes of clarifying what may have been misunderstood—making more applicable that which stands as one of the "three pillars of eternity"[4] upon which rests the whole of the plan of salvation.

NOTES

1. Ladle (2004), 42.

2. Hinckley (1997), 84; Ballard (1997), 49; Kimball (1982), 532; Kimball and Kimball (1977), 344; Gibbons (1993), 176; Gibbons (1992), 242.

3. See Smith (1976), 331; see also Ehat and Cook (1980), 319, 386, n. 18; Madsen (1989), 43; Nibley (n. d.), lecture 6, page 2. The Prophet Joseph Smith remarked that "the Saints are slow to understand." According to him, convincing the members of the Church of an idea that is new to them is akin to trying to split a knot in a piece of wood using a piece of cornbread as your wedge or chisel, and a pumpkin as your sledge hammer. He once observed, "I have tried for a number of years to get the minds of the Saints prepared to receive the things of God; but we frequently see some of them, after suffering all they have for the work of God, will fly to pieces like glass as soon as anything comes that is contrary to their traditions." See Smith (1976), 331.

4. M. McConkie (1998), 190.

ONE

A Common Misunderstanding

PERHAPS NO DOCTRINE has been more misunderstood, and no historical event more misinterpreted, than the Fall of Adam and Eve. Non-LDS Christians traditionally assume that it was an evil, unnecessary act and that Adam and Eve were eternally damned because of their actions.[1] LDS Christians, on the other hand, often struggle to understand why it is that God would give our first parents one commandment ("multiply and replenish the earth") that could only be kept by breaking another commandment ("don't partake of the 'forbidden' fruit"). Regarding these, and other common misunderstandings, Joseph Fielding McConkie wrote:

> From Genesis to Revelation no story in scripture has been the source of more theological mischief than the story of Eden. It is the prime example of scriptural misuse and abuse. The errors that have come from the perversions of this story have given birth in turn to a thousand more. In no story have the figurative and the literal been so thoroughly confused, and in no other story has the absence of "plain and precious" parts caused more to stumble. In the mystery of Eden we have a classic case study of the dangers and difficulties with which uninspired scriptural exegesis is fraught, and the manner in which the scriptures remain a sealed book to all save those who know that same Spirit by which they were originally given.[2]

Although the various revelations of the Restoration[3] greatly clarify the events and doctrine of the Fall, there remains a confusion—even

5

among Latter-day Saints—regarding what really happened in Eden. True, there are certain key doctrines that the story of the Fall teaches, which are clearly articulated and well received by Latter-day Saints. However, aside from these doctrines, there are also popular *interpretations* of the four authorized Fall accounts (Genesis, Moses, Abraham, and the temple),[4] which often contradict the doctrines revealed through the Restoration. That is not to say that these four accounts are in *any* way skewed or inaccurate. On the contrary, the problem lies in the fact that lay Latter-day Saints often read into the story of the Fall inaccurate ideas—ideas that, frankly, would be more at home in other Christian traditions than they are in the restored gospel of Jesus Christ. In part, this may be because "we do not have a complete account" of what happened in Eden—at least not in any single source.[5]

Certain key questions regarding the Eden episode surface time and again. For example, was the choice of Adam and Eve to partake of the "forbidden" fruit a mistake? And in what sense was that act a transgression, rather than a sin? Or what did Adam and Eve know of their purpose while in Eden (such as, what instructions had they been given)? And who was deceived? Eve? Adam? The serpent? Not all Latter-day Saints will answer these questions alike. And yet, an incorrect understanding of the answers to these questions leads to an inaccurate understanding of the Fall.

What follows in the next few pages is an examination of these important questions and a review of the answers as given by prophets—ancient and modern. Via this review, it is hoped that the reader will recognize that popular interpretations may not necessarily be in harmony with the doctrine of the Fall as taught by the Lord's anointed representatives. Thus, the reader should not be surprised to find his or her long-held assumptions about the Fall overturned as he or she reads the remaining pages of this chapter.

DID ADAM AND EVE MAKE A MISTAKE IN EDEN?

Adam and Eve made no mistake in Eden. "Neither Adam nor God regretted that the Fall occurred—in fact, this event is a matter for ultimate rejoicing."[6] They did exactly what God sent them to do—exactly what the Father wanted them to do. Robert L. Millet wrote: "Latter-day Saints view the Fall with an optimism that is uncharacteristic of most of the Christian world. It is an optimism born of the conviction that Adam and Eve went into the Garden of Eden to fall, that the Fall was as much a part of the foreordained plan of the Father as the Atonement. We believe they did precisely what needed to be done."[7] Elsewhere we read:

> There was no mad scramble in heaven when Adam fell. The Fall was part of the plan from the beginning, and those present in the premortal world knew of it and accepted it even before the earth was created. . . . In the premortal council Lucifer proposed that he would "redeem all mankind, that one soul shall not be lost" (Moses 4:1). This suggests that the knowledge of a fall and the need for redemption were known to God's spirit children before the creation of the earth.[8]

From the very inception of the plan, it was clear that a fall would be necessary if God's children were to become like Him.[9] The Fall would change Adam and Eve's bodies so they would have blood, and thus the power of procreation.[10] And the Fall would also remove each of us from God's immediate presence—placing a veil between us and our Creator—which would enable us to walk *entirely* by faith (see 2 Nephi 2:22–25), something we could not do in the premortal world nor in Eden, where mankind walked and talked with God.[11] This is not to suggest that agency did not exist in the premortal world or in Eden. On the contrary, agency is an eternal principle—as is evidenced by the choice of the third part of the hosts of heaven to follow Lucifer instead of God.[12] But the degree to which we can exercise our agency, and the ways in which we can utilize that same gift, are greatly influenced by both the environment in which we are placed and the nature of our knowledge.

For example, had I been privileged to witness the appearance of the Father and Son to the Prophet Joseph Smith, I would know for certain that the Prophet's testimony of the First Vision was true. My testimony would not be based on faith in his witness or simple belief in his claims, but rather on the empirical proof I had of that sacred event. In such a situation it would be impossible for me to walk by faith, because I would know for certain that the event happened. In other words, I would have "a sure knowledge." However, since I was not there, I am forced to develop and walk by faith—trusting in the Spirit, its whisperings, and in the testimonies of living prophets.

In a similar way, the plan of salvation calls for you and me to have a veil of forgetting placed over our memories, removing us from the direct presence of God and Christ, thereby facilitating the experience of walking entirely by faith and believing in that which cannot be seen.[13] Elder Neal A. Maxwell explained it this way:

> We define the veil as the border between mortality and eternity; it is also a film of forgetting that covers the memories of earlier experiences. This forgetfulness will be lifted one day, and on that day we will see forever, rather than "through a glass, darkly" (1 Corinthians 13:12). . . . But mercifully the veil is there! It is fixed by the wisdom of God for our good. . . . [To not have] the veil . . . would interfere with our mortal probation and maturation. Without the veil, our brief, mortal walk in a darkening world would lose its meaning, for one would scarcely carry the flashlight of faith at noonday and in the presence of the Light of the world! Without the veil, we could not experience the gospel of work and the sweat of our brow. If we had the security of having already entered into God's rest, certain things would be unneeded; Adam and Eve did not carry social security cards in the Garden of Eden! . . . Nor could we choose for ourselves in His holy presence among alternatives that do not there exist, for God's court is filled with those who have both chosen and overcome—whose company we do not yet deserve. . . . Fortunately, the veil keeps [us] cocooned, as it were, in order that we might truly choose.[14]

Thus, although the eternal principle of agency is ever in force, you and I are greatly benefited by the additional gift of a veil of forgetting—requiring that we live obedient to God's commands, not because we have seen and thereby *know* there is a reward to be had, but rather because we have placed ourselves in a position to feel God's Holy Spirit confirming to us our *belief* in that promised reward.

Although it is common to read the story of the Fall as suggesting that Adam and Eve acted contrary to God's command, several Presidents of the Church have taught that our parents' choice to partake of the fruit of knowledge of good and evil was exactly what God desired them to do. For example, the Prophet Joseph Smith stated: "Adam did not commit sin in eating the fruits, for God had decreed that he should eat and fall."[15] Likewise, on numerous occasions President Brigham Young broached this subject. Among other things, he taught:

> In my fullest belief, it was the design of the Lord that Adam should partake of the forbidden fruit, and I believe that Adam knew all about it before he came to this earth. I believe there was no other way leading to thrones and dominions only for him to transgress, or take that position which transgression alone could place man in, to descend below all things, that they might ascend to thrones, principalities, and powers; for they could not ascend to that eminence without first descending, nor upon any other principle.[16]

Elsewhere he explained:

> Some may regret that our first parents sinned. This is nonsense. If we had been there, and they had not sinned, we should have sinned. I will not blame Adam or Eve, why? Because it was necessary that sin should enter into the world; no man could ever understand the principle of exaltation without its opposite; no one could ever receive an exaltation without being acquainted with its opposite. How did Adam and Eve sin? Did they come out in direct opposition to God and to His government? No. But they transgressed a command of the Lord, and through that transgression sin came into the world. The Lord knew they would do this, and He had designed that they should.[17]

Similarly, from President Wilford Woodruff, we read: "Adam and Eve came to this world to perform exactly the part that they acted in the garden of Eden; and I will say, they were ordained of God to do what they did, and it was therefore expected that they would eat of the forbidden fruit in order that man might know both good and evil by passing through this school of experience that this life affords us."[18]

Years later, President Joseph Fielding Smith wrote: "The simple fact is, as explained in the Book of Mormon and the revelations given to the Prophet Joseph Smith, the fall was a very essential part of the divine plan. Adam and Eve therefore did the very thing that the Lord intended them to do. If we had the original record, we would see the purpose of the fall clearly stated and its necessity explained."[19]

Finally, a number of General Authorities have taught this same doctrine. Elder B. H. Roberts, for example, indicated that "the 'Fall' was as much a part of God's earth-planned life for man as the 'redemption' provided for him . . . and no redemption would have been provided [in the Grand Council] but for anticipation of the 'Fall.'"[20] In other words, a Savior was chosen and foreordained in the Grand Council in Heaven specifically because God had planned the Fall. Were the Fall unpremeditated, Jesus would not have been chosen "from the foundation of the world" (Mosiah 4:6–7; 15:19). Indeed, there would have been no need for a Messiah. Elder Bruce R. McConkie reasoned: "Just as surely as salvation comes because of the Atonement, so also salvation comes because of the Fall."[21] Elsewhere he wrote:

> Be fruitful, and multiply. "Provide bodies for my spirit progeny." Thus saith thy God. Eternity hangs in the balance. The plans of Deity are at the crossroads. There is only one course to follow: the course of conformity and obedience. Adam, . . . our father, and Eve, our mother, must obey. They must fall. They must become mortal. Death must enter the world. There is no other way. They must fall that man may be. Such is the reality. Such is the rationale. Such is the divine will. Fall thou must, O mighty Michael. Fall? Yes, plunge down from thy immortal state of peace, perfection, and glory to a lower existence; leave the presence of thy God in the garden and enter the lone and dreary world. . . . Yes, Adam, fall; fall for thine own good; fall for the good of all mankind; fall that man may be; bring death into the world; do that which will cause an atonement to be made, with all the infinite and eternal blessings which flow therefrom. And so Adam fell as fall he must.[22]

In the end, death would be Adam's gift to humanity, rather than his curse upon mankind (as so many perceive it).[23] It would be a gift second only to the Atonement of Christ. Like those before him, Elder Jeffrey R. Holland wrote that Adam and Eve were willing to knowingly and consciously transgress they had a full knowledge of the plan of salvation.[24]

As can be seen, numerous General Authorities[25] and many LDS scholars[26] have taught the doctrine that the Fall was God's will and that Adam and Eve, by partaking of the "forbidden" fruit, did exactly what God wanted them to do.[27] From at least as early as the premortal Grand Council, we were aware that God intended that Adam and Eve provoke the Fall of man—for there was no other way to enable the eternal life of God's creations.

To draw from the story of the Fall a belief that God didn't want Adam and Eve to eat the "forbidden" fruit is to misunderstand the plan of salvation, the premortal Grand Council, and the teachings of the prophets of the Restoration. It was God's will and design that Adam and Eve partake![28]

WHAT DID ADAM AND EVE KNOW OF THEIR PURPOSE WHILE IN EDEN?

A simple review of what the restored gospel tells us about Adam and Eve's experiences in Eden should be sufficient to establish that they knew why they were placed in the Garden, and they were not ignorant of the plan, nor of the need for a fall.

We are informed that our first parents walked and talked with God while they dwelt in Eden (see Genesis 3:8–10). President Brigham Young stated that "Adam was as conversant with his Father who placed him upon this earth as we are conversant with our earthly parents."[29] The Father taught them many things during their stay in the Garden—a stay that may have encompassed months or possibly even years.[30] Are we to believe that in all their time in Eden, and in all of their communications with God and Christ, the reason for their placement in Eden was never mentioned by the Father, nor did Adam and Eve ever query as to why they were there? Such goes against reason.[31] Indeed, the cursory account of God's command to not eat of the tree of knowledge of good and evil (see Genesis 2:17; Moses 3:17) is evidence that the discussion of Adam and Eve's purpose in Eden did arise on at least one occasion.

As to what they were told, one author has written: "God the Father walked and talked with His beloved children in the Garden of Eden. Because they were the . . . only ones who could bring to pass mortal life so that His own promises to all His children can be fulfilled, we can feel confident that God did not visit them to speak trifling matters. Each meeting was surely a time of important instruction and learning."[32] Similarly, Elder Jeffrey R. Holland informs us, "They had full knowledge of the plan of salvation" during their stay in Eden.[33]

Alma says, "God gave unto them commandments, having made known unto them the plan of redemption" (Alma 12:32; emphasis mine; see also Moses 7:32). Owing to the fact that God's laws do not change, we must assume that this same principle was in effect in Eden. Indeed, the Lord stated that He gave Adam and Eve their knowledge in the day He created them (Moses 7:32). That being the case, clearly Adam and Eve would have known their purpose in Eden. Indeed, if they had not known their purpose in Eden, they would not have been capable of exercising agency, for, as Elder Bruce R. McConkie has noted, knowledge is a prerequisite to the exercising of agency.[34]

We know from modern revelation that Adam and Eve entered into covenants with God while they were in the Garden.[35] At the very least, they participated in the new and everlasting covenant of marriage—being sealed for time and all eternity by God the Father Himself. It is quite likely that they also received at least part of their endowment in Eden.[36] Covenants, of course, can be entered into by those spiritually and intellectually capable of understanding the promises they are making. Otherwise, they could not be held responsible for the promises and commitments they have made.[37] As President Boyd K. Packer has noted: "Moral law assumes accountability; no accountability, no penalties! Moral law will self-destruct if enforced against those not accountable. It is *not moral* to do so."[38]

Thus, the fact that Adam and Eve did make covenants in Eden prior to their Fall indicates that they were intellectually and spiritually mature and capable of being held accountable for their actions.[39] Indeed, if our first parents were "as little children" in their intellect or level of spirituality, how could they have been held accountable by God when they partook of the fruit of knowledge of good and evil? Such would be contrary to the laws of God and the plan of salvation.[40] As President Packer noted, it wouldn't be moral. We are never accountable for what we do not know or cannot understand.

Elder Gerald N. Lund of the Seventy once noted that "Freedom (agency) + Knowledge = Accountability."[41] It is not enough to be free. One must also be capable of making informed decisions.[42] It is for this reason that children under the age of eight are not accountable nor expected to repent in order to gain forgiveness when they do things contrary to God's laws.[43] Because of their intellectual, experiential, and spiritual level of understanding, they are covered by the Atonement of Christ (see Mosiah 3:16). Indeed, they are "alive in [Christ] because of his mercy" (Moroni 8:19).

> The ordinary explanation of the phrase "good and evil" in the literal sense assumes that God would . . . withhold from man the ability to discern between what is morally right and wrong—a view which contradicts the spirit of Scripture. Moreover, Adam would not have been made "in the image of God" if he did not from the first possess the faculty of distinguishing between good and evil. And if he lacked such faculty, his obedience or disobedience to any command whatsoever could have no moral significance.[44]

Thus, God would have to have made Adam and Eve aware of their purpose in Eden. They would have necessarily been intellectually capable of understanding such if God were to hold them accountable—which He did when He removed them from Eden because of their decision to eat that which had been "forbidden."

Because of the metaphorical aspects of the story of the Fall, some have assumed that Adam and Eve had a veil placed over their minds when they were first placed in Eden—a veil akin to that which you and I currently labor under. However, this does not appear to be the case. In the *Lectures on Faith* traditionally attributed to the Prophet Joseph Smith, we are informed that Adam was "lord or governor of all things on earth, and at the same time enjoying communion and intercourse with his Maker, without a veil to separate between."[45] Likewise, Elder Orson Pratt taught that, while in Eden, there was no veil over Adam and Eve.[46] In an 1842 *Times and Seasons* editorial, we are told that, while in Eden, our first parents "could converse with God face to face as we converse with our friends; [with] no intervening veil."[47] Elder Parley P. Pratt,[48] President John Taylor,[49] and President Joseph Fielding Smith[50] each stated that in Eden there was no "dimming veil between" Adam and God.

On several occasions Elder Milton R. Hunter taught that it was after Adam and Eve's Fall that the veil was placed upon them, thus wiping out their memory of the premortal life and ending their direct access to the presence of God the Father.[51] Elder B. H. Roberts taught that "with the fall of Adam there seems to have come a forgetfulness of the plan of salvation."[52] Many commentators recognize that the notion that Adam and Eve labored under a veil in Eden is illogical.[53] And if there indeed was no veil between them and their God, then how could they have been ignorant as to why they had been sent to the Garden?[54]

President Joseph Fielding Smith once remarked that Adam and Eve's intelligence while they were in Eden was greater than that had by any human today. They were intellectually as adults, having great reasoning powers.[55] Likewise, anciently it was believed that, *prior* to his fall, Adam had prophetic gifts and understanding. The early Church did not perceive father Adam as the equivalent of a child in either his pre-fall intellectual or spiritual capacities.[56] Rather, he was perceived as having wisdom and knowledge beyond that of the serpent (or Satan).[57] Elder Dallin H. Oaks also noted that "our first parents understood the necessity of the Fall."[58] Elder John A. Widtsoe wrote: "The gospel had been taught them during their sojourn in the Garden of Eden. They could not have been left in complete ignorance of the purpose of their creation."[59] One early Christian source states: "Be not deceived. Our father [Adam] was ignorant of nothing."[60] Indeed, Judaism holds that prior to the Fall "God revealed [to Adam] the whole history of mankind. . . . The tale of their years, the number of their days, the reckoning of their hours, and the measure of their steps, all were made known unto him."[61]

The only knowledge Adam and Eve appear to have been void of during their stay in the Garden was experiential knowledge.[62] Certain things, such as spiritual death being the repercussion for partaking of the "forbidden" fruit, could be grasped intellectually—but would only fully be comprehended once experienced. Alma suggests that prior to the Atonement, Christ was in a similar situation regarding sin. He stated: "Now the Spirit knoweth all things; nevertheless the Son of God suffereth according to the flesh that he might take upon him the sins of his people, that he might blot out their transgressions according to the power of his deliverance; and now behold, this is the testimony which is in me" (Alma 7:13). Of this verse Hugh Nibley once noted that, although the Spirit could have shown Christ what being a sinner would be like, Jesus needed to experience this firsthand. He must "go through it himself."[63] Elder Neal A. Maxwell added, "Jesus knew cognitively what He must do, but not experientially."[64] The Atonement provided Christ with this experiential knowledge. And so it was with Adam and Eve. In order to gain their eternal exaltation, they needed experiential knowledge as well as intellectual knowledge. The Fall would be the means of gaining that.[65]

"It is by contrasts that distinctions can best be made. White is whiter when placed next to black. Bitter is more clearly bitter when contrasted with sweet. To learn adequately the difference between good and evil or between God and Satan, mankind must have the full experience of life in a challenging world, a world of comparison and contrasts. Without this opposition of forces . . . the creation would have been 'a thing of naught.'"[66]

If Adam and Eve were ignorant of their purpose while they were in Eden—if they were intellectually and spiritually as little children—then it would go against the nature of God to have held them accountable for partaking of the fruit of the tree of knowledge of good and evil. The Restoration assures us that divine law protects from accountability those who are intellectually "as children" and those who do not know the law (see Moroni 8:22; 2 Nephi 9:25). Adam and Eve understand why they were in Eden and what God wanted them to do.

What Were Adam and Eve's Instructions in Eden?

As we have noted, too often it is assumed that in Eden God gave Adam and Eve two contradictory commandments (meaning, two commandments that were mutually exclusive). It is common in discussions about the Fall to hear commentators suggest that Adam and Eve *had to* break the one command in order to keep the other. However, the Restoration of the gospel makes it quite clear that God does not—indeed, cannot—contradict Himself. There is not a single example in scripture, outside of the story of the Fall, that supports the notion that God gives us commandments that require the breaking of other commandments in order for us to be obedient to the first.

Some would suggest that God's command to Abraham or Nephi (to slay a human being) was a "contradictory command." Those who take this position often cite these words by the Prophet Joseph: "God said, 'Thou shalt not kill;' at another time He said, 'Thou shalt utterly destroy.' This is the principle on which the government of heaven is conducted—by revelation adapted to the circumstances in which the children of the kingdom are placed. Whatever God requires is right, no matter what it is, although we may not see the reason thereof till long after the events transpire."[67]

Although these words relate well to the circumstance in which Abraham and Nephi found themselves, they do not apply to the situation in which we find Adam and Eve. Note that, unlike Adam and Eve, both Nephi and Abraham had the ability to do what God commanded them. They were simply given a new commandment that overrode a previous command. Neither Father Abraham nor the Prophet Nephi were being commanded to keep two mutually exclusive commandments, where the keeping of one required the breaking of the other.

Adam and Eve, on the other hand, were not being given a new command as a replacement of a previous command. Instead, they were given two simultaneous commands that could not both be kept. For God to command Adam and Eve to partake of the fruit of knowledge of good and evil, and also command them to multiply and replenish the earth (which they could do only if they partook of the "forbidden" fruit), is to place them in a logical paradox in which they cannot possibly be obedient. That is contrary to the nature of God (1 Nephi 3:7).

Additionally, for God to then administer repercussions (akin to penalties) for their disobedience to one law—when He Himself had required that they break that law so as to fulfill another law—runs entirely counter to God's nature, to the eternal principle of agency, and to the entire plan of salvation. God simply would not do this—to Adam and Eve or to you and me. To do so would be to act unmercifully, unjustly, and unrighteously.

Of course we must remember that nowhere in scripture do we have a full account of exactly what took place in the Garden surrounding the giving of the command not to partake of the "forbidden" fruit.[68] Something is clearly missing in each of the authorized accounts of the Fall. Something additional must have happened that is unclear in the story of the Fall but revealed through modern prophets.

On several occasions, President Joseph Fielding Smith taught: "The Lord said to Adam, here is the tree of knowledge of good and evil. If you want to stay here then you cannot eat of that fruit. If you want to stay here then I forbid you to eat it. But you may act for yourself and you may eat of it if you want to. And if you eat it you will die."[69] One LDS scholar similarly taught:

> What, therefore, did God really say to them in the garden? I suggest that He might have said something like the following: "If you want to stay in the Garden of Eden with no cares and no possibility of growth, you should not eat from the tree of knowledge of good and evil. However, if you desire to grow and receive all that I have in store for you, you will have to leave the garden. If you eat of the tree, you will be cast out of the garden into the earth and into mortality, and you will die both temporally and spiritually, but you will open the door for yourselves and for all humanity to receive eternal life like I have. The choice is yours." In other words, God gave them information.[70]

Thus, according to President Smith (and many others),[71] God was quite clear with Adam and Eve that they had a choice—and that choice was *not* which of the two contradictory commandments they would keep. On the contrary, the two options given them were as follows: If they wanted to stay in Eden, then the fruit of knowledge of good and evil was forbidden. However, if they wanted to leave, they would have to partake of that fruit. The first couple would have been quite clear on what their options were and what the repercussions of either choice would be. Unlike the common theory of "higher" and "lesser" commandments[72] or "contradictory commandments," President Smith's view is in harmony with the plan and the nature of God.

In What Sense Did Adam and Eve Transgress a Commandment of God?

As seemingly ideal as Eden was, it was not an environment suited for the type of growth and development needed for exaltation. Because it offered direct access to God, it could not serve as the testing ground that the children of God needed in order to become like Him. Thus, as we have already discussed, a removal from that locale was necessary.[73]

But how could God force Adam and Eve out of Eden so long as they were keeping His commandments? Such would be contrary to His law and the pattern set in scripture (see, for example, Ether 3:26; 12:20–21; Doctrine and Covenants 67:10). In addition, God could provide opposition to His *own* plan. This too would be contrary to the nature of deity.[74] Thus, Adam and Eve were given the responsibility of introducing a world filled with opposition, the veil of forgetting, and eventual death—and this they could do in only one way; via intentional partaking of something God had specifically, and formally, forbidden them to partake of. The word *transgress* means literally to "pass over," "step across," or "go beyond" a boundary.[75] God set boundaries in Eden, and then Adam and Eve intentionally "crossed over" those into mortality—not because our first parents were sinful or rebellious in their natures but again, because they needed to formally, or technically transgress God's law in order to introduce the conditions requisite for their growth and exaltation. There was no other way! Elder Dallin H. Oaks wrote:

> This transition, or "fall," could not happen without a transgression—an exercise of moral agency amounting to a willful breaking of a law (see Moses 6:59). This would be a planned offense, a formality to serve an eternal purpose. . . . It was Eve who first transgressed the limits of Eden in order to initiate the conditions of mortality. Her act . . . was formally a transgression but eternally a glorious necessity to open the doorway toward eternal life. Adam showed his

wisdom by doing the same. And thus Eve and "Adam fell that men might be" (2 Nephi 2:25). This suggested contrast between a *sin* and a *transgression* reminds us of the careful wording in the second article of faith: "We believe that men will be punished for their own *sins* and not for Adam's *transgression*" (emphasis added). It also echoes a familiar distinction in the law. Some acts, like murder, are crimes because they are inherently wrong. Other acts, like operating without a license, are crimes only because they are legally prohibited. Under these distinctions, the act that produced the Fall was not a sin—inherently wrong—but a transgression—wrong because it was formally prohibited.[76]

According to Elder Oaks, Father in Heaven labeled some acts—perhaps some "things"—as off limits. In so doing He provided the means by which Adam and Eve could transgress, or technically disobey God, and yet move forward the plan of happiness. In knowingly partaking of the "forbidden" fruit, our first parents technically broke a law of God and thus were forced out of Eden, and a veil was placed between them and God.[77]

In the restored gospel, transgression and sin are traditionally juxtaposed. Admittedly, 1 John 3:4 informs us that "sin is the transgression of the law." Thus, seeking to draw irrefutable, firm definitions of *sin* and *transgression* may be a futile act of hair-splitting. Nevertheless, since so much emphasis is placed on the fact that Adam and Eve transgressed rather than sinned, we will make an effort at explaining that distinction here.

In technical terms, to transgress is to unknowingly or accidentally break one of God's laws.[78] It is akin to what children under the age of eight do. And for such transgressions, as we noted above, they are not held accountable. To sin, on the other hand, is traditionally defined as knowingly going against the will of God.[79] In such cases, the individual breaking the law of God is held accountable for that act or sin until he or she sincerely repents of it. As will be explained below, Adam and Eve were viewed as transgressors rather than sinners, not because they were ignorant of right and wrong, but rather because their intent was perfectly pure (i.e., non-sinful). They chose to partake of that which God had formally or technically forbidden, not because they had a rebellious nature or sinful desire, but rather because they sought to introduce mortality in accordance with the plan and God's will. Elder Orson F. Whitney wrote:

> Sin is the transgression of divine law, as made known through the conscience or by revelation. A man sins when he violates his conscience, going contrary to light and knowledge—not the light and knowledge that has come to his neighbor, but that which has come to himself. He sins when he does the opposite of what he knows to be right. Up to that point he only blunders. One may suffer painful consequences for only blundering, but he cannot commit sin unless he knows better than to do the thing in which the sin consists. One must have a conscience before he can violate it. "Where there is no law given, there is no punishment . . . no condemnation." "He that knoweth not good from evil is blameless."[80]

Similarly, President Brigham Young taught: "If I do wrong knowingly, then I sin. When this people can live and never do a wrong knowingly, if they should sin in their ignorance, God will freely forgive that sin, if they are ready to repent when it is made known to them and refrain from it in the future."[81]

Technically, Adam and Eve were guilty of an act that would, by definition, qualify as a sin. They knowingly went against the declared will of God and thus committed what would usually be termed a sin. However, although they suffered the repercussions of their choice, they were not held accountable for sinning because their intent was not malicious. As we noted, they partook of that which was "forbidden" in an attempt—a successful attempt—at fulfilling the will and plan of their God. Robert J. Matthews, former Dean of Religious Education at Brigham Young University, noted that "Adam was not required to repent of the transgression that he had committed in the garden."[82] Again, in the words of Elder Oaks, Adam and Eve's actions were "legally" or "formally prohibited," but were not "inherently wrong."[83] Thus, although Adam and Eve knowingly acted contrary to the *vocalized* will of God (i.e., the command not to partake of the "forbidden" fruit), their intent was to do what God ultimately desired. For this reason their action is deemed a transgression rather than a sin.

WHO WAS DECEIVED IN EDEN?

A number of the Brethren have taught that Adam and Eve deserve our respect and admiration for bringing to pass the Fall. Elder James E. Talmage wrote: "It has become a common practice with mankind to heap reproaches upon the progenitors of the family, and to picture the supposedly blessed state in which we would be living but for the fall; whereas our first parents are entitled to our deepest gratitude for their legacy to posterity—the means of winning title to glory, exaltation, and eternal lives."[84] Similarly, Elder Dallin H. Oaks stated: "Some Christians condemn Eve for her act, concluding that she and her daughters are somehow flawed by it. Not the Latter-day Saints! Informed by revelation, we celebrate Eve's act and honor her wisdom and courage in the great episode called the Fall."[85] Elder Bruce R. McConkie wrote: "As there are not words to extol the greatness of the Ancient of Days . . . so there is no language that could do credit to our glorious mother Eve."[86] Elder Marion G. Romney called Eve's decision to partake of the fruit "noble."[87] In the LDS Bible Dictionary we are told that "the fall is a blessing, and . . . Adam and Eve should be honored."[88] Numerous Latter-day Saint scholars and commentators have taught this same idea.[89] And, no doubt, this idea will feel comfortable and right to Latter-day Saints. However, if they are literal in their approach to the story of the Fall, this doctrine will seem in error. In other words, a literal reading of the story tells us that the "woman was deceived."[90]

Yet this raises the question: If Eve was deceived, why do we honor her? If she was beguiled into desiring something contrary to God's will—even if it played into God's plans—Eve should not be extolled. She should be seen for what she then would be: a person with sinful desires, whose evil and selfish intent God was able to use to move His work forward. We might note that both Judas Iscariot and Lucifer committed sins that played into God's plans and furthered His purposes. However, we do not honor either of them for their sins.

Thus, the traditional interpretation that Eve was somehow tricked is inaccurate. Such a reading stands in contradiction with the doctrine as taught by living prophets. In Eden, Eve was intellectually and spiritually mature, understood God's will, and then consciously made the informed decision to move the plan forward by eating the fruit that would bring mortality into the world. It is for this reason that we honor her. We do not honor those who sin, *even if* some good comes from their missteps. But with Eve, there was no mistake, no misunderstanding, no succumbing to temptation. She is a heroine because she understood what was right and then chose to do exactly that, not because she was deceived into doing something that, in the end, benefited God's plan. Elder Jeffrey R. Holland wrote: "Adam and Eve made their choice for an even more generous reason than those of godly knowledge and personal progress. They did it for the one overriding and commanding reason basic to the entire plan of salvation and all the discussions ever held in all the councils of heaven. They did it 'that men might be.'"[91] True to form, not so much as a hint of selfishness was present in their decision to partake of the fruit. Elder Holland continued:

> These terrible risks of sorrow and death were facts Adam and Eve were willing to face in order that "men might be.". . . They were willing to transgress knowingly and consciously (the only way they could "fall" into the consequences of mortality, inasmuch as Elohim could not force innocent parties out of the garden and still be a just God) only because they had a full knowledge of the plan of salvation, which would provide for them a way back from their struggle with death and hell.[92]

Lucifer is clearly the one deceived in Eden. Hugh Nibley wrote: "In ancient lore [Eve] is the one who outwits the serpent and trips him up with his own smartness."[93] God wanted Adam and Eve to eat, but Lucifer "knew not the mind of God" (Moses 4:6). It follows, therefore, that Satan—either because he assumed that God desired Adam and Eve to stay in Eden, or because he wanted access to the rest of God's children—offered them that which was "forbidden."[94] But in doing so, he thwarted his own work and furthered God's. Literally, Satan's act helped initiate God's plan, even though the adversary's intent was to frustrate God's will.[95] He set up the very circumstance in which Christ would later "crush" his head (see Genesis 3:15; Moses 4:21).

HISTORY OR METAPHOR?

As can be seen, we are not always accurate in our interpretation of the Fall. One major stumbling block in efforts to correctly understand this sacred and foreordained event is the tendency for many to interpret the story of Adam and Eve (as given in scripture and the temple) as a historical account. True, Adam and Eve existed as real people. There was indeed a garden in which they dwelt. They had actual interactions with God and Christ during their time there. In addition, while in Eden, they dwelt with no other humans—but were surrounded by many animals, fowls, and fish. We know that during that period Satan sought to overthrow the work that Adam and Eve had been sent to do. And, in the end, it is true that a Fall did take place, which introduced a veil of forgetting and eventual death to each person that would live upon the earth. But the vast majority of what is related in scripture and ritual regarding these two is conveyed in metaphorical or symbolic language.[96] Consequently, because we tend to read the story from a strictly historical perspective, the Fall is often misunderstood and misinterpreted.

Inasmuch as the events surrounding the Fall are told in figurative language, the words in the scriptural and temple accounts have been "deliberately chosen" to teach us "more than what is seen on the surface."[97] But how are lay members of the Church to distinguish between what was intended to be understood metaphorically and that which was designed to be interpreted literally? In many cases simple logic will enable us to make the distinction. However, the Lord has not left us to rely solely on our intellect in such matters. In any effort to understand the holy scriptures, the teachings of the living prophets are our best guide, coupled with the assistance of the Lord's Spirit. The Brethren have made quite clear the doctrines of the Church—including those pertaining to the Fall. If we familiarize ourselves with their teachings on the subject, we will be able to distinguish between the symbolic and literal portions of the "story."[98]

In order to illustrate this point, note the following examples wherein both simple logic and the revealed doctrines of the Church clarify what is literal and what is figurative.

- If man was made from the dust (see Genesis 2:7), and woman from a rib (see Genesis 2:22), why is it that men do not have one less rib on either the right or left side of their rib cage? Taken literally, this seems contradictory. However, modern prophets have made it quite clear that we were never intended to read this passage as a literal, historical depiction of what happened in Eden.[99]

- In the story man is commanded to leave his father and mother and cleave to his wife, and to become "one flesh" with her. No one could seriously question the metaphorical nature of such a comment.

- After Adam and Eve partook of the "forbidden" fruit, God is depicted as trying to figure out where they were and how they found out that they were naked. Obviously the Father knew where Adam and Eve were hiding and exactly how they discovered their nakedness. If we understand the nature of God, we cannot assume that the Father could be ignorant regarding any of these matters.

- In His explanation of the penalties to be doled out upon Lucifer, God states that Christ would "bruise" the serpent's head (see Genesis 3:15). Are we to take this comment literally, thereby drawing the conclusion that, because of Satan's actions in Eden, Jesus will bruise the head of the snake? Such a conclusion makes no sense.[100]

- As we noted above, the story of the Fall depicts God as giving Adam and Eve two mutually exclusive commandments. They could not keep both. Thus, if we read this account as literal, we see God as an unjust being who places His children in impossible circumstances. This is contrary to the nature of God. Hence, it is evident that the language is figurative.[101]

- Again, as discussed above, the story of the Fall speaks of Adam and Eve as "little children." If this is literal, then it would be unfair for them to be punished for their transgression. Thus, the language utilized has to be symbolic.

Although many other examples could be given, suffice it to say, as this handful of illustrations shows, much of the story of the Fall cannot possibly be taken as literal. To do so would cause both confusion and potentially the acceptance of false doctrines. Yet, if these passages are figurative, what then are they endeavoring to teach us? What is their symbolic message?

THE COMMON MISUNDERSTANDING

It is generally understood that Adam and Eve were typological symbols for the human race. They serve as representations of each of us and our own personal fall from grace. Indeed, President Gordon B. Hinckley, in speaking of the holy temple and the story taught therein, stated that "we have sketched before us the odyssey of man's eternal journey from premortal existence through this life to the life beyond."[102] Likewise, Elder Bruce C. Hafen expressed the following: "The experience of Adam and Eve is an ideal prototype for our own mortal experience. Their story is our story. The complete cycle of their fall from innocence and their ultimate return to God typifies a general human pattern."[103] BYU's Hugh Nibley wrote this: "The Mormon endowment . . . is frankly a model, a presentation in figurative terms. . . . It does not attempt to be a picture of reality, but only a model . . . setting forth the pattern of man's life on earth with its fundamental whys and wherefores."[104] Echoing the sentiments of these aforementioned brethren, another Latter-day Saint scholar has written:

> What, then, . . . of the Eden story? . . . A rehearsal of the key events of Eden brings the realization that we too are privileged to leave the lone and dreary world and enter the sacred sanctuaries of the Lord, where we participate in essentially the same experiences known to our first parents before the Fall. The temple is to us as Eden was to Adam and Eve. . . . The story of Eden, in fact, [is] a light that reveals the path all must travel to return to the divine presence.[105]

Similarly, in an LDS publication dedicated to an examination of the life of Father Adam, one author informed his readers: "In the mind of first-century Jews and Christians, what Adam was, we are; what Adam could become, we can become."[106] Indeed, it is generally held within Mormonism that Adam and Eve "are symbolic representations of all men and women."[107] Even when in sacred precincts, Latter-day Saints are instructed that, when contemplating the Fall, they should substitute themselves for the persons of Adam and Eve.[108] Clearly their story is our story. The message of the Fall is about us.[109]

This concept is not unique to Latter-day Saints. Even non-LDS scholars and theologians acknowledge that the scriptural story of the Fall is *primarily* designed to teach us about ourselves. As one noted:

> Adam . . . is the Representative of the human race. . . . This story must be taken seriously but not literally. . . . It is a [scriptural story] that accurately reveals the existential situation in which man finds himself in the world. . . . While it is anchored in history, its significance is not limited to a particular history. . . . The language or terminology employed is, for the most part, symbolic. . . . To affirm that there are [figurative and symbolic] elements in Scripture is not to detract from its divine inspiration nor from its historical basis but to attest that the Holy Spirit has made use of various kinds of language and imagery to convey divine truth. . . . The tale in Genesis concerns not only a first fall and first man but a universal fall and universal man. Adam is not so much a private person as the head of the human race. He is a generic as well as first man. He is Everyman and therefore Representative Man. He is the representative of both our original parents and of all humankind.[110]

Similarly, the prolific Jacob Neusner noted that in marriage and life the man is symbolically living out the role of Adam and the woman that of Eve.[111] Our first parents are symbols for the whole of Israel or "the children of Zion."[112] When a man and woman marry, they adopt the roles of Adam and Eve; and they hope that their home can become a new Eden or, better put, a temple.[113]

As we read scripture, it is hard to escape the fact that a recurring Adamic theme is present. The story of Adam and Eve and their Fall appears as the backdrop for numerous scriptural stories. Adam stands as an archetype for other human beings. His story can be seen in their story—and, more important, they are to see themselves in him.[114] For example, Noah steps forth from the ark as the beginning of a race of humans, immediately after God's judgments have been poured out upon the earth. Such was also the case with Adam. As with the first man, Noah was commanded by God to "be fruitful, and multiply, and replenish the earth" (Genesis 9:1). Even Noah's relationship with the animals seems to draw upon the Adamic motif.

And knowing that the great prophet of the deluge was familiar with Adam's story, surely Noah would have recognized these parallels.

Likewise, Abraham's life was also filled with Adamic motifs. He and his seed are promised that they will be fruitful and multiply.[115] In so doing, Abraham's offspring generates Israel, just as Adam and Eve give birth to the human race.

Covenant Israel is no different. Her story is just as saturated with this same Adamic symbolism—from her constant struggle with obedience to God's commands (which reminds us of Adam and Eve's "disobedience") to the architecture of her temples (which mirrors the Garden of Eden). Regarding this last parallel, note the following Adamic symbols. Eden was said to have been filled with gold and onyx,[116] and Israel's temple employed gold and onyx stones abundantly.[117] Adam's garden had its tree of life, and Israel had its branched and flowering lampstand, representative of Eden's tree.[118] In Solomon's temple, plant figures were carved into the walls and doors,[119] creating the appearance of Eden for the priests who served therein. Real animals were constantly in use as sacrifices by ancient Israel, just as animals were constantly present in Eden and used by Adam as sacrifices once he left the Garden.[120] In each of Israel's temples cherubim are found on the veil and atop the ark,[121] reminding us of the cherubim with flaming sword that served to guard or veil Eden from fallen man.[122] The entrance to Jerusalem's temple was oriented toward the east, recalling the situation of Eden's gate. Even the duty of the Levites to guard the sanctuary[123] reminds us of the commission God gave to Adam to till, serve, protect, or guard the garden.[124] Finally, as He did for Adam, God offers to covenant Israel blessings—but He also commands her, "Thou shalt not do that which I forbid you."[125]

Why all of the Adamic parallels? Because Adam and Eve are our pattern. Their story is ours. Noah, Abraham, covenant Israel, and you and I are to consider ourselves as if we were Adam and Eve. We are to see the story of the Fall as the story of our fall. Thus, so much of our lives—and so much of the lives of the ancient patriarchs and prophets—seems saturated in symbols of the paradise that was willingly given up in the hopes of obtaining an inheritance in the celestial kingdom.

The fact of the matter is that the story of the Fall—as told in scripture and the temple—is intended to give us more detail regarding our personal falls (as weak and sinful mortals) than about the Fall of the historical figures, Adam and Eve. Each of the inspired, authorized accounts have been couched in such a way as to serve as a message about need for obedience, the consequences of *our* sins, and desperate need for a Savior to redeem us from *our* fallen condition. To misunderstand this is to misunderstand the Fall.

Summary

In light of our discussion, the following concepts should be clear:

- The Fall of man was planned by God, and taught in the premortal world, even before this earth was created.

- In the Grand Council in Heaven, Adam and Eve were called, sustained, and set apart to bring to pass that Fall.

- When Adam and Eve entered Eden they had direct access to God and frequently conversed with Him regarding the plan and their role in it.

- While in Eden, our first parents understood that God desired them to bring to pass a state of mortality so that the plan of salvation could be initiated for those waiting in the premortal world.

- The only way to introduce mortality, death, and the veil of separation was to intentionally transgress one of God's commands.

- God could not oppose His own plan; He could not instigate death; nor could he force a veil between Himself and His creations. Thus, Adam and Eve functioned as the agents to bring each of these elements into play.

- Adam and Eve are to be honored because they did God's will and, in so doing, provided an opportunity for our exaltation.

- Lucifer was the only participant in the Fall to actually be deluded.

- Finally, for the discussion that is to follow, it is important to realize that the vast majority of what we learn from the scriptural and temple accounts of the Fall is about us and our personal fall—and not about Adam and Eve and their fall from Eden. To miss this distinction is to both misunderstand what the authorized accounts of the Fall are trying to convey and also to potentially misunderstand the doctrines relating to the Fall.

We will now turn our attention to a discussion of the four accounts of the Fall and what they can teach us about the metaphor and doctrine of the Fall. But before doing so, I wish to emphasize that the aforementioned ideas be kept in mind when reading what follows.

Notes

1. See Laffey (1995), 516; Bloesch (2001), 1:103–9.

2. McConkie (1990), 34.

3. By "revelations of the Restoration" the author means both the canonical revelations found in the Doctrine and Covenants and Book of Mormon and also the teachings of the prophets and apostles of The Church of Jesus Christ of Latter-day Saints.

4. Certainly there are other scriptural passages that deal with the Fall—such as 2 Nephi 2 and Alma 12. However, these only refer to the Fall or some aspect of it, while the four "authorized" scriptural accounts mentioned above actually go into detail regarding the vast majority of the events we label "the Fall of man."

5. Jackson (2001), 90; Keller (2004), 103.

6. Matthews (1990), 38.

7. Millet (1997), 11–12. "God's son and daughter had done what needed to be done." Campbell (2003), 101.

8. Parker (2003), 79, 89, n. 3. See also Roberts (1996), 345. "The reason why it is important for us to know that God has a plan for the salvation of man, and that the plan includes the fall of man, is such knowledge dignifies the Fall and gives man a sense of security by removing the idea of chance or happenstance. The idea of a plan of God directs us to the conclusion that the Fall (1) was necessary, (2) was not a surprise to God, (3) was not an outright rebellion, (4) was an actual occurrence, and (5) is an essential part of the journey of man toward perfection." Matthews, "The Fall of Man" (1990), 40–41.

9. Packer (1996), 49–50.

10. Turner (1972), 206; Clark (1997), 27; Parker (2003), 88.

11. It must be remembered that a person or being with a "perfect knowledge" still has agency. Joseph Fielding McConkie put it this way: "Adam needed to transgress in order to be put on probation and be subject to sin, that he might reject sin, overcome, and embrace righteousness. . . . Contrary to the beliefs of traditional Christianity, Adam conformed to the will of the Lord when he partook of the forbidden fruit. . . . The creation of a mortal state of probation was the very reason for the Fall, and it was a state that could not come into being without the transgression of the first man and the first woman." (1990), 32–33.

12. B. McConkie, "Agency" (1979), 26–28.

13. One LDS commentator on the Fall argued that God was eventually going to give Adam and Eve of the fruit of knowledge of good and evil. Their "transgression," according to Gerald Jones, consisted of eating the fruit before God offered it to them. He compares it to premarital intimacy; what is forbidden prior to marriage is commanded after. See Jones (1997), iv-v. One apparent flaw in this argument is that if God gave Adam and Eve the fruit, then there would be no transgression—and thus no obligation for them to leave God's presence or have a veil drawn between them and their Father in Heaven. Were that separation not to take place, the plan would have been frustrated, because they would not be able to walk by faith.

Related to this is the following comment: "Believing men and women [have] indicated that they perceive Eve as a sinner, reasoning that God would have found another, less harsh way for mankind to claim mortality had Eve not partaken of the fruit. The inevitable conclusion was that the Fall, a sacramental symbol foreordained of God, was not necessary. . . . Perhaps the most harmful misperception in the entire Garden saga is the idea that another way for humankind to enter mortality would have been found had [Adam and] Eve not partaken of the fruit of the tree of knowledge." Campbell (2003), 6, 27. 2 Nephi 2:11–12, 15–16 seem to contradict the claim that God was going to give Adam and Eve the forbidden fruit. Opposition was needed, and only Adam and Eve could introduce that.

14. Maxwell (1979), 9, 10–11. See also Maxwell (1982), 37; Cannon, in *Journal of Discourses*, 26:187–93; Hyde, in *Journal of Discourses*, 13:180.

15. Ehat and Cook (1980), 63.

16. Young, in *Journal of Discourses*, 2:302.

17. Young, in *Journal of Discourses*, 10:312. See also 17:143. "Mother Eve partook of the forbidden fruit. We should not have been here today if she had not; we could never have possessed wisdom and intelligence if she had not done it. It was all in the economy of heaven, and we need not talk about it; it is all right. We should never blame Mother Eve, not the least." Young (1998), 103. See also Pratt (2000), 73.

18. Woodruff, in *Journal of Discourses,* 23:126.

19. Smith (1957–1966), 4:80.

20. Roberts (1996), 345.

21. B. McConkie, *Ensign*, 1982, 9. See also B. McConkie (1985), 82; Matthews (1990), "The Fall of Man," 39.

22. B. McConkie (1978), 221.

23. M. McConkie (1998), 179.

24. See Holland (1997), 202–3.

25. In addition to the quotes already given, see also Widtsoe (1998), 103; Pratt (2000): 88; Whitney (1921), 93; Roberts (1996), 344; Talmage (1975), 70; Widtsoe (1960), 192; Widtsoe (1937), 51–52; Clark (1997), 27; Smith (1993), 2:213–15; Smith (1998), 1:109–10, 115; Packer (1996), 49–50; McConkie, "Eve and the Fall" (1979), 68; B. McConkie (1985), 82; Oaks (1993), 73; Hafen (1990), 9; Holland (1997), 204; First Presidency (1995), 102, paragraph 3.

26. For a look at LDS authors and scholars who have advocated this position, see LDS Bible Dictionary (1979), 670, s. v. "Fall of Adam"; Keller (2004), 103; Matthews, "The Fall of Man" (1990), 38–41, 62, 67, 77–78; Millet (1990), 191; Millet (1997), 11–12; McConkie, "The Mystery of Eden" (1990), 32–35; Rasmussen (1993), 14; Jackson (1994), 14; Parker (2003), 79, 88–89, n. 3; Turner (1972), 206; Peterson (1992), 213; Ludlow (1981), 114; Rockwood (1992), 6, 21, 24; Adams (1990), 99; Campbell (2003), 6, 8, 13–14, 23, 27, 29–31, 81, 89, 101, 112–14, 166; Ladle (2004), 47; Bennion (1988), 96–97; Bailey (1998), 23. See also Oden (2001), 100; Lewis (1993), 440; Ryken, Wilhoit, and Longman (1998), 247; Vawter, (1977), 79.

27. Keller (2004), 104–5. "The author [of the Fall account] does not accuse or blame the couple for their transgression. In fact, he seems to imply that the choice they made is good." Rockwood (1992), 21.

28. "Their 'transgression' was . . . a painful but correct, even eternally glorious, choice." Hafen (1990), 9. "The Family: A Proclamation to the World" states that "in the premortal realm, spirit sons and daughters . . . accepted

[God's] plan by which His children could obtain a physical body and gain earthly experience to progress toward perfection." (1995), paragraph 3. That plan that we accepted and sustained consisted, in part, of Adam and Eve coming to earth and partaking of the "forbidden" fruit that each of us might be born. See also Campbell (2003), 8.

29. Young, in *Journal of Discourses*, 9:149. See also Smith (1993), 5:123; Smith (1998), 1:103; *Lectures on Faith*, 2:18; Pratt, in *Journal of Discourses*, 7:257.

30. It is conjectural, but a number of extracanonical texts suggest that Adam and Eve were in Eden for an extended period of time. See, for example, "2 Enoch" in Charlesworth (1983–1985), 1:154; Talmudic tractate Sanhedrin 38b. See also Smith (1949), 67; Reynolds and Sjodahl (1955–1961), 6:86–87.

31. Campbell (2003), 67–68. "Adam and Eve agreed to go to the Garden on an assignment that was known to them and to us before the world was created. . . . As God walked and talked with Adam and Eve in the Garden, they learned that to fulfill this assignment they would have to transgress (go across) the boundary of the place known to them as the Garden of Eden into a mortal state. Blood would have to flow in their veins to accomplish this." Campbell (2003), 112–13.

32. Campbell (2003), 64–65.

33. Holland (1997), 202–3.

34. See B. McConkie (1979), 26, s. v. "Agency."

35. Facsimile 2, Figure 3 in the book of Abraham speaks of "the grand Keywords of the Holy Priesthood, as revealed to Adam in the Garden of Eden." This clearly implies that Adam and Eve had significant knowledge and accountability in Eden, and apparently had some portion of the temple rites prior to their Fall. See also Kimball, in *Journal of Discourses*, 8:330; 9:129–30, 135; Duke (1992), 2:858.

36. See Facsimile 2, Figure 3; McConkie (1989), 80. Reason would have it that, if such were the case, they likely could also have been baptized, confirmed, and Adam would have been ordained—all preparatory to receiving their endowment and sealing. Although Moses 6:64 might be read as implying that Adam's baptism took place after his fall, there is insufficient information to dogmatically draw this conclusion. First of all, it is uncertain if Enoch is reciting these events in chronological order. Second, it is not clear that Adam received the ordinances in the order in which they are traditionally received today. Finally, we do not know if the principle of rebaptism was in place in Adam's day (i.e., is there any chance that Adam was baptized in Eden, then baptized again once he left the

garden?). Thus one must reserve judgment on the timing of the receipt of any of Adam's ordinances, other than his endowment and sealing—both of which appear to have taken place in Eden.

37. See Packer (1990), 13–14. One non-LDS scholar noted that prior to the Fall Adam and Eve are treated as though they are mature and capable of making moral choices or decisions. See Kidner (1967), 63. See also Genesis 2:16–17, which implies this.

38. Packer (1990), 6. President Packer has also written: "There was too much at issue to introduce man into mortality by force. That could contravene the very law essential to the plan." Packer (1991), 78–79. "The Fall, even in light of its paramount importance to the Father's plan, could not be forced on Adam and Eve. They had to voluntarily choose the course themselves. Nor could their choice be made in ignorance, for a choice made in such a state would not be a true exercise of agency." Campbell (2003), 37–38.

39. Hyrum Andrus wrote that, while in Eden, "Man was considered an independent being who could make decisions for himself. But he would also be responsible for his actions." Andrus (1967), 185.

40. It is the position of this author that Adam and Eve were "as little children" only in their levels of experience and purity—but not in their intellect or understanding of their purposes in Eden.

41. Lund (1989), 104.

42. Elder John A. Widtsoe wrote: "The Lord had warned Adam and Eve of the hard battle with earth conditions if they chose to eat of the tree of knowledge of good and evil. He would not subject his son and daughter to hardship and the death of their bodies unless it be of their own choice. They must choose for themselves. They chose wisely, in accord with the heavenly law of love for others." Widtsoe (1960), 194.

43. Robert L. Millet has written: "It is not to say that children cannot do things that are evil, that they cannot perform deeds that under other circumstances would be called sinful. They certainly can do such things. The revelations teach that their actions are covered by the merciful ministry of our Master. In this sense they cannot sin. Thus, 'little children are holy, being sanctified through the atonement of Jesus Christ.'" Millet (1995), 7.

44. Hertz (1962), 10.

45. *Lectures on Faith*, 2:12. In 2 Enoch it is claimed that during their stay in Eden Adam and Eve had heaven completely open to their view and that, among other things, they could hear and see the angels singing praises to God. See 2 Enoch 31:2, in Charlesworth (1983–85), 1:152, 154.

46. Pratt, in *Journal of Discourses*, 21:203–4; see also 7:257.

47. *Times and Seasons* (1843), 672.

48. Pratt (1978), 85.

49. Taylor (1852), 108–9.

50. Smith (1954), 383–84.

51. See Hunter (1949), 70; (1952), 122; and (1952), 36–37. See also Millet (2000), 161–62.

52. Roberts (1907–1912), 2:62–63. See also Roberts (1996), 399–400; Joseph E. Taylor, in *Journal of Discourses*, 23:246.

53. See, for example, John Taylor, in *Journal of Discourses*, 7:363; Smith (1998), 1:95; Millet (2000), 161–62; Matthews, "The Fall of Man" (1990), 46; Bailey (1998), 22; Adams (1990), 102, 105; Reynolds and Sjodahl (1955–1961), 4:219; Ludlow (1975), 314; Campbell (2003), 37–38, 64–68, 112–14; Clarke (n. d.), 1:45, 50; Jamieson, Fausset, and Brown (n. d.), 18; Ginzberg (1967–1969), 1:61. See also Neusner (1985), 264; Robinson (1990), 134–35; Kidner (1967), 63; 2 Enoch 31:2, in Charlesworth (1983–1985), 1:152, 154.

54. In chapter two of this work, we will examine why it is that Adam and Eve are depicted as not recognizing Satan for who he really is.

55. See Smith (1998), 1:94–95. See also *Times and Seasons* (1843), 672. According to Jewish legend, "Adam came from the hands of the Creator fully and completely developed. He was not like a child, but like a man of twenty years of age." See Ginzberg (1967–1969), 1:59. See also Neusner (1985), 154; Oden (2001), 100; Jamieson, Fausset, and Brown (n. d.), 18.

56. See, for example, Chrysostom, "Homilies on Genesis" 15–16, in Oden (2001), 72; Augustine, "On the Literal Interpretation of Genesis" 9.19.36, in Oden (2001), 70.

57. See Ephrem the Syrian, "Commentary on Genesis" 2.15.1, in Oden (2001), 74.

58. Oaks (1993), 73.

59. Widtsoe (1960), 193.

60. Clement of Rome, "The Clementine Homilies" 3:18, in Roberts and Donaldson (1994), 8:241.

61. Ginzberg (1967–1969), 1:61. See also Neusner (1985), 264; Robinson (1990), 134–35.

62. The Hebrew of the Genesis account makes it clear that Adam and Eve were not without an "intellectual" knowledge of "good and evil." Rather,

what they did not have was an "experiential" knowledge. In other words, they understood the difference between good and evil but had no practical experience of the latter of the two. That would come through their disobedience. In the end that is exactly what they had no experience of—disobedience! See Speiser (1962), 26; Clifford and Murphy (1990), 12; Parker (2003), 85.

Admittedly, we humans need the "experiential knowledge" of mortality to fully become like God. But one can mature spiritually and mentally without many of the experiences of life—as Jesus clearly did in the premortal world (where He became a God before He ever experienced mortality, and without ever committing any sins). Of course, in the end Adam and Eve (and you and I) can only become wholly like God via our "experiential knowledge." But clearly Adam and Eve were unique during their stay in Eden—just as Christ was unique when compared to God's other spirit offspring.

63. See Nibley (1988–1990), 2:297.

64. Maxwell (1985), 72.

65. See Pratt (2000), 81.

66. King (1995), s. v. Moses 4:22–25.

67. Smith (1932–1951), 5:135.

68. Keller (2004), 103.

69. Smith (1982), 124. See also Smith (1993), 4:81; Smith (1990), 185–86, in which President Smith stated: "Mortality was created through the eating of the forbidden fruit, if you want to call it forbidden, but I think the Lord has made it clear that it was not forbidden. He merely said to Adam, if you want to stay here [in the garden] this is the situation. If so, don't eat it."

   It seems fair to note that, while President Smith's position that Adam and Eve did not receive "contradictory commandments" finds support in the teachings of a number of the Brethren, various General Authorities have held different opinions on how best to address this issue of the seeming contradiction. In the end, in the opinion of this author, President Smith's interpretation seems to best coincide with the overarching doctrine of the Church.

70. Keller (2004), 104.

71. See, for example, Keller (2004), 104. Also, Elder L. Lionel Kendrick wrote: "Adam and Eve made a conscious decision based upon the two choices that were placed before them. They chose mortality." Kendrick (1996),

31. Elsewhere we read: "You may eat from the forbidden tree if you want the consequence that you will fall and man will come into mortality." Parker (2003), 87. Campbell wrote that the "fruit was forbidden to them only if they wished to stay in the Garden because it contained within it the elements of death." Campbell (2003), 113 (see also 37, 75). One patristic scholar noted that Adam was not sent forth from Eden against his will, but rather willingly left Eden because it was his will or desire to do so. See Oden (2001), 100.

72. Descriptions such as the following are common: "In life all must choose at times. Sometimes, two possibilities are good; neither is evil. Usually, however, one is of greater import than the other. When in doubt, each must choose that which concerns the good of others—the greater law—rather than that which chiefly benefits ourselves—the lesser law. . . . That was the choice made in Eden." Campbell (2003), 167. Yet, again, problematic is the suggestion that God would command both, knowing that it is impossible to keep both the "good" and the "better" commandment—both the "higher" and the "lower" law. Were God to do this, He would place Adam and Eve in an impossible situation.

73. See Harper (2004), 90, 92, in which Steven Harper speaks of the need for mankind to be in a place "outside of God's immediate oversight" and "presence" in order for us to be able to act for ourselves. Harper suggests that this applies to Adam and Eve as well as their posterity.

74. Gerald Lund penned this: "The creation of the world (and man) was done in a perfect, holy, and innocent state. To have done otherwise would have been contrary to the nature of God, which sets up an interesting problem. Opposition is necessary to man's progression, but God could not create it and be true to his perfect nature." Lund (1989), 102.

Kent P. Jackson wrote: "Why did God not simply create the world in such a condition that the plan would be underway from the beginning? Why did God place Adam and Eve in paradise with the anticipation that it and they would need to fall? I suggest a twofold answer. First, all things were created to be very good, because that is the nature of God and his work. God creates things that are organized, spiritual, and in harmony with his order. Second, perhaps man needed to exercise his own agency to fall and die because God would not force those conditions on us. According to Alma, our fallen condition is something we brought on ourselves (see Alma 42:12). Yet if God would not impose the conditions of mortality on us, then it is reasonable to suggest that Adam and Eve, who made decisions that affect every human being, were not acting without our specific approval. Because they were representing us in what they did, it makes sense that in the premortal councils we sustained them to act in our behalf." Jackson (2001), 94–95.

On a related note, Elder Orson Pratt stated: "God did not make a mortal being. It would be contrary to his great goodness to make a man mortal, subject to pain, subject to sickness, subject to death. . . . If he had made them mortal, and subject to pain, there would have been some cause, among intelligent beings, to say that the Lord subjected man, without a cause, to afflictions, sorrows, death and mortality. But he could not do this; it was contrary to the nature of his attributes, contrary to the nature of that infinite goodness which dwells in the bosom of the Father and the Son, to make a being subject to any kind of pain." Pratt, in *Journal of Discourses*, 21:289. See also Pratt (2000), 81–82.

Roger Keller wrote: "Mortality can be forced on no one, since to do so would violate the eternal nature of agency. Thus, Adam and Eve had to choose to become mortal, as did all human beings." Keller (2004), 116.

Robert J. Matthews penned this: "If God had created man mortal, then death, sin, and all the circumstances of mortality would be God's doing and would be eternal and permanent in their nature; whereas if man brings the Fall upon himself, he is the responsible moral agent, and God is able to rescue and redeem him from his fallen state." Matthews, "The Fall of Man" (1990), 60. See also Adams (1990), 100–101.

75. See Random House, *Webster's College Dictionary* (1996), 1415. See also Parker (2003), 86; Campbell (2003), 39–40, 113.

76. Oaks (1993), 73. "This was a transgression of the law, but not a sin in the strict sense, for it was something that Adam and Eve had to do!" Smith (1998), 1:115. "Adam was banished from Paradise on account of violating a light [or insignificant] command." Ginzberg (1967–1969), 2:49.

77. Widtsoe (1937), 51–52.

78. See Ludlow (1982), 494–95.

79. See James 4:17. See also Ludlow (1982), 494–95; Bennion (1959), 64.

80. Whitney (1921), 239–40.

81. Young, in *Journal of Discourses*, 9:220–21.

82. Matthews, "The Revelation of the Gospel to Adam" (1990), 77–78. "After their expulsion from Eden into the earth as it is, Adam exults: '. . . Blessed be the name of God, for because of my transgression my eyes are opened, and in this life I shall have joy, and again in the flesh I shall see God.' And Eve seemed almost jubilant: '. . . Were it not for our transgression we never should have had seed, and never should have known good and

evil, and the joy of our redemption, and the eternal life which God giveth unto all the obedient' (Moses 5:10–11). These were not the words of sinners or of repentant sinners. This was spoken by people who had met and accepted a great challenge, with which, as they imply, God was pleased." Widtsoe (1960), 192.

83. Oaks (1993), 73.

84. Talmage (1975), 70.

85. Oaks (1993), 73.

86. B. McConkie, "Eve and the Fall" (1979), 68. See also 57–68.

87. Romney (1968), 84–89; Rockwood (1992), 12.

88. LDS Bible Dictionary (1979), 670, s. v. "Fall of Adam."

89. Roger R. Keller wrote: "Rather than seeing the Fall as a disaster, we see Eve as a heroine and the Fall as an immense step forward in humanity's eternal progression . . . thanks to the courage of Adam and Eve." Keller (2004), 102, 104 (see also 105). See also Matthews, "The Revelation of the Gospel to Adam" (1990), 66–67; Matthews, "The Fall of Man" (1990), 62; Campbell (2003), 14, 19, 29; Rockwood (1992), 21; McConkie, "The Mystery of Eden" (1990), 35. "Adam and Eve were two of the noblest children of God. For this reason they were chosen to come to earth and to initiate mortal life for others of God's children. . . . The story of the fall of man in scripture is an effort to explain the divine origin and purpose of life and should be read with this thought in mind. The story is . . . figurative and symbolic. . . . Adam and Eve chose the courageous role, the one God wanted them to choose. . . . They 'fell' in the sense that they left the presence of God and became subject to the limitations of mortality, including death, ignorance, and sin. . . . As Latter-day Saints, we honor Adam and Eve because they had the courage and faith to become mortal and so to assume moral responsibility. We believe . . . they were doing God's will." Bennion (1988), 96–97.

90. Some readers will be reminded of Paul's comment to Timothy (in 1 Timothy 2:12–14). According to Stephen E. Robinson, Paul's comments regarding Eve being "deceived" are culturally conditioned, reflecting the normative social practice of his day, more so than the doctrine of the early Church. See Robinson (1990), 132–33. Another LDS scholar noted that in his epistles Paul speaks of the status and conduct of women and utilizes the Adam and Eve account "out of its context to illustrate a point. . . . Paul's advice on issues involving women was usually a mixture of Christian principles boldly sprinkled with Jewish customs." For example, in 1 Timothy Paul says that Adam was not deceived, but rather

Eve was (see 1 Timothy 2:12–15). However, in Romans he says the Fall was Adam's fault (see Romans 5:12; see also 1 Corinthians 15:22). Thus, Paul is using the story of the Fall to suit the needs of his audience and the message he is trying to share. See Rockwood (1992), 7–8.

Like Paul, a number of LDS General Authorities have also used the story of the Fall in a variety of ways, contingent upon the individual need of their audience. Some have interpreted these variant applications of the Fall as contradictory. However, in reality there is no contradiction. These are simply attempts by leaders to apply a familiar scriptural story to a variety of situations.

On a separate point, it is noteworthy that Jesus never suggests that Eve sinned. Indeed, he never uses Adam or Eve as models of sinners in His teachings. Rockwood also noted: "The Midrash, Talmud, and apocryphal and pseudepigraphal literature were all in use by the Jews at the time of Christ and shaped the society into which he was born. His mother took him to the temple after her days of purification. He studied the Torah along with other boys. The four Gospel accounts of his ministry depict him as having a thorough knowledge of the scriptures and the law of Moses as found in such Jewish works as the Talmud and Midrash. Yet in none of the Gospels is Jesus seen using the Adam and Eve story as an explanation for either the origin of sin or the respective roles of men and women," as the Jews would have. Rockwood (1992), 6. "The tradition of Eve as a temptress . . . is wholly a product of post-biblical traditions. . . . In 1 Timothy 2:14 . . . there is no trace of the archetype that has been so powerful in the postbiblical tradition of Eve as a seducer to sin." Ryken, Wilhoit, and Longman (1998), 247. See also Vawter (1977), 79.

91. Holland (1997), 204.

92. Holland (1997), 202–3. See also Harper (2004), 91; Keller (2004), 103–4; Faust (1990), 132.

93. Nibley, Old Testament and Related Studies (1986), 88–89. See also Campbell (2003), 77.

94. One commentator conjectured that since Satan's "motive was the destruction of mankind; he must gain access to the spirits of men, and the earth as his dominion (Moses 4:6; 2 Nephi 2:18)." Adams (1990), 101. Elsewhere Adams stated: "Satan, not knowing the mind and will of God, sought to destroy God's plan. He sought to get them to partake of the fruit so that they would have children so that he would have access to those spirits too." Adams (1991). Similarly, Elder Milton R. Hunter

wrote: "It was not only God's will that the earth become filled with His sons and daughters, but it was also in harmony with the devil's desires. Satan had done all the damage to the plan of salvation and to God's spirit-children that he could in the spirit world [or premortal life] before he was cast out; and now if he [wished to continue] to destroy God's sons and daughters, it was necessary for them to become mortals and dwell upon the earth. For these reasons Lucifer was anxious for Adam and Eve to partake of the forbidden fruit." Hunter (1951), 118. See also Campbell (2003), 97.

95. Bailey (1998), 23; Campbell (2003), 97. Adam and Eve would have chosen to fall anyway, regardless of Satan's enticements in Eden. But Lucifer was providing the necessary opposition to the plan that you and I, along with the fallen Adam and Eve, would need in order to become as God is. In this way, the devil inadvertently played into the hands of God. "Hugh Nibley has suggested that by the time they were tempted by the being who symbolically is called a serpent, Adam and Eve had concluded that they must partake of the fruit of the tree of knowledge of good and evil." See Campbell (2003), 65.

96. "The story of the Fall is not a myth. It is a record, in poetic, highly-figurative language, of an actual occurrence," Reynolds and Sjodahl (1955–1961), 2:68. One early understanding of the Fall was as follows: "The story was never meant to be taken literally but should be understood as spiritual allegory." See Pagels (1989), 64.

97. Jackson (2001), 81–82, 84.

98. Of course, we do not draw doctrine from metaphors or symbols. Rather, only by correctly understanding the doctrines can we accurately interpret the metaphors and symbols of the scriptures and temple.

99. See Young, in *Journal of Discourses* 2:6; 3:319; 7:285; Kimball (1976), 71. Elder Russell M. Nelson of the Quorum of the Twelve indicated that this is a figurative element in the story, intended to signify a greater gospel truth. It is not a description of the way in which Eve was actually created. See Nelson (1987), 87.

100. It is common knowledge that this comment foreshadows (in figurative language) Christ's eventual destruction of Satan's work and influence. See, for example, B. McConkie (1978), 472; Nyman (1985), 95; Adams (1990), 103–4.

101. We will discuss below what the intended metaphor is.

102. Hinckley (1997), 636. Elsewhere we read: "The Endowment ceremony . . . portrays the journey of individuals from the premortal existence

through mortal life and death to life after death. . . . Dramatic presentations, special clothing, and symbolic instruction during the temple ceremonies represent various stages in an individual's eternal progression." Cooper (1992), 3:1430–31. See also Pagels (1989), xx–xxi, xxiv.

103. Hafen (1989), 37. "All of us, like Adam and Eve, must leave God's presence in the quest for knowledge and growth through personal experience. . . . The story of Adam and Eve is our story." Hafen (1989), 33, 50.

104. Nibley (1975), xiii.

105. McConkie, "The Mystery of Eden" (1990), 29, 30, 23.

106. Robinson (1990), 128.

107. Rockwood (1992), 18.

108. Scott (1996), 74; Holland (1997), 203–4; Hafen (1990), 10; Hafen (1989), 33, 37–39, 50; Nibley (1989), 6; McConkie, "The Mystery of Eden" (1990), 30; Matthews, "The Revelation of the Gospel to Adam" (1990), 67; Rockwood (1992), 18; Cooper (1992), 3:1430–31; Adams (1990), 85; Campbell (2003), 7, 96, 123, 166; Robinson (1990), 138; Lundquist (1989), 88; Hutchinson (1988), 69.

109. Steven Harper wrote "We are akin to Adam and Eve." Harper (2004), 92. In the mind of this author, that may be an understatement. The metaphor does not appear to be secondary, but rather primary in the standard accounts of the Fall.

110. Bloesch (2001), 1:104–5, 106. See also Pagels (1989), xxi, 74.

111. Neusner (1991), 53–65.

112. Neusner (1991), 62. See also Neusner (1985), 174, 208, 209, 211, 213, 224, 230. "The story of the 'fall' is a paradigm of human conduct in the face of temptation." Vawter (1977), 81, 90.

113. Neusner (1991), 62. One LDS author suggested: "We in essence enter Eden when we enter the temple, for there, as in Eden, we are in a place wherein God can dwell, wherein we can make covenants, receive ordinances, and learn all that is necessary to find our way back to our heavenly home." Campbell (2003), 57.

114. This discussion of Adam as the archetype for other scriptural figures is drawn from comments made by Ryken, Wilhoit, and Longman (1998), 11–12.

115. See Genesis 12:2–3; 17:2, 6, 8; 22:16–18; 26:3–4; 28:3; 35:11–12; 47:27; 48:3–4.

116. See Genesis 2:12; Ezekiel 28:13; Moses 3:12.

117. The gold and onyx were used in both the architecture of the temple and the clothing of the high priest. See Exodus 25:7; 28:9–20; 35:9, 27; 38:24; 39:6, 13; Numbers 7:86; 1 Chronicles 29:2.

118. See Exodus 25:31–40.

119. See 1 Kings 6:29–35.

120. See Moses 5:6.

121. See Exodus 25:18–22; 26:1, 31; 36:8, 35; 37:7–9; Numbers 7:89; 1 Samuel 4:4; 2 Samuel 6:2; 1 Kings 6:23–35; 8:6–7; 2 Kings 19:15; 1 Chronicles 13:6; 2 Chronicles 3:7–14; 5:7–8; Psalm 80:1; 99:1; Isaiah 37:16; Ezekiel 41:18–25, and so on.

122. See Genesis 3:24 ; Moses 4:31; Alma 12:21; 42:2–3.

123. See Numbers 1:53.

124. See Genesis 2:15; Moses 3:15; Abraham 5:11.

125. Compare, for example, the directive in Genesis 2:17 with those in Exodus 20:1–17.

TWO

You and Me as Adam and Eve

A NUMBER OF years ago I was sitting with a former student of mine discussing various gospel questions he had. As we neared what I thought to be the end of our discussion, he asked a question that obviously had been eating at him for some time, but which he was reluctant to ask. "Why did God make Adam from dust, but Eve from Adam's rib?" I was *nearly* speechless and, frankly, shocked that he had missed the fact that this story has elements that are simply figurative.

As I began to address his concern, and as he added to the discussion, it became evident that this brother perceived the story of the Fall, as recorded in the holy temple and in scripture, as a literal, historical account void of symbolism or metaphorical intent. While I have no doubts as to the existence of Adam and Eve as historical figures and as to the historicity of the event we refer to as the Fall, nevertheless I had never supposed that one attending the temple would take as entirely literal every detail of the story told therein. In other words, I had always assumed that the fact that the temple and scriptural accounts of the Fall were laden with symbols went without saying.[1] Apparently it is not as self-evident as I had thought.

Keep in mind that the primary purpose of scripture is not to recount a historical message but rather to bring men unto Christ.[2] Prophets are, first and foremost, teachers—not historians rehearsing mundane facts and data. We cannot fully do justice to any scriptural passage if we fail to see its significance in our own lives or the life of the Church. As is so often quoted, Nephi encouraged his people to "liken" all scripture unto themselves so that the words would have profit and meaning in their lives (see 1 Nephi 19:23). Although we should not assume that *everything* in scripture is symbolic or figurative, we *should* be sensitive to the fact that to read scripture *only* for its historical content is to severely limit the power of the word in our lives. Scripture, inspired by God and given through divinely chosen prophets, is not a record of useless and insignificant details. Rather, it is instruction profitable for life and salvation. When believers read the standard works of the Church, they should look for the spiritual message—the personal application that will help them draw closer to Christ—even in passages that may seem primarily historical in nature. For example, one biblical scholar stated that the Mosaic laws and regulations are "offensive and ridiculous" if not seen in light of their "deeper symbolical meaning," that is, to make Israel more like and obedient to her God.[3]

Thus, to draw an analogy, scripture is like an ear of corn. The husk is part of the ear, but it is not the nourishing or desirable portion. It is to be peeled off, making available the more important or beneficial part of the ear—the kernels. Similarly, scripture often contains historical narratives, sacrificial rites, lengthy genealogies, and so on. But if scripture is to be of benefit to the reader, he or she must seek for application by "peeling off the husk," so to speak.[4] As interesting as the historical facts are, the spiritual message of the scriptures far outweighs their temporal message. The reader should always be on the lookout for a more profound meaning. Such is certainly the case when reading the story of the Fall—an event so important that literally hundreds of references are made to it throughout the standard works.

As noted in chapter one of this work, LDS and non-LDS scholars alike consistently describe the story of Adam and Eve as a metaphor about the personal fall of each of God's children.[5] As one Latter-day Saint scholar wrote,

From the early days of the Mormon church to the present Latter-day Saints have quite consistently taught that the text is figurative rather than literal. . . . Teachings in the doctrine of the church and the accounts given in the books of Moses, Abraham, and Genesis differ from the depiction of the . . . fall in the temple ceremony. The intent of the temple ceremony seems to be much the same as the intent of the Genesis account: to present ideas through symbols and figurative language which have many layers of meaning. . . . To interpret the visual (film) depiction of the . . . fall as only history rather than also as a figurative representation of underlying truths would deviate from the intent of the temple experience as a whole.[6]

Another commentator penned the following: "The fall [is] a prototype of all sins. . . . The snake, the woman, and the man are depicted as individuals involved in a personal crisis; rather, they are representatives. We are left with the impression that this is not their story so much as it is our story, the story of humankind."[7] Likewise, one popular Christian author wrote:

The whole story of the Fall is a parable of every sinner's experience. . . . It is generally accepted that the details [of the Fall] are to be interpreted symbolically rather than literally. . . . They are in marvelous agreement with the real facts of human nature and experience. Adam is the representative of the human race. . . . When [a man] reads this narrative, his conscience says to him, like a prophet of God: "Thou art the man; the story is told of thee!"[8]

With this notion that the story of the Fall is about you and me and our personal fall from grace, what follows in the remaining pages of this chapter is an examination of the scriptural accounts of the Fall. In light of the overwhelming evidence that this is story, our intent is to examine the story in order to find personal meaning in the Fall. We will examine verse by verse this oft-told story in an effort to see what it is the story of the Fall can teach us about how we might return to the God who gave us life.

The Creation of Adam and Eve

Genesis 1:27	Moses 2:27	Moses 6:9
So God created man In his own image, in the image of God created he him; male and female created he them.	And I, God, created man in mine own image, in the image of mine only Begotten created I him; male and female created I them.	In the image of his own body, male and female, created he them, and blessed them, and called their name Adam, in the day when they were created and became living souls in the land upon the footstool of God.

Created in the image of God. As with Adam and Eve, you and I were created in the image of God. President Spencer W. Kimball stated on numerous occasions: "We are gods in embryo."[9] Indeed, we are God's creations, His children, His offspring. Our resurrected Father in Heaven made us in His image—in the image "of his own body" (Moses 6:9). President Ezra Taft Benson noted: "As God's offspring, we have His attributes in us. We are gods in embryo, and thus have an unlimited potential for progress and attainment."[10] C. S. Lewis once wrote: "It is a serious thing to live in a society of possible gods and goddesses, to remember that the dullest and most uninteresting person you can talk to may one day be a creature which, if you saw it now, you would be strongly tempted to worship."[11] Living up to this potential—this divine commission—is our great quest and challenge. Is it not appropriate to ask, in what we say and do, can others see in us a strong resemblance to our Father? And just as the fish, birds, and beasts were to be "after their kind" (Genesis 1; 6; Moses 2; Abraham 4), we too are called to be "after our kind" (i.e., to be like God and Christ).[12]

Called their name Adam. Here it is evident that the name is not always a personal name. Prior to the Fall, its use in Eden was traditionally calculated to mean both the man and the woman— Adam Eve. Similarly, the scriptures often use the name-title *Adam* in reference to the whole of the human race. Thus, the Lord calls "their name" Adam (Moses 6:9). And hence, you and I are represented by those two divinely chosen beings.

Genesis 2:7	Moses 3:7	Abraham 5:7
And the Lord God formed man of the dust of the ground, and breathed into his nostrils the breath of life; and man became a living soul.	And I, the Lord God, formed man from the dust of the ground, and breathed into his nostrils the breath of life; and man became a living soul, the first flesh upon the earth, the first man also; nevertheless, all things were before created; but spiritually were they created and made according to my word.	And the Gods formed man from the dust of the ground, and took his spirit (that is, the man's spirit), and put it into him; and breathed into his nostrils the breath of life, and man became a living soul.

From the dust of the ground. Many biblical scholars have noted that the name *Adam* means literally "earth" or "soil."[13] Thus, Philo of Alexandria suggested that when we hear the name *Adam* in the scriptures, it is to remind us of that which is perishable, earthly, or temporary.[14] And so it is with us. We are each appropriately called Adam because we are earthly and perishable. From the dust we were made, and to that dust our mortal bodies will one day return (see Genesis 3:19). In addition, since the earth is a standard symbol for things that are temporal, worldly, or temporary in nature,[15] it is possible that this figurative description of the origin of man serves to highlight both our carnal or worldly nature and also the temporary nature of the mortal experience.

A living soul. The placement of our spirits in our tabernacles is that which gives us mortal life. But even as mortals, we are but dust—indeed, less than the dust of the earth (see Mosiah 4:2; Helaman 12:7). It is the receipt of the Holy Spirit that makes us most fully "alive." Having that Spirit breathed into our lives makes us "alive in Christ" (2 Nephi 25:25; see Moroni 8:12, 22). Thus, one third-century Christian writer wrote:

> Man . . . was made from different and opposite substances [i.e., dust and spirit] . . . [and] these two things contend against each other in man: so that if the [spirit of man], which has its origin from God, gains the mastery, it is immortal, and lives in perpetual light; if, on

the other hand, the body shall overpower the [spirit], and subject it to its dominion, it is in everlasting darkness and death . . . [and will subject] them to everlasting punishment.[16]

After his placement in Eden, Adam is said to be like a little child. We have already established that Adam and Eve were not as little children in their intellect or understanding, either during their time in Eden or after the Fall.[17] They were, however, as little children in their purity, humility, righteousness, and closeness to the Father. You and I, on the other hand, are aptly represented by the phrase "having become as a little child." When each of us is sent to this mortal proving ground we forget all and begin our mortal journey as little children. All memory of our premortal existence is erased, and we are placed under the watchful care of the Father and also under the protective covering of Christ's Atonement—at least until we reach the age of accountability. Thus, Adam's creation is really a foreshadowing of our creation and of the state of innocence in which we enter this world.

Genesis 2:8–9	Moses 3:8–9	Abraham 5:8–9
And the Lord God planted a garden eastward in Eden; and there he put the man whom he had formed, And out of the ground made the Lord God to grow every tree that is pleasant to the sight, and good for food; the tree of life also in the midst of the garden, and the tree of knowledge of good and evil.	And I, the Lord God, planted a garden eastward in Eden, and there I put the man whom I had formed. And out of the ground made I, the Lord God, to grow every tree, naturally, that is pleasant to the sight of man; and man could behold it. And it became also a living soul. For it was spiritual in the day that I created it; for it remaineth in the sphere in which I, God, created it, yea, even all things which I prepared for the use of man; and man saw that it was good for food. And I, the Lord God, planted the tree of life also in the midst of the garden, and also the tree of knowledge of good and evil.	And the Gods planted a garden, eastward in Eden, and there they put the man, whose spirit they had put into the body which they had formed. And out of the ground made the Gods to grow every tree that is pleasant to the sight and good for food; the tree of life, also in the midst of the garden, and the tree of knowledge of good and evil.

Eastward in Eden. In ancient times the direction east commonly represented God's abode or God's presence.[18] Thus, that which came from the east was perceived as coming from God, being godly in nature, or having been sent by God.[19] Here we learn that Eden was in the east, or, in other words, it was in the presence of God. Thus, Adam and Eve walked with, talked to, and were instructed by the Father while there. Eden functioned as a temple for our first parents.[20] For us, the temple is Eden, and it is the earthly abode of God. It is a place of communion for those who are worthy to enter. And, as Eden was for Adam and Eve, the temple (for us) can function as a refuge from "the lone and dreary world," as well as a school in which we can be taught the will of the Lord.

In the midst of the garden. Each of our accounts indicates that at the center of Eden was found the "tree of life" and the "tree of knowledge of good and evil"—highlighting the fact that good and evil are ever present before us during this mortal probation. We need the opposition provided by the "tree of knowledge of good and evil," or the principle of agency could not fully function, and you and I could not grow as God intended. One commentator wisely noted: "Observe that the tempting fruit was placed in the midst of the garden, not in some secluded corner. It was not God's plan to exclude the forbidden fruit from man's view. The plan of life requires that man meet temptation and overcome it."[21] This doctrine is clearly taught in the Book of Mormon (see 2 Nephi 2:11).

As much as we need the enticement of the "tree of knowledge" as a central part of the plan, we also need Christ (symbolized by the "tree of life," 1 Nephi 11:8–21) at the center of our lives so that we are not overcome by the enticings of Satan. Christ's central role in the plan of salvation, the scriptures, and the temple highlights for the observant Christian the imperative need to ever keep him at the center of all we think and do.

The tree of life and the tree of knowledge. Eden had many trees. However, only two are highlighted—the tree of knowledge of good and evil, and the tree of life. These two trees represent our two choices: obedience to God or obedience to our own will. Partaking of the fruit of each tree has a consequence. Elder Bruce C. Hafen wrote:

The *tree of knowledge* (learning through mortal, sometimes bitter, experience) and the *tree of life* (the Father's sweet bestowal of forgiveness and a divine character) are necessary for us to find fulfillment and meaning. Neither tree—neither force—is sufficient unless completed by the other. . . . In the beginning, the Lord God taught this vision of life's nature and purpose to Adam and Eve. To symbolize these teachings, he placed two trees in the Garden of Eden: *the tree of knowledge and the tree of life.* The fruit of the first tree seemed desirable, but it became bitter as it led to the knowledge of good and evil. The second tree was sweet, and it led to a fulness of Godlike life. We, like Adam and Eve, taste the bitter fruit of the first tree that we may know to prize the sweet fruit of the second tree. . . . The mortal learning experience, represented by the *tree of knowledge*, is so necessary that God placed cherubim and a flaming sword to guard the way of the *tree of life* until Adam and Eve completed, and we, their posterity, complete this preparatory schooling. Our tutorial is the gospel, a schoolmaster that brings us to Christ. But he cannot fully receive us and give us the gift of celestial life—partaking of God's very nature—until we have *learned by our own experience* to distinguish good from evil.[22]

THE FIRST COMMANDMENT

Genesis 1:28	Moses 2:28	Abraham 4:28
And God blessed them, and God said unto them, Be fruitful, and multiply, and replenish the earth, and subdue it; and have dominion over the fish of the sea, and over the fowl of the air, and over every living thing that moveth upon the earth.	And I, God, blessed them, and said unto them: Be fruitful, and multiply, and replenish the earth, and subdue it, and have dominion over the fish of the sea, and over the fowl of the air, and over every living thing that moveth upon the earth.	And the Gods said: We will bless them. And the Gods said: We will cause them to be fruitful and multiply, and replenish the earth, and subdue it, and to have dominion over the fish of the sea, and over the fowl of the air, and over every living thing that moveth upon the earth.

Multiply and replenish the earth. We live in a time when modern society sees these words as antiquated and irrelevant. Indeed, in a twist of irony, those who curtail their families for selfish reasons—careers and money being chief among them—claim that those who are obedient to this command are the selfish ones. Cries of "overpopulation" and "the depletion of resources" are heard, even though numerous countries actually have a zero or negative population growth.[23] Contrary to the reasoning of man, the Lord has said:

> I, the Lord, have decreed to provide for my saints, that the poor shall be exalted, in that the rich are made low.
>
> For the earth is full, and there is enough and to spare; yea, I prepared all things, and have given unto the children of men to be agents unto themselves.
>
> Therefore, if any man shall take of the abundance which I have made, and impart not his portion, according to the law of my gospel, unto the poor and the needy, he shall, with the wicked, lift up his eyes in hell, being in torment. (Doctrine and Covenants 104:16–18)

Selfishness often keeps us from being obedient to God's commands. And yet through that selfishness we actually rob ourselves of the very blessings the commandments were designed to provide. One commentator noted: "The greatest opportunity of all, to learn eternal values and achieve heavenly potentials, resides in the responsibility and the privilege to create bodies for others of God's spirit children."[24] We grow and become more like God when we are obedient to His command to each of us to create tabernacles for our brothers and sisters who are awaiting their chance at mortality. The First Presidency of the Church wrote:

> The Lord has told us that it is the duty of every husband and wife to obey the command given to Adam to multiply and replenish the earth, so that the legions of choice spirits waiting for their tabernacles of flesh may come here and move forward under God's great design to become perfect souls, for without these fleshly tabernacles they cannot progress to their God planned destiny. Thus, every husband and wife should become a father and a mother in Israel to children born under the holy, eternal covenant.[25]

Genesis 2:10	Moses 3:10	Abraham 5:10
And a river went out of Eden to water the garden; and from thence it was parted, and became into four heads.	And I, the Lord God, caused a river to go out of Eden to water the garden; and from thence it was parted, and became into four heads.	There was a river running out of Eden, to water the garden, and from thence it was parted and became into four heads.

A river parting into four heads. We are told that a river flowed from Eden into four different directions. In Hebrew culture the number four meant "geographic fullness" or "totality."[26] Thus, the experiences of Eden apply to the totality of mankind.[27] All have fallen, and all must get back to the presence of God in order to partake of the tree of life. One commentator noted that this Edenic river is a fine symbol of the vitality, strength, and life that flows from holy ground.[28] Thus, if we are found on holy ground (e.g., the temple, the Church, a service project, and eventually Zion), we too shall enjoy spiritual vitality, strength, and life.

Genesis 2:15	Moses 3:15	Abraham 5:11
And the Lord God took the man, and put him into the garden of Eden to dress it and to keep it.	And I, the Lord God, took the man, and put him into the Garden of Eden, to dress it, and to keep it.	And the Gods took the man and put him in the Garden of Eden, to dress it and to keep it.

God placed Adam in the garden. While in its native environment (the ocean), the chambered nautilus—a mollusk distantly related to the snail—can withstand upwards of nine hundred pounds of pressure per square inch without sustaining any harm to its shell or the organism within. However, when removed from the ocean it becomes extremely fragile and is easily broken.[29] By analogy, we are informed that Adam was not made in Eden, but rather was brought to this earth to dwell and be tried.[30]

Adam and Eve do not belong in this telestial world. They increasingly feel like "strangers and pilgrims" in proportion to their understanding of their plight and their potential (Hebrews 11:13; see also 1 Peter 2:11; Doctrine and Covenants 45:13). Still, this dangerous environment helps them exercise agency, and thus they gain the knowledge that only independent experience brings (see Doctrine and Covenants 93:30–31).[31]

The earth was not Adam's home. He was a visitor; a temporary resident. Such is the case with each of us. We are not home. We are visitors here in this foreign land. We are dwelling in a world, an environment, that makes us fragile indeed.[32] It has been noted that when Adam and Eve fell, humans lost certain powers and gifts that they had originally possessed—powers and gifts that would have made us stronger and protected us from the dangers of this fallen world.[33] True, through the Fall mankind has gained the power of procreation. However, certain spiritual gifts and powers that were originally ours have been forfeited. As a result, mankind finds itself subject to certain mortal influences prevailing in this telestial world.

> Spiritual powers which were part of his original organization were powers of life, and he therefore had vigor of body and power of mind that he no longer enjoys. As a physical-spiritual being, he was organized to endure forever. But now he has no power, in the ultimate sense, over death and its deteriorating influences; and sickness and disease at times reduce him to a state of misery and pain. While man resided in the presence of God, he had access to the spiritual powers and attributes that constitute God's glory. For this reason, he probably had the ability to see as Moses saw while upon the mountain and to learn as other great prophets have learned when quickened by the glory of God. But as a temporal being, man is largely reduced to the ability to learn only through the physical senses, unless he has or acquires faith to obtain the revelations of the Holy Spirit.[34]

One Latter-day Saint author noted, "To Adam and Eve, accustomed to dwelling in . . . light, this mortal world must have seemed a frightening, unenlightened place."[35] So it is with us.

Dress and keep it. A number of messages can be seen in God's command to Adam to "dress" and "keep" the garden. One commentator suggested that it means no one was sent to earth to be idle. In addition, it may well suggest that secular employment can be compatible with a spiritual life; for clearly the passage indicates that the occupations of farmer, agronomist, or horticulturist are ancient and honorable.[36] An individual can find true pleasure in whatever business God calls him or her to.[37] Also note that "the place appointed for Adam's residence was a garden, not an ivory house nor a palace overlaid with gold, but a garden . . . intended for the mansion and estate of this great lord, the palace of this prince."[38] Like the Savior, Adam too was born into humble circumstances. And in these humble circumstances he was to take delight (for *Eden* means "delight"). This is a clarion call to the Saints to live lives of simplicity rather than excess, humility rather than extravagance. They are to delight in the things of God and be content with the simple things of life.

Commentators on the Hebrew have noted that the words translated in the King James Version as "dress" and "keep" can also be translated "to worship and obey."[39] As one of the repercussions of the Fall was to have to till and take care of the earth (Genesis 3:23; Moses 4:29), this alternate translation makes more sense. Hence, we read: "To till and keep the garden means to believe in God and to keep the commandments."[40] It means to cultivate the virtues God has commanded and to resolve to never desert them.[41] One fifth-century Christian text states: "Tilling the earth, keeping the commandments of God and fidelity to those commandments was the 'labor' of God. . . . 'Work' was keeping the spiritual words. . . . The text says 'work' [i.e., 'till'] and 'protect it.' From what? There were no thieves, travelers or people with bad intentions. 'Protect it' from what? From himself. Do not lose it by transgressing the command."[42] You and I have been sent here for this same purpose—to see if we will "till and take care," or "worship and obey." We must be cautious that we, through transgression, do not lose the blessings God has in store for us. Finally, we are also stewards over this earth; a stewardship for which we will have to someday give an accounting before God.[43]

The Second Commandment

Genesis 2:16–17	Moses 3:16–17	Abraham 5:12–13
And the Lord God commanded the man, saying, Of every tree of the garden thou mayest freely eat: But of the tree of knowledge of good and evil, thou shalt not eat of it: for in the day that thou eatest thereof thou shalt surely die.	And I, the Lord God, commanded the man, saying: Of every tree of the garden thou mayest freely eat, But of the tree of the knowledge of good and evil, thou shalt not eat of it, nevertheless, thou mayest choose for thyself, for it is given unto thee; but, remember that I forbid it, for in the day thou eatest thereof thou shalt surely die.	And the Gods commanded the man saying: Of every tree of the garden thou mayest freely eat, But of the tree of knowledge of good and evil, thou shalt not eat of it; for in the time that thou eatest thereof, thou shalt surely die. Now I, Abraham, saw that it was after the Lord's time, which was after the time of Kolob; for as yet the Gods had not appointed unto Adam his reckoning.

Thou shalt not eat of it. Scripture records two commandments given by the Father to Adam and Eve. The first command was for our first parents to "multiply" and "replenish" the earth (see Genesis 1:28; Moses 2:28; Abraham 4:28). The second command, given here, was that they were not to eat of the fruit of the tree of knowledge of good and evil.[44]

As we have noted, all too frequently these two dictates (Genesis 1:28; 2:16–17) have been labeled as "contradictory commandments." However, if this metaphor is about you and me, then there is no contradiction in these two commandments. Although Adam and Eve *had to* partake of the "forbidden" fruit in order to multiply, you and I, on the other hand, needn't do so. On the contrary, we are commanded to multiply and replenish the earth, all the while being expected to *avoid* partaking of that which has been forbidden. And you and I *are* capable of keeping both of these commandments at the same time.

Significantly, the two commandments that they were given are the same two options all of Adam's posterity are given when they kneel at an altar in the temple and enter into the new and everlasting covenant of marriage.

Adam and Eve's first option was to stay in Eden and enjoy themselves and their paradisiacal surroundings. This, of course, might bring them some small degree of pleasure. However, it would also prevent humankind from being born. Similarly, our first "option"— if it can even be called such—is to be self-serving and put off having a family until we've done all that we want to do and have obtained all that we wish to obtain.

Adam and Eve's second option was to sacrifice the luxury and ease of Eden so that you and I could be born. Likewise, the second option for you and me is to sacrifice what we want and what the world tells us that we should and must have, in order that others may have a chance at mortality and exaltation. Adam and Eve's choice was really to have a family or not have a family. Hence, Adam says, "I will partake that man may be!"[45]

It was mentioned above that prior to partaking of the fruit of the tree of knowledge of good and evil, Adam could not die. Thus, when he ate of the other fruits of the Garden, he did so not to sustain his life, but for enjoyment or pleasure. Thus, the eating of the "forbidden" fruit aptly symbolizes our choice to do things that are forbidden but that we *think* will bring us pleasure.[46] In the end, however, sinful choices rob us of the pleasures God has in store. As one early church father noted: "It was not the tree, as some think but the disobedience, which had death in it."[47]

At about the same time as Christ was fulfilling His mortal ministry, Philo of Alexandria wrote: "The recommendations that [God] addresses to [Adam] are as follows: 'Of every tree that is in the Paradise thou mayest freely eat.' [In other words, God] exhorts the soul of man to derive advantage not from one tree alone nor from one single virtue, but from all the virtues; for eating is a symbol of the nourishment of the soul, and the soul is nourished by the reception of good things, and by the doing of praiseworthy actions."[48] As Peter encouraged:

> Add to your faith virtue; and to virtue knowledge;
> And to knowledge temperance; and to temperance patience; and
> to patience godliness;

And to godliness brotherly kindness; and to brotherly kindness charity.

For if these things be in you, and abound, they make you that ye shall neither be barren nor unfruitful in the knowledge of our Lord Jesus Christ.

But he that lacketh these things is blind, and cannot see afar off, and hath forgotten that he was purged from his old sins.

Wherefore the rather, brethren, give diligence to make your calling and election sure: for if ye do these things, ye shall never fall. (2 Peter 1:5–10)

The Lord invites us to freely partake of the virtues offered us through the restored gospel. Only by so doing can our election be made sure. We must be "anxiously engaged" in bringing to pass "much righteousness," not only in the world, but in our own lives (see Doctrine and Covenants 58:27). We have been commanded to "seek . . . earnestly the best gifts" (Doctrine and Covenants 46:8). As in Eden, so also in our own lives, these are freely available to us as we, like Adam and Eve, keep ourselves on hallowed ground.

Genesis 2:18	Moses 3:18	Abraham 5:14
And the Lord God said, It is not good that the man should be alone; I will make him an help meet for him.	And I, the Lord God, said unto mine Only Begotten, that it was not good that the man should be alone; wherefore, I will make an help meet for him.	And the Gods said: Let us make an help meet for the man, for it is not good that the man should be alone, therefore we will form an help meet for him.

A help meet for man. Traditionally the title *help meet* is understood to mean "a helper fit for him,"[49] "a helper like-the-opposite-of-him,"[50] or "a help corresponding to him."[51] In other words, it suggests an equal, but opposite, half of the whole. It does not, as some have supposed, mean a servant-helper or an inferior.[52] Thus the ideal relationship, as depicted in Eden, consists of man and woman—husband and wife—being perfectly one: two halves of the same whole! Adam and Eve represent the ideal marriage, the marriage each of us is commissioned to seek. The wife is to be a blessing to her husband, and the husband a blessing to his wife. Each will have different roles, and each will be a blessing to the other in entirely different ways. The blessings they willingly—not begrudgingly—shower upon each other will make them one in every sense of the word. In the third century AD, one staunch defender of the Christian faith noted that God provided Adam with Eve because He knew what a blessing woman would be to man and to the Church.[53] More recently, one Protestant commentator penned the following: "He who has a good God, a good heart, and a good wife, to converse with, and yet complains he lacks conversation, would not have been easy and content in paradise."[54]

Genesis 2:19–20	Moses 3:19–20	Abraham 5:20
And out of the ground the Lord God formed every beast of the field and every fowl of the air; and brought them unto Adam to see what he would call them: and whatsoever Adam called every living creature, that was the name thereof. And Adam gave names to all cattle and to the fowl of the air, and to every beast of the field; but for Adam there was not found an help meet for him.	And out of the ground I, the Lord God, formed every beast of the field, and every fowl of the air; and commanded that they should come unto Adam, to see what he would call them; and they were also living souls, for I, God, breathed into them the breath of life, and commanded that whatsoever Adam called every living creature, that should be the name thereof. And Adam gave names to all cattle, and to the fowl of the air, and to every beast of the field; but as for Adam, there was not found an help meet for him.	And out of the ground the Gods formed every beast of the field, and every fowl of the air, and brought them unto Adam to see what he would call them; and whatsoever Adam called every living creature, that should be the name thereof.

Adam named every living creature. Adam's naming of the animals is said to have taken place "in order that God might make known [both] the wisdom of Adam and [also] the harmony that

existed between the animals and Adam before he transgressed. . . .
They were neither afraid of him nor were they afraid of each other. A
species of predatory animals would pass by with a species of animal
that is preyed upon following safely right behind."[55] Such will be
the case again when this earth returns to its Edenic or paradisiacal
splendor during the Millennium. Animals will no longer have need
to fear you and me, nor will we seek shelter from the predatory or
the poisonous.

Allegorizing the passage in the late fourth-century, Ambrose
suggested that the beasts of the field and the birds of the air can
symbolize our "irrational senses" and the "diverse passions of the
body"—both those impassioned and those temperate. According to
Ambrose, God brings them to our attention, just as He brought the
animals to the attention of Adam, all in the hopes that we will realize that we are superior to those base cravings that provoke our fall
from grace.[56]

One commentary on this passage notes: "In giving names to
earth's creatures, [Adam] would establish his dominion over them."[57]
Although God gave Adam (or mankind) dominion over the animals,
with that stewardship comes responsibility and accountability.[58]
Notice that the animals were formed Adam and Eve. Of this reality,
one Jewish scholar wrote: "The world was made for man, though he
was the last-comer among its creatures. . . . Man's late appearance on
earth is to convey an admonition to humility."[59] We too are called
to a life of humility and selflessness; in relation to each other and in
relation to God's other creations.

The fact that Adam came after the animals can also highlight
that humans are the only ones created in God's image. As royalty
always enters a scene last, you and I, being made in the image of the
divine King, are ourselves divinity or royalty in embryo.

Finally, as each of the animals passed by Adam, surely he could
see both his superiority to them and also that he was the only one
who was like God. We too are to remember that only we are created
in the image of God; and thus the Father has an expectation as to
how we will live our lives (i.e., in the image and pattern of His life
and that of His Only Begotten Son).

Genesis 2:21–24	Moses 3:21–24	Abraham 5:15–18
And the Lord God caused a deep sleep to fall upon Adam, and he slept: and he took one of his ribs, and closed up the flesh instead thereof; And the rib, which the Lord God had taken from man, made he a woman, and brought her unto the man. And Adam said, This is now bone of my bones, and flesh of my flesh: she shall be called Woman, because she was taken out of Man. Therefore shall a man leave his father and his mother, and shall cleave unto his wife: and they shall be one flesh.	And I, the Lord God, cased a deep sleep to fall upon Adam; and he slept, and I took one of his ribs and closed up the flesh in the stead thereof; And the rib which I, the Lord God, had taken from man, made I a woman, and brought her unto the man. And Adam said: This I know now is bone of my bones, and flesh of my flesh; she shall be called Woman, because she was taken out of man. Therefore shall a man leave his father and his mother, and shall cleave unto his wife; and they shall be one flesh.	And the Gods caused a deep sleep to fall upon Adam; and he slept, and they took one of his ribs, and closed up the flesh in the stead thereof; And the rib which the Gods had taken from man, formed they a woman, and brought her unto the man. And Adam said: This was bone of my bones, and flesh of my flesh; now she shall be called Woman, because she was taken out of man; Therefore shall a man leave his father and his mother, and shall cleave unto his wife, and they shall be one flesh.

Deep sleep. The "deep sleep" referred to here has been taken, among other things, as a representation of Adam's resignation to God's will and His divine and wise counsel.[60] There is no struggle or fight against God. You and I too must resign ourselves to God's will. We must not fight His workings in our lives. The oft-quoted words of Elder Neal A. Maxwell seem germane:

> The submission of one's will is really the only uniquely personal thing we have to place on God's altar. The many other things we "give" . . . are actually the things He has already given or loaned to us. However, when you and I finally submit ourselves, by letting our individual wills be swallowed up in God's will, then we are really giving something to Him! It is the only possession which is truly ours to give![61]

Adam's rib. Late in the fourth-century Ambrose penned this: "Not without significance, too, is the fact that woman was made out of the rib of Adam. She was not made out of the same earth with which he was formed."[62] Thus from the very beginning it became clear that men and women are different in their makeup and nature.

Augustine reasoned that the fact that the man was made first, and that the woman was made from the man, indicates that from the beginning the patriarchal ordering of families was intended. The man was to preside in righteousness in the home. Were such not the case, he suggested, the woman would have been made first.[63]

Drawing on his training as a medical doctor, Elder Russell M. Nelson of the Council of the Twelve stated:

> From the rib of Adam, Eve was formed (see Genesis 2:22; Moses 3:22; Abraham 5:16). Interesting to me is the fact that animals fashioned by our Creator, such as dogs and cats, have thirteen pairs of ribs, but the human being has one less with only twelve. I presume another bone could have been used, but the rib, coming as it does from the side, seems to denote partnership. The rib signifies neither dominion nor subservience, but a lateral relationship as partners, to work and to live, side by side.[64]

Similarly, Judaism holds that the woman was made from the rib of man so that man would remember to love his wife as himself. Thus, Paul said: "So ought men to love their wives as their own bodies. He that loveth his wife loveth himself" (Ephesians 5:28). The following has become somewhat of a colloquial interpretation of the rib metaphor: Eve was "not made out of his head to rule over him, nor out of his feet to be trampled on by him, but out of his side to be equal with him, under his arm to be protected, and near his heart to be beloved."[65]

Others have seen in this rib metaphor—and Eve's symbolic origins in Adam's body—a message about the "indissoluble" oneness of husband and wife. The metaphor suggests that human existence is intended to be a partnership of man and woman. As noted above, "the story of the creation of Eve . . . is symbolical of marriage."[66]

Genesis 2:25	Moses 3:25	Abraham 5:19
And they were both naked, the man and his wife, and were not ashamed.	And they were both naked, the man and his wife, and were not ashamed.	And they were both naked, the man and his wife, and were not ashamed.

Naked and yet not ashamed. When the metaphorical or symbolic aspects of the scriptural accounts of the Fall are missed, readers tend to interpret the nakedness of Adam and Eve as evidence that they were intellectually infantile. However, scripture is intending to make no such claim about our first parents. On the contrary, God held them accountable for their choices in Eden, which establishes that Adam and Eve knew what they were doing. You and I, on the other hand, begin this mortal test "naked and unashamed." In our childhood we are innocent, unassuming, and infantile.

Nakedness can also be a symbol for being unashamed. Scripture informs us that when we are righteous our "confidence [will] wax strong in the presence of God" (Doctrine and Covenants 121:45). We feel no fear of judgment or condemnation. One fourth-century Christian commentary states: "They were not ashamed because of the glory with which they were clothed. It was when this glory was stripped from them after they had transgressed the commandment that they were ashamed because they were naked."[67] The nakedness of Adam and Eve, without shame, prior to the Fall, highlights our feelings of confidence when we are keeping the Lord's words, commands, and covenants.

The Temptation of Adam and Eve

Genesis 3:1–5	Moses 4:5–11	2 Nephi 2:17–18
Now the serpent was more subtil than any beast of the field which the Lord God had made, And he said unto the woman, Yea, hath God said, Ye shall not eat of every tree of the garden? And the woman said unto the serpent, We may eat of the fruit of the trees of the garden: But of the fruit of the tree which is in the midst of the garden, God hath said, Ye shall not eat of it, neither shall ye touch it, lest ye die. And the serpent said unto the woman, Ye shall not surely die: For God doth know that in the day ye eat thereof, then your eyes shall be opened, and ye shall be as gods, knowing good and evil.	And now the serpent was more subtle than any beast of the field which I, the Lord God, had made. And Satan put it into the heart of the serpent, (for he had drawn away many after him,) and he sought also to beguile Eve, for he knew not the mind of God, wherefore he sought to destroy the world. And he said unto the woman: Yea, hath God said—Ye shall not eat of every tree of the garden? (And he spake by the mouth of the serpent.) And the woman said the serpent: We may eat of the fruit of the trees of the garden; But of the fruit of the tree which thou beholdest in the midst of the garden, God hath said—Ye shall not eat of it, neither shall ye touch it, lest ye die. And the serpent said unto the woman: Ye shall not surely die; For God doth know that in the day ye eat thereof, then your eyes shall be opened, and ye shall be as gods, knowing good and evil.	And I, Lehi, according to the things which I have read, must needs suppose that an angel of God, according to that which is written, had fallen from heaven; wherefore, he became a devil, having sought that which was evil before God. And because he had fallen from heaven and had become miserable forever, he sought also the misery of all mankind. Wherefore, he said unto Eve, yea, even that old serpent, who is the devil who is the father of all lies, wherefore he said: Partake of the forbidden fruit, and ye shall not die, but ye shall be as God, knowing good and evil.

The serpent approached Adam and Eve. In chapter five of this work we will examine who it was that approached Adam and Eve (i.e., Lucifer or the serpent). However, as the story pertains to our personal fall, "the gliding stealthy movement of the serpent is a fitting symbol of the insidious progress of temptation."[68] According to one legend, Satan was restricted to the outside of Eden until Eve "opened the gate" and let him in.[69] Such is certainly the case in our own lives. As the Prophet Joseph noted, "The devil has no power over us only as we permit him."[70] Satan seeks invitation from each of us that he might enter our lives. As soon as we open the door, he seeks to wreak havoc. But if we keep the door to temptation locked tight, the adversary of all mankind has no access to our hearts. President Spencer W. Kimball stated: "The powerful Lucifer has his day. He whispers into man's ears. Some reject his enticing offers, others yield. Satan whispers, 'This is no sin. You are no transgressor. I am no devil. There is no evil one. There is no black. All is white.'"[71]

Augustine noted that Satan, the father of sin, fell from grace in the premortal world through giving in to pride. He has since taken his own vice and utilized it against God's children here in mortality. It is commonly thought that Satan's words to Adam and Eve (i.e., "Ye shall be as gods") were an effort at appealing to their pride or vanity.[72] Augustine wrote: "Whoever seeks to be . . . self-sufficing, . . . retreats from the One who is truly sufficient for him."[73] It is our prideful desires that cause us to sin against God and to lose our inheritance in the Eden that God has in store for each of us. The story of the Fall indicates that it is through pride that each of us falls. Thus, the posterity of Adam and Eve will be able to return to God only through displacing their pride with Spirit-born humility.[74] "For man sinned in wishing to . . . be free from [God's] dominion, as God is free from all dominion, since he is the Lord of all."[75]

Neither shall ye touch it. As the story is told, Adam and Eve were not only commanded to abstain from eating the forbidden fruit, they were also prohibited from even touching it "lest they become entrapped."[76] It is very much the old adage, "Don't play with fire." Those inclined toward an allegorical interpretation of scripture tend to see Eve's eating the fruit as symbolic of thinking about sinning or entertaining sinful thoughts. Adam's eating, according to that school of thought, might then symbolize the physical act of sin that only comes because of the previous act of pondering sin.[77] One follows the other. If you can control your thoughts, you'll control your actions. Thus, Ambrose taught that the serpent is a symbol for the pleasures of the body. The woman stands for our senses and the man for our minds. Pleasure stirs the senses, which in turn have their effect on the mind.[78] Similarly, Protestant commentator Matthew Henry wrote, "Those who would not eat the forbidden fruit must not come near the forbidden tree."[79] On a related note, there is a popular Jewish legend that is found in a number of sources.

The serpent pushed Eve against the tree, and [then] said: "Thou seest that touching the tree has not caused thy death. As little will it hurt thee to eat the fruit of the tree. . . ." To give due weight to these words, the serpent began to shake the tree violently and bring down its fruit. He [then] ate thereof, saying: "As I do not die of eating the fruit, so wilt thou not die." . . . [Eve then] made a compromise with her conscience. First she ate only the outside skin of the fruit, and then, seeing that death did not fell her, she ate the fruit itself.[80]

This is what Satan seeks to get us to do, namely, watch others sin with what appears to be no consequence, all in the hope that we will heed his devilish promptings and partake of that which has been forbidden. We must remember that the Lord has forbidden us to flirt with temptation just as much as He has forbidden us to give in to temptation. Lucifer's methodology in tempting Eve has a very familiar ring to it. It mirrors his techniques in tempting each of us.

First of all, the devil seeks to raise questions regarding the integrity of God. He "sows discord between man and his maker by misrepresenting God's character."[81] He attacks our mental picture of the Father. God is a fiend, rather than a friend, the devil suggests. How selfish of Him to put limitations on what we can eat. Does he not understand how to share?[82] Commentators have noted Lucifer's incredulous tone—"So God has actually said . . . ?" Satan seeks to incite a reassessment of God's instructions and commands.[83] This is his daily attack plan with each of us. He wants each of us to see God, His commandments, and those appointed to enforce them (e.g., priesthood leaders and parents) as oppressive dictators, selfishly trying to control us.

His second technique, very much related to this first one, is to encourage autonomy. You have agency! You have the right to choose for yourself. Lucifer suggests that God and His agents are simply trying to oppress you, and so His commandment is absurd and irrelevant.[84] You know just as well as the prophet, the bishop, or your parents what's best for you. Matthew Henry described Lucifer's methodology this way:

1. Satan calls into question the idea that eating the fruit is indeed a sin, suggesting perhaps Eve has misunderstood (Genesis 3:1). "It is the subtlety of Satan to blemish the reputation of the divine law as uncertain or unreasonable, and so to draw people to sin."

2. The devil denies that there is any danger in eating the fruit (Genesis 3:4). "Satan teaches men first to doubt and then to deny; he makes them skeptics first, and so by degrees makes them atheists."

3. Our adversary suggests that there are great advantages to be had by eating the fruit (Genesis 3:5). "After all, how do you think God got so smart? Eat this and you'll become just like Him!"

Thus, that which is depicted regarding Eve is clearly the experience of every man and every woman.[85] Satan acts no differently with us. Yet, tragically, so many never seem to learn the lesson taught in Eden.

In actuality, there is no scriptural record of the Father saying "ye shall not touch" the tree. Thus, you and I are depicted as Eve being drawn in by the adversary's criticism of the Father, adding the phrase herself, in an apparent attempt at magnifying or adding to God's strictness.[86] Such is the tendency of most of us.[87] When we are unhappy with one of the commands of God we tend to exaggerate God's unfairness and strictness. The ever-popular C. S. Lewis wrote:

> How did the Dark Power [Lucifer] go wrong? . . . The moment you have a self at all, there is a possibility of putting yourself first—wanting to be the center—wanting to be God, in fact. That was the sin of Satan [in the premortal Grand Council]: and that was the sin he taught the human race [during the Fall]. . . . What Satan put into the heads of our remote ancestors was the idea that they could "be like gods"—could set up on their own as if they had created themselves— be their own masters—invent some sort of happiness for themselves outside God, apart from God. And out of that hopeless attempt has

come nearly all that we call human history—money, poverty, ambition, war, prostitution, classes, empires, slavery—the long terrible story of man trying to find something other than God which will make him happy.[88]

The sin is *not* in wishing to become like God. The sin is in attempting to do so without God, in attempting to usurp His position over us, and in attempting to do so aside from the path He has laid out for us through entrance into covenants and obedience to commandments.

Genesis 3:6–8	Moses 4:12–14	Doctrine and Covenants 29:39
And when the woman saw that the tree was good for food, and that it was pleasant to the eyes, and a tree to be desired to make one wise, she took of the fruit thereof, and did eat, and gave also unto her husband with her; and he did eat. And the eyes of them both were opened, and they knew that they were naked; and they sewed fig leaves together, and made themselves aprons. And they heard the voice of the Lord God walking in the garden in the cool of day: and Adam and his wife hid themselves from the presence of the Lord God amongst the trees of the garden.	And when the woman saw that the tree was good for food, and that it became pleasant to the eyes, and a tree to be desired to make her wise, she took of the fruit thereof, and did eat, and also gave unto her husband with her, and he did eat. And the eyes of them both were opened, and they knew that they had been naked. And they sewed fig leaves together and made themselves aprons. And they heard the voice of the Lord God, as they were walking in the garden, in the cool of the day; and Adam and his wife went to hid themselves from the presence of the Lord God amongst the trees of the garden.	And it must needs be that the devil should tempt the children of men, or they could not be agents unto themselves; for if they never should have bitter they could not know the sweet.

Their eyes were opened, thereby giving them new knowledge.
This is Satan's false promise to each of us. We take the fruit and eat
of it—so simple an act, and yet so hard its undoing. The story depicts
Adam and Eve as being sold the false notion that evil is really wisdom
and sophistication.[89] The devil is peddling that same bill of goods
today, and business is very good! There is a growing trend in modern
society to call good evil, and evil good. "The nature of man is to
want something he cannot have," to desire that which is forbidden.[90]
The story foreshadows the fall of many of God's children because
they succumb to Satan's pernicious lies. They eat of the fruit because
Satan tells them that in so doing they will become "like God." The
irony of the situation is that once they partake of the forbidden fruit
many realize that they were much closer to God before eating but
have now fallen from that state.[91] This is what Satan seeks to do to
each of us. "The history of every temptation, and of every sin, is the
same; the outward object of attraction—the inward commotion of
mind—the increase and triumph of passionate desire; ending in the
degradation, slavery, and ruin of the soul."[92] The fruit seems not only
good for food but also desirable to look at. What a perfect parallel
to so much of what the adversary tempts us with—the vain, hollow,
empty, meaningless things of this materialistic world.[93]

Taste the bitter in order to know the sweet. Church Patriarch
Eldred G. Smith once noted that life is designed so that we might
have experiences akin to those had by our Father and Mother in
Heaven, thereby making us like Them. Drawing on Doctrine and
Covenants 29:39, he stated:

> So it is with us today, we must also have the bitter in order to know
> the sweet. Sometimes some of us think we have the bitter and not
> enough of the sweet. This is normal. We all have our trials of life to
> strengthen us. Each thinks he has the hardest or most severe trials.
> It may be that they are the most difficult only because they are the
> hardest or most difficult for you. The diamond is enhanced and made
> more valuable with polishing. Steel is made harder and more valuable
> through tempering. So also opposition builds the character of man.[94]

Eve gave some of the fruit to her husband. Once Eve had
partaken, Satan immediately coaxed her to also get Adam to eat

of that which was forbidden. This is no different with us. When we adopt a sinful practice, the devil encourages us to entice others to sin—or, at the very least, to rationalize to those around us that our behavior is appropriate. This somehow soothes the souls of the sinful and gives them a false sense of either "security in numbers" or propriety of belief. In reality, however, it only serves to show whose attributes they have developed. Is the "image of God engraven upon your countenances?" (Alma 5:19). Or is it the image of the devil that you radiate?

Augustine also noted that the "first sin" highlights the tragedy of all sin. The story of the Fall highlights two people with everything they needed—and then some—provided for them. There was no need, nor any justification, for taking more (i.e., partaking of the "forbidden" fruit) when so much was already theirs. Augustine put it this way, "Every possible need of our first parents had been met, and the command to abstain from one tree out of the entire garden was minuscule."[95] So it is with us; we lack so little. So much has been given us. There really is no rationalization for the selfishness of sin!

The fact that Eve ate of the fruit first is taken by some as a metaphor for the Latter-day disease of role reversal. Society encourages women to abandon their divinely appointed callings in an effort to usurp the divinely appointed role of men.[96] The Fall of Adam and Eve teaches us that there is an order to all things—an order instituted by God, not man. The man, by covenant and divine decree, is obligated to preside in his home and family; and he will be held accountable if he does not do so (and do so in righteousness). His wife, also by divine decree, is to function as a counselor and adviser to her husband and as the nurturer of the children they jointly bear. To seek to reverse those roles or usurp either one is to seek to overthrow or correct the plan of God. Similarly, when the members of the Church (the bride) seek to correct or counsel Christ (the bridegroom), they are seeking to usurp His divinely appointed role. In so doing, they will lose blessings and face accountability.

They made themselves fig-leaf aprons. Symbols can have multiple meanings. For example, blood can have a negative connotation (such as sin) and a positive one (life). Similarly, eagles are sometimes positive symbols (representing maternal instincts and protection, for example) and sometimes negative symbols (scavengers). Commentators tend to highlight both negative and positive symbols in the fig and its leaves. Since Adam and Eve did what was right, the symbolism attached to them can only be positive. Since you and I tend to do what's wrong, the symbolism would be (in the cases where we do wrong) negative.

Thus, these aprons symbolized one thing for our first parents and another for us (as fallen Adams and Eves). For you and me the donning of aprons is a symbol of our fallen state—a symbol of the desire to cover our guilt.[97] Anciently, to be naked meant to be innocent or exposed.[98] To cover one's nakedness symbolized the effort to make excuses for one's actions.[99] When we sin, we are symbolically naked or exposed in our sins before God. Thus, we tend to seek to cover ourselves (i.e., cover our sins) by making excuses, depicted by the donning of the aprons. One modern typologist wrote: "Those fig leaves were but a picture of themselves; for, plucked from the parent stem, death had set in, and though for a time they might remain glossy and beautiful, they would soon be withered and dead."[100] Adam and Eve's nakedness is often associated with a loss of the Spirit, which left them outside of the scope of the Atonement—having nothing to cover their guilt. It is the realization that they are without God's protection.

In Judaism their nakedness symbolizes that "they became aware that they were bare of good deeds."[101] Jacob Neusner wrote: "The word 'naked' is associated with 'being clothed by the merit accruing from the performance of religious duties.'"[102] Similarly, Philo of Alexandria stated that nakedness symbolized the state of being "wholly deficient in and destitute of virtue."[103] Are we as Latter-day Saints ever found "bare of good deeds"? Are we living Christlike lives of service, virtue, and faithfulness? Are we attending to our covenant responsibilities at home, at Church, and in the temple? Or will we be found at the judgment day standing before God naked of the very virtues, attributes, and acts He commanded us to develop and perform here in mortality?

In the cool of the day. The early Christians saw as significant the idea that Adam and Eve heard the sound of God walking toward them after they had partaken of the "forbidden" fruit. The sound of

God's footsteps brought Adam and Eve to a consciousness of their guilt. And just as footsteps are a subtle informant that someone is approaching, for the early Christians they symbolized the reality that God has placed around each of us small experiences designed to remind us of Him and to provoke in us repentance.[104] As one fourth-century document states, God "wished to benefit them by the sound of his feet . . . that Adam and Eve might be prepared, at that sound, to make supplication before him."[105] And so it is with us. If we are attentive, we will recognize the subtle signs of His coming, and they will help us to be prepared for that day when we will stand before His face to be judged as to who we have become and what we have chosen to love.

One other curious application of this phrase comes to us from the early Church. Jerome saw the "cool of the day" as a reference to "the evening"—stating that, because of his sins, "Adam had lost the sunlight, for his high noon was over."[106] Augustine made a similar observation, noting that, because of their transgression, "It is fitting that he comes toward evening, that is, when the sun was already setting for them, that is, when the interior light of the truth was being taken from them."[107] May our time of judgment not come when the light of the Spirit is absent from our lives. If we lose the light of God's Spirit, we will be relegated to eternal darkness.

They hid themselves amongst the trees. This aptly stands as a symbol of our tendency, when saturated in guilt, to hide among the things of this world or fill our lives with such things, in the hope that somehow our sins or mistakes will not be noticed.

THE REPERCUSSIONS OF THE FALL

Genesis 3:9–12	Moses 4:15–18
And the Lord God called unto Adam, and said unto him, Where art thou? And he said, I heard thy voice in the garden, and I was afraid, because I was naked; and I hid myself. And he said, Who told thee that thou wast naked? Hast thou eaten of the tree, whereof I commanded thee that thou shouldest not eat? And the man said, The woman whom thou gavest to be with me, she gave me of the tree, and I did eat.	And I, the Lord God, called unto Adam, and said unto him: Where goest thou? And he said: I heard thy voice in the garden, and I was afraid, because I beheld that I was naked, and I hid myself. And I, the Lord God, said unto Adam: Who told thee thou wast naked? Hast thou eaten of the tree whereof I commanded thee that thou shouldst not eat, if so thou shouldst surely die? And the man said: The woman thou gavest me, and commandest that she should remain with me, she gave me of the fruit of the tree and I did eat.

Hast thou eaten of the tree? The tree of the knowledge of good and evil represents our sins and our acts of rebellion. In a sense, it is the poison that destroys our spirituality and steals from our grasp eternal life. The sacrament, on the other hand, "is the remedy against the poison that ruined human nature when Eve and Adam ate of the fruit."[108]

Of course, we need both the tree of life and the tree of knowledge of good and evil if we are to return to God, having become like Him. However, as badly as we need this mortal experience (in which, because of our fallen natures, we are cut off from the Father), we must over time remove ourselves as much as possible from the tree of knowledge (meaning from sin and the ways of this fallen world), while drawing closer to the tree of life (meaning Christ and his gospel).

The woman whom thou gavest me. Remember, this is you and me speaking, rather than Adam. Faithful Father Adam was unwavering in his resolve to do the will of the Father. What is depicted here is about you and me. Thus, notice that there is no confession described by the man and woman—only excuses.[109] This is not a statement about Adam and Eve. It is an indictment of our tendency as fallen men and women. Adam, who stood next in power, might, and dominion to Christ,[110] is here depicted in a metaphorical exchange *representative of our tendency* to blame others for our trials and occasionally even for our sins. Although Paul is quite clear in stating that we are never tempted above that which we can withstand (see 1 Corinthians 10:13),[111] nevertheless, the tendency in hard times is to assume that God has abandoned us. Occasionally we stoop to blaming Him, and His plan, for our difficulties. Or, as President N. Eldon Tanner noted, we "are inclined to . . . blame someone else."[112]

One scholar noted, "By saying that he sinned because of the woman given to him by God, Adam [a metaphorical representation of you and me] tries to attribute his sinning to God. [The metaphorical] Eve also fails to confess her sin and says that the serpent beguiled her. These evasions and attempts at self-justification show an unwillingness to repent."[113] Instead of confessing what he had done wrong, which would have actually helped him, he related what had been done to him, which didn't help at all. Of course, this is not a representation of Adam's actual response, but rather a symbolic reenactment of yours and mine. Adam is figuratively depicted as failing to confess his folly and as casting blame on Eve.[114] How common a practice this is. We frequently see our weaknesses, failings, and sins as someone else's fault! One commentator added:

> As is quite common in cases of pride, he does not accuse himself of having consented to the woman but pushes the fault off upon the woman. Thus, as if out of cleverness the poor fellow had conceived, he cunningly tried to attribute his sinning to God, himself. For he did not just say "the woman gave to me," but added on, "the woman you gave to me." Nothing is as characteristic of sinners as to want to attribute to God everything for which they are accused. This arises from . . . pride.[115]

Adam, where art thou? President N. Eldon Tanner stated: "God . . . called: 'Where art thou?' a question which can and does apply to every one of us individually and collectively, and one which we might well be asking ourselves as it applies to our relationship to God and our fellowmen."[116]

"Adam, Eve . . . Where art thou?" and "Who told thee that thou wast naked?" stand as two of the most significant questions posed by God to our original parents in the Garden of Eden (Genesis 3:9, 11). And if God asks such questions to [the] first man and first woman, by implication, we too are asked. . . . Essentially, life is a journey from "the tree of life . . . in the midst of the garden" (Genesis 2:9) to "the tree of life, which is in the midst of the paradise of God" (Revelation 2:7). The "fruit" of the tree in Eden . . . can be eaten by those who have ears, eyes, and a will to discover how to overcome ignorance—to know, to become. The temple ceremony provides the clearest indications of what is required of each initiate—how, through voluntarily accepting and living covenant laws, one can move from Eden, through mortality, into the presence of God. In order to take full advantage of the Atonement of Jesus Christ, we must individually and collectively answer the questions posed to Adam and Eve, and, like Adam and Eve, eat the fruit of these trees. By so doing, we can become "sons and daughters of the Gods."[117]

It will be noted that the Moses account changes God's query from "Adam . . . where art thou?" (Genesis 3:9) to "Adam . . . where goest thou?" (Moses 4:15). It is a rhetorical question asked by God, designed to provoke in Adam (i.e., you and me) introspection regarding the path being pursued. Ambrose wrote: "What then does he mean by 'Adam, where art thou?' Does he not mean 'in what circumstance' are you; not, 'in what place'? It is therefore not a question but a reproof. From what condition of goodness, beatitude and grace . . . have you fallen into this state of misery?"[118] Elsewhere we read, "'Where are you, Adam?' Are you trapped in the imagined godlikeness that the serpent falsely promised you? Or are you prepared for the death that I, the Lord, decreed for you" should you partake of that which was forbidden?[119] Matthew Henry wrote, "If sinners [would] but consider where they are [going], they [would] not rest until they [returned] to God."[120] This is the Lord's message to us. We are to ask ourselves: Where are we going? In what direction, and down what path, are we headed? "It cannot be denied, the words 'Where art thou?'. . . were intended to bring home to Adam the vast difference between his latter and his former state, . . . between the lordship of God over him then and the lordship of the serpent over him now."[121]

Because I was naked. Two different Hebrew words are used for "naked" in the scriptural story of the Fall. The first, found in Genesis 2:25, refers to physical nakedness. The second word, found in Genesis 3:7, refers to being exposed or "under God's judgment."[122]

St. Augustine makes an interesting point regarding Adam's awareness that he was naked. He wrote: "When Adam heard God's voice, he answered that he hid because he was naked. His answer was a wretched error, as if a man naked, as God had made him, could be displeasing to [God]. It is a distinguishing mark of error that whatever anyone finds personally displeasing he imagines is displeasing to God as well."[123] How true this is. If I tend to be critical and unforgiving, I will perceive God as critical and unforgiving. If I am impatient, I will perceive God as impatient. If I am short-tempered, I will perceive God as short-tempered. We project our sinful characteristics upon God and, in so doing, often distort our perception of Him whom we must emulate.

When Adam realizes he has transgressed, and that he is about to be caught, he is immediately seized with terror and hides himself—not that he can hide from God but, rather, because he feels unworthy to converse with God.[124] This depicts each of us in our fallen condition.[125] When we sin we should draw *closer* to God. However, the devil tells us we should hide.[126] And this has become the natural instinct of nearly all of God's children. Rather than drawing closer to God and seeking to regain the companionship of His Holy Spirit, we withdraw and seek to avoid Him, only making our condition worse. In 2 Nephi 32:8 we read, "For if ye would hearken unto the Spirit which teacheth a man to pray ye would know that ye must pray; for the evil spirit teacheth not a man to pray, but teacheth him that he must not pray." One biblical scholar wisely noted, "When Adam has been caught in his transparent attempt at evasion, Yahweh speaks to him as a father would to his child."[127] Even when we fall short of what God has commanded us to be, His response to our state of inadequacy and sinfulness is not rejection, but rather nurturing and care. In the story of the Fall we are taught that when we sin we will be tempted to listen to the voice of Satan as much after our sin as we did before we committed it. The narrative of the Fall invites us to recognize this and to turn to God, our Father, and live.

Genesis 3:13	Moses 4:19
And the Lord God said unto the woman, What is this that thou hast done? And the woman said, The serpent beguiled me, and I did eat.	And I, the Lord God, said unto the woman: What is this thing which thou hast done? And the woman said: The serpent beguiled me, and I did eat.

The serpent beguiled me. To "beguile" is to "delude by false promises or by craft; to deprive of proper reason by deceit; to cheat."[128] Scripture and rite tells us that Satan promised Eve two things: (1) that she would not die and (2) that, by partaking of the fruit, she would become as God is. It is commonly said that the promise that she would not die was false. However, the Hebrew rendered "ye shall not surely die" is more accurately translated, "in dying ye shall not die, but shall be as the gods."[129]

Thus, although traditionally we assume that Satan lied to Adam and Eve, it appears (from the Hebrew) that he was actually quite accurate in what he told them. As President Brigham Young put it, "He told the truth"![130] In physically dying, you will not die (i.e., permanently die) but will become as the gods (living eternally and potentially becoming as they are). "True to form, Satan had taken a truth and applied it in such a way as to achieve his unrighteous purposes."[131] Hence, although Eve was not beguiled in the proper sense of the word, the devil seeks daily to beguile you and me. And in the premortal world he successfully beguiled a third part of the host of heaven, likely by "false promises" and "deceit."

In this passage (Genesis 3:13; Moses 4:19), Eve, like Adam, is depicted as placing the blame for her actions upon the shoulders of someone else. She is a perfect symbol of fallen humanity. She is represented as blaming the serpent and, in so doing, indirectly blaming God, who created the snake![132] Of course, Eve did not do this. She is symbolically depicted as doing so in an effort to remind us of our wrongful behavior. In many cases the problem isn't that we've been deceived; the problem is that we love darkness more than light. We value the advice of the world more than the commandments of God.[133]

[Adam] replied, "The wife that you gave me"—mark you, not "my wife"—"deceived me." "The wife that you gave me," as if to say, "this disaster you placed on my head." So it is, my brethren, when a man has not the guts to accuse himself, he does not scruple to accuse God. . . . Then God came to Eve and said to her, "Why did you not keep the command I gave you?" as if saying, "If you would only say, Forgive me, to humble your soul and be forgiven." She only answered, "The serpent deceived me!"—as if to say, if the serpent did wrong, what concern is that to me? . . . Neither [Adam nor Eve] stooped to self-accusation, no trace of humility was found in either of them. And now look and consider how this was only an anticipation of our own state! . . . This self-justification, this holding fast to our own will, this obstinacy in being our own guide.[134]

Eve reminds us of those who commit multiple sins. In partaking of that which God has forbidden, we sin against our Creator. Then, in enticing others to partake, we do the devil's work and become partially guilty for other's sins, an accessory to the crime, as it were.[135] Finally, in refusing to repent and acknowledge our guilt, we damn ourselves. The story of the Fall warns us of the dangers of these three acts; it cautions us not to be the source of sin's access to our own lives or to the lives of others.

Dust shalt thou eat. As noted previously, anciently, dust or earth carried the symbolic connotation of things temporal, worldly, or fleeting.[136] Hence, commentators have seen in the dictate that the serpent—a characterization of the devil—shall "eat dust" a representation that he will seek out, possess, and destroy those who are "earthly minded" or place their trust in the things of this world.[137] He will captivate and have power over, both here and in eternity, those who find the ways of the world more enticing than the commandments of God.[138] This is not to suggest that all such shall become sons of perdition. Rather, it implies that the adversary's influence over them will be eternal; for, whether they end up in the telestial kingdom or outer darkness, they will, for eternity, live under conditions imposed on them because they hearkened to his teachings and loved his ways. And, just as God relegated Lucifer to spend an eternity with such souls, those who place their hope and trust in the things of this world and the philosophies and ethics of man will be relegated to spend eternity with like-minded souls—sinful and untrustworthy! The eternal abode of the worldly and faithless will be either with Satan and his minions or with those who loved the devil and his ways. Highlighting this idea are the words of one sixth-century Christian bishop, who wrote:

> God said to the devil: "Dust you shall eat." Is it the earth that we tread underfoot that the devil eats, brethren? No, it is people who are earthly minded, sensual and proud, who love the earth and place all their hopes in it. They labor entirely for carnal advantages, . . . and think little or nothing of the salvation of their souls. People like these, then, the devil seeks. . . . They were assigned to him at the beginning of the world when it was said to him, "Dust you shall eat." Therefore let each one look to his own conscience. If he sees that he has greater care for his body than for his soul, let him fear that he will become the food of the serpent.[139]

Thus, with Ambrose we admonish the Saints not to walk down worldly paths, so that the serpent will be unable to harm you. Rather, put on the "sandals of the gospel" that "shut out the serpent's poison and blunt his bites."[140]

I will put enmity. Drawing on this passage, and the fact that it highlights Christ's ultimate power over the adversary, one Latter-day Saint author wrote:

> The words metaphorically spoken to the "serpent" can reassure all of us, for though Satan has the power to tempt us, we have been given power to resist him. If we need help to resist, or if we are overwhelmed by him, we may be aided to stand firm, or to recover, through the administration of those who bear priesthood powers to cast out Satan in the name of Jesus Christ. Thus we see that both Satan's freedom to act and his power to overcome people are curbed by the curse he received (James 4:7; Matthew 10:1; Mark 3:15; Doctrine and Covenants 24:13).[141]

As to the shift in the relationship between the woman and the serpent, and how that relates to you and me, one seventeenth-century commentator wrote: "Observe here, the serpent and the woman had just now been very familiar and friendly in discourse about the forbidden fruit, and a wonderful agreement there was between them; but here they are irreconcilably set at variance. Note, sinful friendships justly end in mortal feuds: those who unite in wickedness will not unite long."[142]

Genesis 3:16	Moses 4:22
Unto the woman he said, I will greatly multiply thy sorrow and thy conception; in sorrow thou shalt bring forth children; and thy desire shall be to thy husband, and he shall rule over thee.	Unto the woman, I, the Lord God, said: I will greatly multiply thy sorrow and thy conception. In sorrow thou shalt bring forth children, and thy desire shall be to thy husband, and he shall rule over thee.

I will greatly multiply thy sorrow and thy conception. There may be both literal and symbolic meaning in this phrase. In the more literal sense, Eve, and all women after her, suffer physically during childbirth because of the Fall and the changes it brought to the physical body. However, the pain of giving birth has also been seen as a symbol of the members of Christ's Church struggling to give "birth to temperance in their soul."[143] Augustine wrote: "Carnal desire . . . does not [cause] pain in the beginning, until [a] habit is bent toward improvement. . . . In order that this [good] habit might be born, there was a painful struggle with [the] bad habit."[144] The pains of giving birth not only remind us of the Fall. They are also a sign of impending joy. Just as the pains bring forth a child—which the parents rejoice in—our trials can bring forth change and redemption—which will be the source of eternal joy for all who are willing to experience the "labor pains" of the mortal test.[145] Change does not come easily. If we are to overcome sinful desires or habits, there must be significant travail preceding our being "born again."

Thy desire shall be to thy husband. This phrase has been interpreted variously by commentators and may indicate a number of things about you and me and our relationships with our spouses and with Christ.

First of all, some have seen the dictate that Eve's "desire" or "urge" (as the Hebrew reads) would be to her husband as a reference to sexual desire.[146] According to some commentators, this refers to the fact that women will act contrary to reason, in that they will have children even though they know it will cause them excruciating pain. And, although they understand what causes them to be pregnant, they will continue to desire their husbands, when reason would tell them to avoid the source of pain and suffering. This "desire" or "urge" God places in them in order to ensure the continuance of the human race. And, although this comes because of the Fall, in the end it is a blessing to the man and the woman, as through this "desire" they can eternally become one.

A second interpretation of the phrase suggests that, in spite of the suffering she knows will accompany pregnancy and childbirth, the longing for motherhood remains a most powerful instinct in woman.[147] The reason for this "urge" or "desire" is the same as the aforementioned theory—that mankind may be. Again, the blessings of eternal families are the direct product of this God-given "desire."

A third interpretation of the clause "thy desire shall be to thy husband" is that, because of her childbearing, she will also desire her husband's protection against the dangers of a fallen world. Eden offered its own protections to the man and the woman. However, now that they are inhabitants of the "lone and dreary world," the woman's desire would be for her husband's protection—and his desire would be to protect his cherished partner.

Finally, a fourth interpretation, which seems to have a great deal of applicability in modern society, relates to the woman's post-Fall social status. In Eden the man and woman are depicted as one—equal partners with different roles, per se.[148] One is not characterized as ruling over the other, but rather God is shown to be the ruler over all. However, after the Fall and throughout history, women have lived with men in a state of inequality. In the opinion of some commentators, the Lord is informing Eve that, because of the Fall, women would lose their prior Edenic status, which they would desire and fight to regain.[149] The Lord states: "Thy desire shall be to thy husband, *and he shall rule over thee*" One commentary on the passage records: "From being the helpmeet of man [i.e., the mate equal to him] and the partner of his affections, her condition would hence-forth be that of humble subjection."[150] Indeed, some commentators have taken this "desire" or "urge" for the man as a reference to the prevalent female longing for the male social status and position.[151] Although Latter-day Saint women have not been as susceptible to this temptation as have been others, the world does shout the familiar sophistry that success in the corporation is to be valued above success in the clan. The desire by *some* women to dominate in the world and in the marriage may be a fulfillment of this divine declaration.[152]

If marriages are to be as they were in Eden, and as God desires they be now and throughout eternity, then the man and woman must be equal and also willing to accept their divinely appointed roles. One non-LDS commentator noted that too often "'to love and to cherish' becomes 'to desire and to dominate.' While . . . marriage can rise far above this, the pull of sin is always towards it."[153] Whether by the man the woman, an effort to dominate, control, coerce, or usurp divinely appointed roles is a sin.

One may perceive much of this as highly negative. However, it is not intended to be such. During their time in Eden the relationship of Adam and Eve was perfect. Although they could not have children there, we cannot assume that their love for each other was anything less than full and perfect. But as a result of the Fall, something changed. No doubt in Eden Eve desired to love and be with her husband. But after the Fall something about the nature of her desire evolved. This new "desire" or "urge" would serve the purposes of God while requiring Eve and her daughters to grow and overcome the effects of the Fall.

Genesis 3:17–19	Moses 4:23–25
And unto Adam he said, Because thou hast hearkened unto the voice of thy wife, and hast eaten of the tree, of which I commanded thee, saying, Thou shalt not eat of it: cursed is the ground for thy sake; in sorrow shalt thou eat of it all the days of thy life; Thorns also and thistles shall it bring forth to thee;	And unto Adam, I, the Lord God, said: Because thou hast hearkened unto the voice of thy wife, and hast eaten of the fruit of the tree of which I commanded thee, saying—Thou shalt not eat of it, cursed shall be the ground for thy sake; in sorrow shalt thou eat of it all the days of thy life. Thorns also, and thistles shall it bring forth to thee, and thou shalt eat the herb of the field. By the sweat of thy face shalt thou eat bread until thou shalt return unto the ground—for thou shalt surely die—for out of it wast thou taken: for dust thou wast, and unto dust shalt thou return.

Hearkened unto the voice of thy wife. This is in no way a pejorative declaration regarding women. The greatness of Eve has already been established, as has the equality of husband and wife. But in the story of the Fall we learn of one of the great weaknesses of mankind, that is, the tendency to hearken to the counsel of other humans, over and above the counsel and commands of God. And in every case, when we choose to do so, the consequences are that we suffer and bring upon ourselves trials that would otherwise not be necessary. It is we, not God, who introduces the thorns, thistles, briars, and noxious weeds into our lives, and it is we who nurture them so that they grow. Finally, however, it is we who must do the weeding.

Cursed shall be the ground for thy sake. Whereas in Eden the flowers and fruits came forth spontaneously, so also it appears that in our premortal state righteousness came more naturally than it does to fallen mortals. Similarly, Moses informs us that God "cursed" the ground, that it would yield good fruit only upon cultivation and hard work. Such is the case with each of us. Our lives require "cultivation" in order to bring forth good. Yet, it is "for our sakes" that God has chosen to institute such conditions.

Thorns and thistles. God placed "enmity" between the man and the earth he would till, just as enmity was placed between the offspring of the woman and the adversary of all mankind. The man's "toil" by which he would eat of the earth's yield corresponds with the "pain" or "suffering" of woman's childbearing.[154] Fallen man's life is to be hard, the very opposite of the idyllic existence that was Adam's in Eden.[155]

One commentator noted: "The thorns that grow on earth symbolize the sins of humankind removed by Christ."[156] God's promise of "thorns and thistles" represents the fact that we will have tests and trials as part of being mortal.[157] He informs Adam that these new conditions came because he partook of the fruit of the tree of knowledge of good and evil and "for his sake," or in other words, "for his own good." Several elements in this passage are significant.

Mortality will be filled with sorrow. The Hebrew translated "sorrow" in the King James Version means literally "travail" or "pain." Thus, the Lord is indicating that this life will be one of trials and pain. But, says He, this is for our own good. "Thorns and thistles" will spontaneously come forth to afflict and torment man. These thorns and thistles represent the divinely sent trials and tests of life, which seemingly spontaneously come forth at nearly every turn of mortality. They afflict and torment us (i.e., stretch and try us) that we might grow and have our characters sanctified.

Adam is encouraged to eat of the herbs of the field. Both anciently, and in modern times, herbs have been used for medicinal purposes. We must do the spiritually medicinal things that the Lord has given us to overcome our sins and weaknesses.

Only by the "sweat of his face" will man be able to eat his "daily bread." The "sweat of the brow" is suggestive of the difficulty of the task. That task can be compared to the hard work required to repent or change our nature. Through this repentance we are enabled to partake of our "daily bread"—the Bread of Life, which is Christ, the Lord.

Finally, this condition will continue until man dies ("till thou return unto the ground . . ."). The tests and trials of this life will persist throughout our mortal probation. We will all be required to struggle and fight for change throughout our lives.

Thus, the Lord's description to Adam pertains to the purpose of mortality—to deal with our daily trials by relying upon Christ and the things He has given us to overcome our fallen state. This struggle will not end prior to our deaths. It is not something we can totally overcome in mortality. Indeed, it is the very thing requisite for our exaltation. It is, as the Lord stated, "for our sake" that He requires this of us. As Matthew Henry put it: "The toils and sweat suggest the difficulty which, through the weakness of the flesh, man labors under, in the service of God and the work of religion. . . . The curse of barrenness which was brought upon the earth, and its produce of briars and thorns, are a fit representation of the barrenness of a corrupt and sinful soul."[158]

One commentator astutely noted: "It is . . . an incorrect interpretation which sees in these words of God to Adam and Eve primarily a punitive message. . . . Like a surgeon who cuts with his scalpel only that he may heal, God initiates a means of redemption to reclaim the prodigals. . . . These 'sentences' are not the prescribed impositions of a volatile deity. Rather, they are gifts of love, strewn in the pathway of man, to bring him back to God."[159] Elsewhere we read:

Through [man's] suffering he might then get rid of the disease which had come upon him in the midst of paradise. By punishing us with death, the lawgiver cut off the spread of sin. And yet through that very punishment he also demonstrated his love for us. . . . He ordered things in such a way that the punishment might itself serve the goal of salvation. For death brings about separation from this life and brings evil works to an end. It sets us free from labor, sweat and pain, and ends the suffering of the body.[160]

In addition to all of this, President Marion G. Romney noted that "the stern command, 'In the sweat of thy face shalt thou eat bread . . .'" is a call to every Saint to be willing to work and "labor with all his might to [be] self-sustaining."[161]

Man's obligation to till the dust of the earth in order to provide his daily bread highlights a transition in the focus of his daily life. In Eden, man's focus was on the things of God. He walked and talked with Him on a daily basis. His cares were not the cares of the world, but the cares of God (i.e., that which matters in an eternal sense). Now he is told that, because of his actions, his daily concerns will be worldly (i.e., of the "dust of this earth"), and, if he is not careful, they will potentially blur what is really important and eternal. For the vast majority of us, one of the great challenges of mortality is the need to remember to place the things of God—things eternal—before the things of this world—things mundane. Spirituality is no longer found in ease and comfort, as it was in Eden. Now it comes only at a price—the sacrifice of the things of this world. And it is only by that sacrifice that we can hope to inherit eternal life. The *Lectures on Faith* record:

A religion that does not require the sacrifice of all things never has power sufficient to produce the faith necessary unto life and salvation; for, from the first existence of man, the faith necessary unto the enjoyment of life and salvation never could be obtained without the sacrifice of all earthly things. It was through this sacrifice, and this only, that God has ordained that men should enjoy eternal life; and it is through the medium of the sacrifice of all earthly things that men do actually know that they are doing the things that are well pleasing in the sight of God.[162]

BANISHMENT FROM GOD'S PRESENCE

Genesis 3:20–21	Moses 4:26–27
And Adam called his wife's name Eve; because she was the mother of all living. Unto Adam also and to his wife did the Lord God make coats of skins, and clothed them.	And Adam called his wife's name Eve, because she was the mother of all living; for thus have I, the Lord God, called the first of all women, which are many. Unto Adam, and also unto his wife, did I, the Lord God, make coats of skins, and clothed them.

Adam called his wife's name Eve. It was from Eve that all mankind has sprung. She has become the archetype, the pattern for each of her daughters after her. Women have been divinely appointed to serve as the "mothers of all living." Of this reality, and the subsequent responsibilities of those who become mothers, Elder Bruce R. McConkie once stated: "I rate Eve also as one of the greatest women among all of those who have or will come to earth. She, as the mother of all living, set the pattern for all future mothers with reference to bringing up their children in light and truth. . . . Thus, in the beginning, the perfect pattern is set for perfecting the family."[163]

Coats of skins. In the context of the story of the Fall as our story, these garments have several applicable meanings.

At least in part, these skins were a replacement covering for the glory Adam and Eve once possessed but lost because of their Fall.[164] They are a commission to our first parents, and to us, to seek to regain and retain the Spirit and light that radiates from God, Christ, and all resurrected celestial beings. They are a reminder of what awaits all the faithful. And they serve as an admonition to each of us to seek to become as God is by seeking to live as He commands.

In the book of Hebrews we are told that the veil of the temple is the flesh of Christ (see Hebrews 10:19–22). This being the case, when in the endowment one ceremonially acts out his or her ascent back to God, at the final stages it is Christ who stands between the patron and the Father. Christ is, of course, our mediator or go-between (see 1 Timothy 2:5; 2 Nephi 2:27). Since it is Christ who is our mediator through whom we communicate with our Father (both at the veil and in prayer)—and through whom we gain access to the celestial kingdom—then it is also Christ who is symbolized by the clothing Adam and Eve received as they left Eden.[165] This clothing represents the crucified flesh of Christ; it should be received with a covenant and reminder to always live in accordance with what that newly procured covering represents. This should give new meaning to the idea of taking upon oneself the name (see 2 Nephi 31:13; Mosiah 5:8) or image (see Alma 5:19; 1 John 3:1–3) of Christ. One text states: "God had clothed them in coats or garments of skin as a token of the protection provided them through Christ . . . so they were to clothe themselves in his name by faith."[166]

Likewise, the garments covered the nakedness (i.e., the sins) of the man and woman. The Hebrew word for *Atonement* means "to cover."[167] One author noted: "Clothes were provided by God to shield and protect us against not only the harsh elements of nature but also the temptations of our fallen natures, which the adversary seeks to exploit."[168] Elder Carlos E. Asay wrote:

> The heavy armor worn by soldiers of a former day, including helmets, shields, and breastplates, determined the outcome of some battles. However, the real battles of life in our modern day will be won by those who are clad in a spiritual armor—an armor consisting of faith in God, faith in self, faith in one's cause, and faith in one's leaders. The piece of armor called the temple garment not only provides the comfort and warmth of a cloth covering, it also strengthens the wearer to resist temptation, fend off evil influences, and stand firmly for the right.[169]

Thus, the "coats of skins" remind us that God has not sent us out into the "lone and dreary world" without assistance. The Atonement of Christ is there to aid us and cover our sins as we struggle to regain the glory of God's presence.

Even though in the story Adam and Eve were expelled from God's presence for transgressing His law, He nevertheless clothed them first. One commentator noted that this is a demonstration of God's continued love for His creations, despite all their sins and weaknesses. "Even when on the point of banishing the man and woman from his presence in the garden, God manifests his care for their progress and well being."[170] He is our *Father* in Heaven and ever treats us as a truly loving father would. Elder Richard G. Scott noted, "You can learn how to be more effective parents by studying the lives of Adam and Eve."[171]

Finally, it has been suggested that God's act of making "coats of skins" for Adam and Eve is a call to all Saints to be aware of those in need and to act accordingly (e.g., I was "naked, and ye clothed me" Matthew 25:36).[172] King Benjamin's admonition seems pertinent:

And also, ye yourselves will succor those that stand in need of your succor; ye will administer of your substance unto him that standeth in need; and ye will not suffer that the beggar putteth up his petition to you in vain, and turn him out to perish.

Perhaps thou shalt say: The man has brought upon himself his misery; therefore I will stay my hand, and will not give unto him of my food, nor impart unto him of my substance that he may not suffer, for his punishments are just—

But I say unto you, O man, whosoever doeth this the same hath great cause to repent; and except he repenteth of that which he hath done he perisheth forever, and hath no interest in the kingdom of God.

For behold, are we not all beggars? Do we not all depend upon the same Being, even God, for all the substance which we have, for both food and raiment, and for gold, and for silver, and for all the riches which we have of every kind?

And behold, even at this time, ye have been calling on his name, and begging for a remission of your sins. And has he suffered that ye have begged in vain? Nay; he has poured out his Spirit upon you, and has caused that your hearts should be filled with joy, and has caused that your mouths should be stopped that ye could not find utterance, so exceedingly great was your joy.

And now, if God, who has created you, on whom you are dependent for your lives and for all that ye have and are, doth grant unto you whatsoever ye ask that is right, in faith, believing that ye shall receive, O then, how ye ought to impart of the substance that ye have one to another.

And if ye judge the man who putteth up his petition to you for your substance that he perish not, and condemn him, how much more just will be your condemnation for withholding your substance, which doth not belong to you but to God, to whom also your life belongeth; and yet ye put up no petition, nor repent of the thing which thou hast done. (Mosiah 4:16–22.)

Genesis 3:22–24	Moses 4:28–31
And the Lord God said, Behold, the man is become as one of us, to know good and evil: and now, lest he put forth his hand, and take also of the tree of life, and eat, and live for ever: Therefore the Lord God sent him forth from the garden of Eden, to till the ground from whence he was taken. So he drove out the man; and he placed at the east of the garden of Eden Cherubims, and a flaming sword which turned every way, to keep the way of the tree of life.	And I, the Lord God, said unto mine Only Begotten: Behold, the man is become as one of us to know good and evil; and now lest he put forth his hand and partake also of the tree of life, and eat and live forever, Therefore I, the Lord God, will send him forth from the Garden of Eden, to till the ground from whence he was taken; For as I, the Lord God, liveth, even so my words cannot return void, for as they go forth out of my mouth they must be fulfilled. So I drove out the man, and I placed at the east of the Garden of Eden cherubim and a flaming sword, which turned every way to keep the way of the tree of life.

God drove out the man. For transgression of God's law, mankind was driven out. One Jewish commentator aptly noted: "Sin drives man from God's presence; and when man banishes God from his world, he dwells in a wilderness instead of a Garden of Eden."[173] In the story of the Fall we are warned what the consequences will be for those who reject God's word and will. We will be banished from His presence until we repent. And if we procrastinate the day of our repentance until it is everlastingly too late (see Helaman 13:38), we will spend eternity banned from the presence of God, our Father.

The man is become as one of us. This is an indicator of our potential—our destiny—and not so much a statement about our current condition.

Cherubim and a flaming sword. In biblical Hebrew one oriented oneself by facing the east. Thus, the movement of Adam and Eve into mortality, and seemingly away from God's presence, was a movement forward—toward God.[174] Rather than a negative event, Adam and Eve's Fall was progression in the truest sense. And so it is for us. Leaving God's presence in the premortal world was the only way that we could move toward Him in our nature, attributes, knowledge, and so on.

At the point that the first of the human family were removed from the Garden of Eden, Jehovah placed "cherubim and a flaming sword" to guard the way of the tree of life (Alma 12:21; 42:2; Moses 4:31). The Lord did this to keep Adam and Eve safe. It was to keep them from partaking of the tree in their fallen state and thereby causing them to "live forever in their sins."[175]

Of cherubs, typologist Patrick Fairbairn indicated that they are the angels who have become like God and dwell in His presence in eternity.[176] One theological dictionary noted that the Hebrew word *cherub* is likely related to the idea of an "intercessor."[177] Dictionaries, religious and secular alike, often define cherubs as "celestial beings."[178] Joseph Fielding McConkie wrote that cherubs are placed to ensure that the "holiness of God is not violated by those in transgression or those who have not complied with the proper rituals."[179]

The tree of life was that from which God chose to shelter fallen man. Trees have several standard symbolic meanings. Green trees often represent the righteous, whereas dry trees can symbolize the wicked.[180] M. Catherine Thomas noted that "most often in scripture . . . the tree is an anthropomorphic symbol. A tree serves well as such a symbol because it has, after all, limbs, a circulatory system, the bearing of fruit, and so forth. Specifically, scriptural trees stand . . . for Christ and his attributes."[181] Elsewhere we read, "In ancient times, sacred trees . . . were [the] attributes of the gods."[182] Susan Easton Black wrote: "The tree of life is connected with the cross, the two having somewhat the same significance. Both related to the resurrection, eternal life, the Lord, and the 'Love of God.' . . . Before the crucifixion of Christ, the *tree of life* symbol was used extensively. After the crucifixion the cross seems to have replaced it to a degree."[183] When Nephi wished to know the meaning of the tree that his father saw in his dream (see 1 Nephi 11:9–24), the angel showed him a vision of the birth of Christ. The angel then asked Nephi, "Behold the Lamb of God, yea, even the Son of the Eternal Father! Knowest thou the meaning of the tree which thy father saw?" (1 Nephi 11:21). To this Nephi responded, "It is the love of God" (1 Nephi 11:22). Jesus is the tree of life and also the love of God (John 3:16).

Note that it was acceptable to partake of the tree of life as long as Adam and Eve were keeping the commandments, just as Jesus' glory was permissible to partake of so long as they were obeying the commandments.[184] God placed the cherubim with their flaming swords to protect Adam and Eve from the direct presence of Christ while they were in their fallen state. One author suggested that the sword-wielding angels in this episode symbolize sentinels that guard the way.[185] The placement of the cherubs with flaming swords, along with their symbolic meaning, illuminates this further.

Flames conjure up images of sanctification or purging. However, there are numerous other connotations associated with this relatively popular symbol. Flames are a manifestation of the godly or celestial nature of a thing.[186] They represent holiness, illumination, inspiration, enlightenment, and purification.[187]

As for swords, standard symbolic interpretations include the word of God—meaning covenants, commandments, teachings, and so on.[188] Swords also symbolize discernment,[189] and that which separates.[190]

Curiously, there appears to be a linguistic connection between these two seemingly separate and unrelated symbols. The early twentieth-century linguist and typologist Harold Bayley wrote, "The symbolism of the sword as the word of God is enshrined in the word Sword, i.e. se-word or is-word [meaning] 'the fire or light of the word.' The Anglo-Saxon for a sword was *seax* [which meant] 'the fire of the great fire.' Similarly the Italian *spada* resolves into *sepada* [which translates] the fire of the shining father, and the German *sabel* into 'fire of bel.'"[191]

Thus, in the flaming sword it appears that we have a symbol of the celestial and divinely revealed words, commands, or covenants used to discern, protect, and separate the righteous from the disobedient. The placement of the cherubs with flaming swords in the Genesis and Moses accounts serves as a representation of those beings who will test us regarding those things we were to learn in this life, which are requisite for us to enter the presence of God. President Brigham Young once stated:

Let me give you a definition in brief. Your endowment is, to receive all those ordinances in the house of the Lord, which are necessary for you, after you have departed this life, to enable you to walk back to the presence of the Father, passing the angels who stand as sentinels, being enabled to give them the key words, the signs and tokens, pertaining to the holy Priesthood, and gain your eternal exaltation in spite of earth and hell.[192]

Similarly, in Doctrine and Covenants 132 we are told that, if we keep the covenants we make in relation to eternal marriage, we will "pass by the angels, and the gods, which are set there, to [our] exaltation and glory in all things, as hath been sealed upon [our] heads" (Doctrine and Covenants 132:19).

The placement of these sentinels in front of the tree of life indicates our need for the ordinances and covenants of the temple in order to regain the presence of the Father and the Son—Jesus being the tree of life![193] Hence, one eighth-century Christian text states: "Through the water of [baptism], the flickering flame—by which the cherubim guardian blocked the entry into paradise when the first Adam was expelled—would be extinguished."[194]

Moses 5:5–8

And he gave unto them commandments, that they should worship the Lord their God, and should offer the firstlings of their flocks, for an offering unto the Lord. And Adam was obedient unto the commandments of the Lord. And after many days an angel of the Lord appeared unto Adam, saying: Why dost thou offer sacrifices unto the Lord? And Adam said unto him: I know not, save the Lord commanded me. And then the angel spake, saying: This thing is a similitude of the sacrifice of the Only Begotten of the Father, which is full of grace and truth. Wherefore, thou shalt do all that thou doest in the name of the Son, and thou shalt repent and call upon God in the name of the Son forevermore.

Adam offered sacrifice. Owing to their transgression of God's law, Adam and Eve were cast out of His presence. When you and I break God's laws, we too are metaphorically "cast out," in that God's Spirit withdraws and we are left to stew in our guilt. However, in this

Adam and Eve have shown us the way; they have set the example for us to follow. When they found themselves unworthy to be in God's presence, they offered a sacrifice, as He required. They conformed to God's will and, in so doing, received communion from on high in the form of an angel. If we follow suit, we are promised that the Father's Holy Spirit, a messenger from His presence, will attend us, and we too can again commune with God. Elder Bruce C. Hafen wrote:

> James E. Talmage believed that the physiological cause of Christ's death was, literally, a broken heart. This element in our Lord's sacrifice suggests two differences between animal sacrifices and the sacrifice of a broken heart. First is the difference between offering one of our possessions, such as an animal, and offering our own hearts. Second, one who offers an unblemished animal, the firstling of a flock, acts in similitude of the Father's sacrifice of his unblemished, firstborn Son. By contrast, one who offers his own broken heart acts in similitude of the Son's terribly personal sacrifice of himself. Thus, the figurative breaking of our own hearts, represented by our repentance and our faithful endurance of the mortal crucible—our own taste of a bitter cup—is a self-sacrifice that mirrors the Savior's own self-sacrifice.[195]

I know not save the Lord commanded me. Adam's act is not one of blind obedience, but rather one of faith and trust—one of submission. He didn't ask, "Lord, should I?" only, "Lord, *how* should I?" If we are to expect God's blessings, we must act in faith, as Adam and Eve did. God does not desire that we act out of blind obedience, as this shows a lack of desire to know God's will, which He willingly reveals to those who seek Him. Indeed, acting out of blind obedience presupposes a degree of spiritual laziness not pleasing to God. On the contrary, what God desires of each of us, as He did of Adam and Eve, is that we be spiritually attuned so that we might heed the commands given through His prophets.

Conclusion

So much of the story of Eden relates to our own lives, because in reality the main message of the story of the Fall is about you and me. In summarizing this idea, Elder Bruce C. Hafen wrote:

[We] can identify with the lost feelings and the sorrows of Adam and Eve so fully as to say, "That is the story of my life." When we see how much their story is our story, perhaps we too will exclaim, as Adam might have said, "Blessed be the name of God! Because Christ came, mortality is not my enemy—it is precisely because of my mortality that, in this life, I shall find joy, understanding, and even the presence of God."[196]

Notes

1. It is quite evident from the New Testament that the story of Adam and Eve is based on historical events surrounding two historical persons. However, scholars acknowledge the symbolic telling of the story, comparing it to other clearly symbolic recitations of historical events. See, for example, the historical account of David's sin (in 2 Samuel 11) as retold metaphorically or symbolically (in 2 Samuel 12:1–6).

2. See, for example, Ricks (1992), 1:205; Matthews (1989), 13.

3. Goppelt (1982), 46.

4. See Davidson (1981), 21, n. 1.

5. See, for example, Hinckley (1997), 636; Scott (1996), 74; Holland (1997), 203–4; Hafen (1990), 10; Hafen (1989), 33, 37–39, 50; Nibley (1989), 6; McConkie, "The Mystery of Eden" (1990), 23, 29–30; Matthews, "The Revelation of the Gospel to Adam (1990), 67; Rockwood (1992), 18; Cooper (1992), 3:1430–31; Adams (1990), 85; Campbell (2003), 7, 96, 123, 166; Robinson (1990), 128, 138; Lundquist (1989), 88; Hutchinson (1988), 69. See also Bloesch (2001), 1:104–5, 106; Pagels (1989), xx–xxi, xxiv, 74; Neusner (1991), 53–65.

6. Rockwood (1992), 22, 34–35.

7. Sailhamer (1992), 105–6. See also Sailhamer (1976–1992), 2:54–55.

8. Dummelow (1936), 9, 6.

9. Kimball (1998), 170; Kimball (1969), 286.

10. Benson (1998), 21.

11. Lewis (1980), 18.

12. See King (1995), s. v. Moses 2:26–27.

13. Speiser (1962), 16; Cornwall and Smith (1998), 6, s. v. "Adam"; Sweet (1995), 15; Hertz (1962), 5; Neusner (1985), 183.

14. See Philo of Alexandria, "Allegorical Interpretation" 1:29, in Yonge (1997), 35.

15. See Fontana (1994), 34; Todeschi (1995), 289.

16. Lactantius, "The Divine Institutes" 2:13, in Roberts and Donaldson (1994), 7:61.

17. See our discussion of this issue in chapter one of this work. See also Young, in *Journal of Discourses*, 9:149; Smith (1993), 5:123; Smith (1954–1956), 1:94–95, 103; Holland (1997), 202–3; Kimball, in *Journal of Discourses*, 8:330; 9:129–130, 135; Duke (1992), 2:858; J. McConkie (1989), 80; Packer (1990), 6; Lund (1989), 104; *Lectures on Faith*, 2:12, 18; Oaks (1993), 73; Widtsoe (1960), 193.

18. See Cirlot (1962), 245; Holzapfel and Seely (1994), 17; Gaskill (2003), 150–156.

19. See Cooper (1995), 59; Drinkard (1992), 2:248; McConkie and Parry (1990), 44; Meyers and Meyers (1987), 300; Ryken, Wilhoit, and Longman (1998), 225.

20. Parry (1994), 133.

21. Andrus (1967), 186.

22. Hafen (1989), 29–30.

23. As an example, in 2003 the following countries actually recorded a negative birthrate: Austria, Belarus, Botswana, Bulgaria, Czech Republic, Estonia, Georgia, Germany, Greece, Hungary, Italy, Latvia, Lithuania, Romania, Russia, Sweden, and Ukraine. Many other countries had negative birthrates or nearly zero birthrates. These are but a few examples.

24. Rasmussen (1993), 7–8.

25. Grant, Clark, and McKay (1965–1975), 6:177. See also Hunter (1951), 147–48; Young, in *Journal of Discourses*, 4:56.

26. Gaskill (2003), 119. See also Draper (1991), 24, 77, 94; Neusner (1985), 173.

27. See Clifford and Murphy (1990), 12.

28. See Kidner (1967), 63.

29. See Wani (2004), 113–23.

30. Young, in *Journal of Discourses*, 1:50; Church (1992), 6.

31. Harper (2004), 94.

32. The author wishes to acknowledge that this idea is not original. It was drawn from a talk heard early in the 1990s. However, after several months of fruitless searching for the source of this idea, the author is unable to determine the originator of this analogy.

33. Andrus (1967), 194–95.

34. Andrus (1967), 194–95.

35. Campbell (2003), 111.

36. The Lord is not necessarily suggesting that these are more honorable than other professions. But this verse does highlight the reality that such secular occupations existed at the beginning of time and were honorable in the eyes of God.

37. Church (1992), 6–7.

38. Church (1992), 6.

39. Sailhamer (1992), 101; Sailhamer (1976–1992), 2:45, 47, n. 15. Brown, Driver, and Briggs give as possible definitions for the Hebrew word translated as dress in the KJV, "perform acts of worship," "obey," "serve with [a] peace-offering and grain-offering," "Levitical service," "caused to serve God," and so on; and for the Hebrew word translated as keep in the KJV, "observe," "keep [the] covenant," "keep commands," "observe," and so on. See Brown, Driver, and Briggs (1999), 712–13, 1036–37.

40. Oden (2001), 59.

41. See Philo of Alexandria, "Allegorical Interpretation" 1:28, in Yonge (1997), 35.

42. Severian of Gabala, "On the Creation of the World" 5:5, in Oden (2001), 60. See also Theophilus of Antioch, "Theophilus to Autolycus" 2:24, in Roberts and Donaldson (1994), 2:104; Ginzberg (1967–1969), 1:70.

43. See Nibley, "Subduing the Earth" (1988), 85–99; Nibley (1994), 3–101.

44. President N. Eldon Tanner noted: "God has pointed out to us, as to Adam, that if we are to enjoy life to the full, there are things we must do and things we must not do. In other words, we are given everything for our benefit and blessing but we must remember that there are a few 'forbidden fruits' that will deprive us of full enjoyment and bring sorrow and regret to us if we partake." Tanner (1971), 32.

45. B. McConkie (1978), 221.

46. Nachmanides (1971–1976), 1:76.

47. Theophilus of Antioch, "Theophilus to Autolycus" 2:25, in Roberts and Donaldson (1994), 2:104.

48. Philo of Alexandria, "Allegorical Interpretation" 1:31, in Yonge (1997), 36.

49. Ryken, Wilhoit, and Longman (1998), 247; Clifford and Murphy (1990), 12; Hertz (1962), 9. Beverly Campbell defines "help meet" as "a power or strength equal to" man. See Campbell (2003), 24.

50. Rasmussen (1993), 12. See also Neusner (1985), 180; Clarke (n. d.), 1:45.

51. Kidner (1967), 65; Speiser (1962), 17; Sailhamer, (1976–1992), 2:46; Hertz (1962), 9; Adams (1990), 97. Jolene Edmunds Rockwood translates the Hebrew for help meet as "a power or strength equal to man." See Rockwood (1992), 16.

52. Rockwood (1992), 16.

53. See Tertullian, "Against Marcion" 2:4, in Oden (2001), 64.

54. Church (1992), 7.

55. Ephrem the Syrian, "Commentary on Genesis" 2.9.3, in Oden (2001), 65. See also Parley P. Pratt, as cited in Andrus (1967), 203–4.

56. See Ambrose, "Paradise" 11:51–52, in Oden (2001), 66. See also Ginzberg (1967–1969), 5:65, n. 6.

57. Hertz (1962), 9. Anciently, to give one a name, or to know one's name, placed the individual with that knowledge in power over the thing or person named. See Gaskill (2003), 219–20.

58. See Jones (2003).

59. Ginzberg (1967–1969), 1:49.

60. Church (1992), 7.

61. Maxwell (1995), 30.

62. Ambrose, "Paradise" 10:48, in Oden (2001), 68.

63. See Augustine, "On the Literal Interpretation of Genesis" 9:5–9, in Oden (2001), 69.

64. Nelson (1987), 87.

65. See Church (1992), 7. See also Holland and Holland (1989), 107; Ginzberg (1967–1969), 5:90, n. 47. See also Burton (1986), 154; Pfeiffer and Harrison (1962), 5–6; Jamieson, Fausset, and Brown (n. d.), 19. Hertz records the saying as follows: "The woman is formed out of the man's side; hence it is the wife's natural duty to be at hand, ready at all times to be a 'help' to her husband; it is the husband's natural duty ever to cherish and defend his wife, as part of his own self." Hertz (1962), 9. "We should not create her beginning with the head, so that she not be frivolous, nor from the eye, that she not be a starer (looking at men), nor from the ear, that she not be an eavesdropper, nor from the mouth, that she not talk too much (as a gossip), nor from the heart, that she not be jealous, nor from the hand, that she not be light-fingered [or a thief], nor from the foot, that she not be a gadabout [one who roams about aimlessly or without purpose and direction], but from a covered up place on man." Neusner (1985),

191. See also McConkie, "The Mystery of Eden" (1990), 26.

66. Hunter (1951), 145. See also Ginzberg (1967–1969), 1:66; Sailhamer (1976–1992), 2:47.

67. Ephrem the Syrian, "Commentary on Genesis" 2.14.2, in Oden (2001), 72.

68. Hertz (1962), 10. In the Apocalypse of Abraham it suggests that the connection between the serpent and Satan is simply a metaphorical expression indicating that the devil had the appearance of a serpent. See Ginzberg (1967–1969), 5:123–24, n. 131.

69. "Life of Adam and Eve," Greek version, 19:1, in Charlesworth (1983–1985), 2:279.

70. Ehat and Cook (1980), 60.

71. Kimball (1967), 30.

72. See Augustine, "On Nature and Grace" 29:33, in Oden (2001), 77. See also Ephrem the Syrian, "Commentary on Genesis" 2:16, in Oden (2001), 77; Oden (2001), 74.

73. Augustine, "City of God" 14:13, in Oden (2001), 77.

74. See Augustine, "On Faith and the Creed" 4:6, in Oden (2001), 77. See also Oden (2001), 74.

75. Augustine, "Two Books on Genesis against Manichaeans" 2.17.25, in Oden (2001), 86.

76. Ephrem the Syrian, "Commentary on Genesis" 2.20.1, in Oden (2001), 75–76.

77. Philo of Alexandria certainly saw Adam and Eve as a representation of the "two elements within human nature"—the mind and the body. See Pagels (1989), 64–65.

78. See Ambrose, "Paradise" 15:73, in Oden (2001), 89.

79. Church (1992), 8.

80. Ginzberg (1967–1969), 1:72, 73–74. See also Neusner (1985), 201; Clarke (n. d.), 1:50.

81. Dummelow (1936), 9.

82. Hamilton (1982), 47.

83. Kidner (1967), 67. See also Andrus (1967), 186; Hertz (1962), 10; Rasmussen (1993), 14.

84. Hamilton (1982), 47.

85. Church (1992), 8–9.

86. Kidner (1967), 67–68; Speiser (1962), 23; Hertz (1962), 10; Pfeiffer and Harrison (1962), 7; Peake (1919), 140; Dummelow (1936), 9; Neusner (1985), 201–2; Clarke (n. d.), 1:50.

87. It should be noted that faithful Mother Eve would never have done this. She was true to God's word, and correct in her interpretation of it. However, owing to the fact that this story is about us, the addition of (or changing of) the command highlights what we tend to do and not what Eve would have done.

88. Lewis (1996), 53–54.

89. See Kidner (1967), 69.

90. Reynolds and Sjodahl (1980), 136.

91. See Sailhamer (1992), 104; Sailhamer (1976–1992), 2:51.

92. Jamieson, Fausset, and Brown (n. d.), 19.

93. Reynolds and Sjodahl (1980), 136–37.

94. Smith (1974), 63, emphasis in original. See also 62.

95. See Augustine (1950), 460. See also Keller (1990), 156.

96. See Oden (2001), 74, 92. Ancient Jewish belief held that Adam was created before Eve in order to send a message about the divinely established roles of men and women. See Ginzberg (1967–1969), 5:88, n. 41. One fourth-century source states: "She hastened to eat before her husband that she might become head over her head, that she might become the one to give command to that one by whom she was to be commanded." Ephrem the Syrian, "Commentary on Genesis" 2.20.3, in Oden (2001), 78.

97. Augustine, "Two Books on Genesis against the Manichaeans" 2.15.23, in Oden (2001), 81; Bede the Venerable, "Homilies on the Gospels" 1:17, in Oden (2001), 82.

98. See Wilson (1999), 17, 289.

99. See Ryken, Wilhoit, and Longman (1998), 320; Charles (1997), 59.

100. Habershon (1974), 104.

101. This is a common Hebrew idiom in the Talmud. See Ginzberg (1967–1969), 5:121–22, n. 120; "Life of Adam and Eve," in Charlesworth (1983–1985), 2:281, note 20a.

102. Neusner (1985), 205.

103. Philo of Alexandria, "Allegorical Interpretation" 3:18, in Yonge (1997), 56.

104. Chrysostom, "Homilies on Genesis" 17:3–4, in Oden (2001), 82.

105. Ephrem the Syrian, "Commentary on Genesis" 2.24.1, in Oden (2001), 82.

106. Jerome, "Homilies" I, in Oden (2001), 82.

107. Augustine, "Two Books on Genesis against the Manichaeans" 2.16.24, in Oden (2001), 83.

108. Oden (2001), 74.

109. Ginzberg (1967–1969), 1:76–77; Vawter (1977), 81; Kidner (1967), 70; Jamieson, Fausset, and Brown (n. d.), 19.

110. B. McConkie, "Eve and the Fall" (1979), 58.

111. We're never tempted above our ability to withstand, so long as we do not place ourselves—physically, or in our thoughts—in tempting situations. However, if we choose to do otherwise, we can (and likely will) be tempted far above our strength to resist.

112. Tanner (1971), 33. Adam and Eve's posterity imitate their passing of the buck. Clarke (n. d.), 1:52.

113. Oden (2001), 84. Thus, one text claims that "God's calling, and saying, Where art thou, Adam?" was God's way of offering you and me (represented by Adam) "an opportunity of repentance and confession"—an opportunity fallen men (symbolized by Adam) too often do not take. See Theophilus of Antioch, "Theophilus to Autolycus" 2:26, in Roberts and Donaldson (1994), 2:105.

114. See Ephrem the Syrian, "Commentary on Genesis" 2.27.1–2, in Oden (2001), 85.

115. Augustine, "Two Books on Genesis against the Manichaeans" 2.17.25, in Oden (2001), 86. See also Vawter (1977), 81; Nachmanides (1971–1976), 1:83; Sailhamer (1992), 106; Sailhamer (1976–1992), 2:54; Jamieson, Fausset, and Brown (n. d.), 19; Church (1992), 10; Hertz (1962), 11; Pfeiffer and Harrison (1962), 8; Peake (1919), 140; Dummelow (1936), 10; Clarke (n. d.), 1:52; Rockwood (1992), 20; Keller (1990), 172–73; Reynolds and Sjodahl (1980), 138–39.

116. Tanner (1971), 33.

117. Lundquist (1989), 88.

118. Ambrose, "Paradise" 14:70, in Oden (2001), 84. See also Philo of Alexandria, "Allegorical Interpretation" 3:17, in Yonge (1997), 56.

119. Ephrem the Syrian, "Commentary on Genesis" 2.26.1–2, in Oden (2001), 84.

120. Church (1992), 10.

121. Ginzberg (1967–1969), 1:76.

122. Sailhamer (1992), 103; Sailhamer (1976–1992), 2:49–50.

123. Augustine, "Two Books on Genesis against the Manichaeans" 2.16.24, in Oden (2001), 85.

124. See Irenaeus, "Against Heresies" 3.23.5, in Roberts and Donaldson (1994), 1:457.

125. Kidner (1967), 70.

126. President N. Eldon Tanner put it this way: "We are all like Adam in that when we partake of 'forbidden fruits' or do the things we are commanded not to do, we are ashamed, and we draw away from the Church and from God and hide ourselves, and if we continue in sin, the Spirit of God withdraws from us." Tanner (1971), 33.

127. Speiser (1962), 25.

128. Reynolds and Sjodahl (1980), 134. See also King (1995), s. v. Moses 4:6.

129. See footnote 3:4a in the LDS edition of the King James Version of the Bible. See also Irenaeus, "Against Heresies" 5:23, in Roberts and Donaldson (1994), 1:551; Clarke (n. d.), 1:44, 54; Pagels (1989), 67.

130. Widtsoe (1998), 107; Young, in *Journal of Discourses*, 15:126.

131. Andrus (1967), 187–88.

132. See Vawter (1977), 81.

133. See Symeon the New Theologian, "Discourses" 5:6, in Oden (2001), 87.

134. Dorotheus of Gaza, "Spiritual Instruction" I, in Oden (2001), 87. Like Eve, our tendency is to blame the devil—suggesting that his temptations were either too great, or his methodology too subtle. However, "Satan's subtlety will not justify us in sin: though he is the tempter, we are the sinners; and indeed it is our lust that draws us aside and entices us." See Church (1992), 10. "Man is always inclined to blame the outward incitement to sin, rather than the inward inclination." See Dummelow (1936), 10. See also Hunter (1951), 118.

135. See Church (1992), 10.

136. See Fontana (1994), 34; Todeschi (1995), 289; Caesarius of Arles, "Sermons" 136, in Oden (2001), 90; Gaskill (2003), 272.

137. Oden (2001), 88.

138. Augustine, "Two Books on Genesis against the Manichaeans," in Oden (2001), 89.

139. Caesarius of Arles, "Sermons" 136, in Oden (2001), 90.

140. Ambrose, "Flight from the World" 7:43, in Oden (2001), 90.

141. Rasmussen (1993), 16–17.

142. Church (1992), 10.

143. Oden (2001), 92.

144. Augustine, "Two Books on Genesis against the Manichaeans" 2.19.29, in Oden (2001), 93.

145. See Sailhamer (1992), 108; Sailhamer (1976–1992), 2:56.

146. Nachmanides indicated that the Hebrew word translated "desire" refers to "cohabitation." See Nachmanides (1971–1976), 1:84. In the Genesis Rabbah we read: "When a woman sits down on the birthstool, she says, 'I shall never again have sexual relations with my husband.' Then the Holy One, blessed be He, says to her, 'You will return to your lust, you will return to having lust for your husband.' " See Neusner (1985), 221.

147. Hertz (1962), 12.

148. Vawter (1977), 85.

149. Rockwood (1992), 21. Nachmanides noted that some rabbis interpret the phrase "thy desire shall be unto thy husband" as meaning "you will be placed under your husband's authority, and expected to do what he desires, rather than what you desire." See Nachmanides (1971–1976), 1:84; Church (1992), 12.

150. Jamieson, Fausset, and Brown (n. d.), 19. See also Vawter (1977), 84–85.

151. See Peake (1919), 140.

152. See Schlessinger (2004).

153. Kidner (1967), 71. Sailhamer put it this way: "In Genesis 4:7 the 'longing' carries the sense of a desire to overcome or defeat another. . . . The sense of 'desiring' in 3:16 should be understood as the wife's desire to overcome or gain the upper hand over her husband. . . . This statement stands in sharp contrast to the picture of the man and the woman as 'one flesh.' . . . The Fall has had its effect on the relationship of the husband and wife." Sailhamer (1976–1992), 2:58, n. 16. Matthew Henry interprets the passage as saying, because of the Fall, women would "despise," "disobey," and seek to "dominere" their husbands. Church (1992), 11.

154. The words toil and suffering are closely related in Hebrew, and in the Samarian Pentateuch they are the same. See Vawter (1977), 85.

155. Vawter (1977), 85.

156. Oden (2001), 92.

157. Judd King wrote: "The thorns, thistles, and sweat become symbols for the challenges and difficulties all of mankind experience on earth as they live out their days." King (1995), s. v. Moses 4:23–25.

158. Church (1992), 12.

159. Hamilton (1982), 48. It is also interesting that Eve, while being "tempted" by Satan, doesn't see clearly (i.e., she doesn't see Lucifer for what he truly is). However, upon partaking of the fruit of the tree of knowledge of good and evil, the Luciferic veil that prohibited her from seeing Satan for what he is was withdrawn and she exclaims, "I know thee now. . . ." Such is the case with each of us when we are tempted to sin. Satan veils our minds and clouds our vision regarding the repercussion of our actions and the feelings we will have if we succumb. When we sin, however, not only does God's Spirit withdraw, but so does Satan's veil, and—with Eve—we metaphorically exclaim, "I know thee now" (i.e., "How could I have not seen this for what it was?"). We traditionally recognize that it was Satan influencing us right after we do what he was tempting us to do. But in the midst of the temptation he so very successfully veils the truth. "Satan wishes to blur our knowledge of the absolutes of good and evil." Campbell (2003), 40.

160. Theodoret of Cyr, "On the Incarnation of the Lord" 6:1, in Oden (2001), 96.

161. Romney (1943), 27–28. See also Benson (1980), 32.

162. *Lectures on Faith*, 6:7.

163. B. McConkie (1997), 64.

164. Ginzberg (1967–1969), 1:79; 5:97, 103–4. See also Tvedtnes (1994), 651–52. The two Hebrew words for "light" and "skin" differ in only the initial letters, and are pronounced alike in modern Hebrew. This explains why some traditions have the garments of Adam and Eve made of light while others have them made of skin. See Tvedtnes (1994), 651. See also Robinson (1990), 138; Adams (1990), 98. "God killed certain animals in order to furnish Adam and Eve with clothes." Ginzberg (1967–1969), 5:104, n. 93. See also J. McConkie (1985), 202; Tvedtnes (1994), 649–50.

165. Blake Ostler wrote: "It should be noted that the ancient garment bore the same tokens as the veil of the temple at Jerusalem. . . . Many ancient texts confuse the garment with the veil of the temple, such as Ambrose of Milano's Tractate of the Mysteries or the Hebrew Book of Enoch where the 'garment' and 'veil' are used interchangeably." Ostler (1982), 35. "Linen fabric possesses several symbolic aspects that are relevant. . . . The fine linen worn by heavenly beings is described as 'clean and white' or 'pure and white' and is therefore an appropriate symbol of worthiness or righteousness (see Revelation 3:4–5; 15:6; 19:8). Since linen is not the product of an animal that is subject unto death, or 'corruption' as it is called, it is also a fitting

symbol of immortality, which is also called 'incorruption' (see 1 Corinthians 15:52–54)." Brown (1999), 81–82. See also Habershon (1974), 104.

166. J. McConkie, "The Mystery of Eden" (1990), 30.

167. Brown, Driver, and Briggs (1999), 497–98.

168. Tanner (1992), 44.

169. Asay (1997), 21.

170. Vawter (1977), 87.

171. Scott (1996), 74.

172. Kidner (1967), 72.

173. Hertz (1962), 13.

174. See, for example, Holzapfel and Seely (1994), 17; Gaskill (2003), 150–56.

175. O. McConkie (1975), 59.

176. Fairbairn (1989), 1:227. See also 1:218, 221, 223.

177. Myers (1987), 204.

178. Unger (1966), 192; Random House, *Webster's College Dictionary* (1996), 233, s. v., "cherub"; Douglas (1971), 208.

179. J. McConkie (1985), 256. McConkie is drawing on Doctrine and Covenants 132:19. See also Unger (1966), 192.

180. J. McConkie (1985), 274. See also Cooper (1995), 178. Joseph Fielding McConkie (1985) also noted that "the Tree of Life . . . contained the power of everlasting life." J. McConkie (1985), 274.

181. Thomas (1994), 13.

182. Julien (1996), 462. See also Cirlot (1962), 347.

183. Black (1988), 123, n. 7.

184. Fairbairn (1989), 2:208.

185. J. McConkie (1985), 255–56.

186. Julien (1996), 149–50.

187. J. McConkie (1985), 259. See also Cooper (1995), 66–67; Todeschi (1995), 108; Fontana (1994), 139.

188. Barth (1974), 800; McConkie and Parry (1990), 102; J. McConkie (1985), 272–73; Cirlot (1962), 324; Doctrine and Covenants 6:2; 27:18; 1 Nephi 21:2; Ephesians 6:17; Hebrews 4:12; Revelation 1:16; 19:15.

189. Cooper (1995), 167; Fontana (1994), 72.

190. Todeschi (1995), 250.

191. Bayley (1990), 2:74.

192. Widtsoe (1998), 416.

193. "Only through the covenant can human fellowship with God be restored. . . . In the covenant, human beings returned to the state they enjoyed in Genesis 2:15—serving God, obeying his will, and enjoying his blessing." Sailhamer (1992), 110.

194. Bede the Venerable, "Homilies on the Gospels" 1:12, in Oden (2001), 102.

195. Hafen (1989), 32.

196. Hafen and Hafen (1994), 79.

THREE

Adam and Eve as Types for Christ and His Church

THIS CHAPTER IS really but an appendage to our last chapter— "You and Me As Adam and Eve." It is an extension of that concept, based on the reality that scripture frequently highlights Christ's covenant relationship with His Church by employing the symbols of bride and bridegroom for the Church and Messiah respectively.[1] Therefore, this chapter will focus on aspects of the story of the Fall that appear to highlight that relationship between Christ and His covenant people. In this section the man Adam will stand as a representation of God the Father, His Son (and our Savior) Jesus, and their prophets. Eve, on the other hand, will serve as a typological symbol of the Church, the bride of Christ, or covenant Israel.

THE CREATION OF ADAM AND EVE

Genesis 1:27	Moses 2:27	Abraham 4:27
So God created man In his own image, in the image of God created he him; male and female created he them.	And I, God, created man in mine own image, in the image of mine Only Begotten created I him; male and female created I them (see also Moses 6:9)	So the Gods went down to organize man in their own image, in the image of the Gods to form they him, male and female to form they them.

God created man in His own image. Just as Adam was the first human to be created, Christ is the Firstborn of the Father (see Doctrine and Covenants 93:21). Adam was created in the image of God,[2] as was Jesus, who is said to be in the express image of the Father (see Hebrews 1:3). Michael became the "first . . . Adam" and Jesus is the "last Adam" (1 Corinthians 15:45).

Genesis 2:15	Moses 3:15	Abraham 5:11
And the Lord God took the man, and put him into the garden of Eden to dress it and to keep it.	And I, the Lord God, took the man, and put him into the Garden of Eden, to dress it, and to keep it.	And the Gods took the man and put him in the Garden of Eden, to dress it and to keep it.

God put the man in Eden. Eden was the first of earthly temples.[3] The temple is the house of the Lord. Christ's Spirit dwells there. Adam was placed in this prototype temple by God Himself. Similarly, during His mortal ministry—in compliance with the law—Christ regularly went to the temple, where He both taught and participated in the rites of His day.

Dress and keep it. As noted previously, commentators often suggest that the phrase to "dress" and "keep" might better be translated "to worship and obey"[4]—or, in other words, to follow God's laws and commandments. In the same way that God expected Adam to be strictly obedient to all of His commands (thereby setting an example for all of his posterity), so also Christ was sent to earth to set the example of "worship" and "obedience" for the rest of God's children.

A garden. Much like Christ, Adam was born into humble circumstances. He was given a mortal inheritance of simplicity—a garden. There was to be no castle for Michael, the "prince of all" (Doctrine and Covenants 27:11; 107:54–55), and no palace for Christ, the "Prince of Peace" (Isaiah 9:6; 2 Nephi 19:6). Personal opulence distracts from the work of God. The complexities of this life, particularly when in conjunction with living a life of self-indulgence, afford us many opportunities to forget God, His commandments, and our divinely dictated priorities. There is safety in the simple life Adam and Christ were called to live.

A COMMANDMENT

Genesis 2:16–17	Moses 3:16–17	Abraham 5:12–13
And the Lord God commanded the man, saying, Of every tree of the garden thou mayest freely eat: But of the tree of the knowledge of good and evil, thou shalt not eat of it: for In the day that thou eatest thereof thou shalt surely die.	And I, the Lord God, commanded the man, saying: Of every tree of the garden thou mayest freely eat, But of the tree of the knowledge of good an devil, thou shalt not eat of it, nevertheless, thou mayest choose for thyself, for it Is given unto thee; but, remember that I forbid it, for In the day thou eatest thereof thou shalt surely die.	And the Gods commanded the man, saying: Of every tree of the garden thou mayest freely eat, But of the tree of knowledge of good and evil thou shalt not eat of it; for in the time that thou eatest thereof, thou shalt surely die. Now I, Abraham, saw that it was after the Lord's time, which was after the time of Kolob; for as yet the Gods had not appointed unto Adam his reckoning.

Thou shalt not eat of it. In the scriptural accounts of the Fall, Eve is not present when the Father gives the commandment for them to avoid eating of the "forbidden" fruit. Adam receives God's word and then conveys it to Eve. She then is expected to exercise faith in the divinity of the command and be obedient to it. Similarly, God gives to Christ and His prophets commandments, which they in turn convey to us. We do not receive these directly from the Father, but rather through mediators He has chosen. We are then expected to exhibit faith in the divinity of these revealed dictates and be obedient to them. Hence, Ambrose noted that, in the scriptural accounts of the Fall, Satan "aimed to circumvent Adam [i.e., the Christ] by means of the woman [i.e., the Church]. He did not accost the man who had in his presence received the heavenly command. He accosted her who had learned of it from her husband and who had not received from God the command which was to be observed."[5]

So it is with us, Christ's Church. Satan tempts us in order to get at God and Christ. We are susceptible to his enticings, but They are not.

The story of the Fall informs us that Adam (representing Christ) fell, not because he was tricked, but because Eve (symbolic of the members of the Church) gave in to the serpent's enticings (i.e., the devil's temptations), and thus Adam (Christ) needed to come to mortality to fix what Eve (God's other children) had done. Adam's act clearly mirrors Christ's choice to redeem us (His bride or Church) from sin and spiritual death.

Genesis 2:18	Moses 3:18	Abraham 5:14
And the Lord God said, It is not good that man should be alone; I will make him an help meet for him.	And I, the Lord God, said unto mine Only Begotten, that it was not good that the man should be alone; wherefore, I will make an help meet for him.	And the Gods said: Let us make an help meet for the man, for it is not good that the man should be alone, therefore we will form an help meet for him.

I will make him an help meet. This is Christ's work. It is His Church. But it was not in the design and will of the Father that He do it alone. As Eve was Adam's help and support, Christ's bride—the Church—serves as His help and support. Her members aided Him in the creation, in the writing of scripture, in the preaching of His message, in the administration of ordinances, and so on. Their hands are His hands. Their work is His work. Adam and Eve were commanded to be one, and, in a like manner, Christ and His Church are to be one.

Genesis 2:21–24	Moses 3:21–24	Abraham 5:15–18
And the Lord God caused a deep sleep to fall upon Adam, and he slept: and he took one of his ribs, and closed up the flesh instead thereof; And the rib, which the Lord God had taken from man, made he a woman, and	And I, the Lord God, caused a deep sleep to fall upon Adam; and he slept, and I took one of his ribs and closed up the flesh in the stead thereof; And the rib which I, the Lord God, had taken from man, made I a woman, and	And the Gods caused a deep sleep to fall upon Adam; and he slept, and they took one of his ribs, and closed up the flesh in the stead thereof; And of the rib which the Gods had taken from man, formed they a woman, and brought

brought her unto the man. And Adam said, This is now bone of my bones, and flesh of my flesh: she shall be called Woman, because she was taken out of Man. Therefore shall a man leave his father and his mother, and shall cleave unto his wife: and they shall be one flesh.	brought her unto the man. And Adam said: This I know now is bone of my bones, and flesh of my flesh; she shall be called Woman, because she was taken out of man. Therefore shall a man leave his father and his mother, and shall cleave unto his wife; and they shall be one flesh.	her unto the man. And Adam said: This was bone of my bones, and flesh of my flesh; now she shall be called Woman, because she was taken out of man; Therefore shall a man leave his father and his mother, and shall cleave unto his wife, and they shall be one flesh.

She was taken out of man. The Church is called "Christian" because it comes out of the Man, Christ. And the covenant relationship between the bride and the Bridegroom is the most important of all eternal relationships. Adam and Eve were to become one; husbands and wives are all commanded to become one; and Christ and His Church are to be one. One typologist wrote: "[Eve is] a type of the church as Adam is a type of Christ. As Eve was made out of a part of Adam, so the church is a part of the Lord Jesus. The church is called His bride as Eve was Adam's bride."[6]

It is significant that the man calls the woman "bone of my bone and flesh of my flesh," a statement he could not have made about the animals. In Hebrew, these phrases indicate a closeness, a blood relationship between the two parties, and in this case a unified companionship between the man and the woman. But the phrases are also used in other places in the Old Testament to describe two parties who are not necessarily blood relatives but who have made a covenant with each other, such as when the northern tribes of Israel made a covenant with David, their new king, and confirmed: "Behold, we are thy bone and thy flesh." David makes a similar covenant with the elders of Judah: "Ye are my brethren, ye are my bones and my flesh." Some of the participants may have been related, but the phrase refers to a mutual covenant the two parties have made with each other.[7]

There is a covenant relationship between Christ and His Church. This is foreshadowed by Adam's relationship with Eve. That the man was made first and the woman was made from the man has been seen as a statement about the covenant people's dependence upon Christ, who was the Firstborn of Father's spirit offspring.[8] The rib metaphor suggests that human existence is intended to be a partnership of man and woman[9]—or Christ and His bride.[10]

And they shall be one flesh. Jewish thought holds that one reason why Eve was taken from Adam's body was to teach that man and woman were to be "indissoluble" or "one."[11] The phrase "one flesh" has reference to the fact that in Eden Adam and Eve were sealed for time and all eternity. Again, their union is said to foreshadow our union to Christ—He being the Groom and we His bride.[12]

Deep sleep. Commentators have suggested that the "deep sleep" that came upon Adam foreshadowed Christ's sacrifice on our behalf. Augustine put it this way: "Adam's sleep was a mystical foreshadowing of Christ's death, and when his dead body hanging from the cross was pierced by the lance [in] his side."[13] In addition, just as through that sleep Eve was "formed or builded," so also through Christ's death the Church was built up or given strength.[14] "Since Eve had been created from the side of the sleeping Adam, . . . from the side of Christ hanging on the cross the church . . . must be created. In fact the church is 'the woman.' "[15] Christ's bride, the covenant people, certainly existed before His Atonement. However, it was the death of Christ that gave their work efficacy and turned a localized religion of ancient Israel into the worldwide faith of Christianity.

This "deep sleep" coming upon Christ (represented by Adam) may highlight the fact that Christ came here, took upon Himself a mortal body, and subjected Himself to the veil of forgetting and the trials and tests of mortality. However, through His exact obedience and perfect faithfulness, that veil of forgetting—that "deep sleep"—was rent and His communion with the Father was made possible. In this Christ sets for us the perfect example.

Dust versus rib. Late in the fourth century, Ambrose noted that Eve was not made in the same way Adam was. She was created from a rib, whereas Adam came from the dust.[16] Similarly, Christ's mortal birth (represented by Adam's creation) was different from that of each of us (typified by Eve's creation). Whereas we have come entirely from another mortal (symbolized by the rib), Christ's origin is clearly different (as highlighted by the dust utilized in the creation of Adam). It is this difference in His origin and makeup that enables Him to atone—and us to exercise faith in Him.

THE TEMPTATION OF ADAM AND EVE

Genesis 3:1–5	Moses 4:5–11	2 Nephi 2:17–18
Now the serpent was more subtil than any beast of the field which the Lord God had made. And he said . . . Yeah, hath God said, Ye shall not eat of every tree of the garden? . . . Ye shall not surely die: For God doth know that in the day ye eat thereof, then your eyes shall be opened, and ye shall be as gods, knowing good and evil.	And now the serpent was more subtle than any beast of the field which I, the Lord God, had made. And Satan put it into the heart of the serpent, (for he had drawn away many after him,) and he sought also to beguile . . . for he knew not the mind of God, wherefore he sought to destroy the world. And he said . . . Yea, hath God said—Ye shall no eat of every tree of the garden? (And he spake by the mouth of the serpent.) . . . Ye shall not surely die; For God doth know that in the day ye eat thereof, then your eyes shall be opened, and ye shall be as gods, knowing good and evil.	And I, Lehi, according to the things which I have read, must needs suppose that an angel of God, according to that which is written, had fallen from heaven; wherefore, he became a devil having sought that which was evil before God. And because he had fallen from heaven, and had become miserable forever, he sought also the misery of all mankind . . . wherefore he said: Partake of the forbidden fruit, and ye shall not die, but ye shall be as God, knowing good and evil.

Adam was approached first. The book of Hebrews informs us that Christ "was in all points tempted like as we are, yet without sin" (Hebrews 4:15). In the temple account of the Fall, Adam is approached by the devil before Eve is. However, the man rejects Satan's enticements. Therefore, Lucifer moves on to Eve—and she succumbs. So it is with Christ and His Church. He was tempted or tried in all things, but did not fall. We (His bride), on the other hand, too often do give in to the allures of the adversary. Thus, just as Adam is depicted leaving Eden to reverse the effects of what Eve had done, so also Christ left His Father's abode in the heavens in order to rectify what wrongs we have committed.[17] Had Adam not chosen to leave Eden, the plan would have been left incomplete—it would have been thwarted. And had Christ not chosen to leave the Father's presence (in the premortal world), the plan would have been left incomplete—it would have been thwarted. Thus, Adam's actions mirror Christ's.

Genesis 3:6–7	Moses 4:12–13
And when the woman saw that the tree was good for food, and that it was pleasant to the eyes, and a tree to be desired to make one wise, she took of the fruit thereof, and did eat, and gave also unto her husband with her; and he did eat. And the eyes of them both were opened, and they knew that they were naked; and they sewed fig leaves together, and made themselves aprons.	And when the woman saw that the tree was good for food, and that it became pleasant to the eyes, and a tree to be desired to make her wise, she took of the fruit thereof, and did eat, and also gave unto her husband with her, and he did eat. And the eyes of them both were opened, and they knew that they had been naked. And they sewed fig leaves together and made themselves aprons.

Eve ate of the fruit first. As will be recalled, according to the scriptural accounts, Adam received from God the commandment to not partake of the "forbidden" fruit. He then conveyed this commandment to Eve (who was not present at the giving of the divine instructions). Thus, one early Christian commentator suggested that Eve's partaking mirrors the tendency of some Christians to desire to be the ruler of their own lives, rather than allowing Christ to rule and direct them.[18] Adam, standing as a representation of Christ, should rule the woman or Church. But her partaking of the fruit without a directive from him to do so echoes our temptation to take things into our own hands.

Again, according to the scriptural accounts, Eve had less information than Adam—she could not see as clearly, as it were—and thus Adam was to be her guide, to whom she was to cling. Similarly, you and I have less information about the things of salvation than do Christ and His prophets—we labor under a veil, as it were—and hence they must be our guides, to whom we must cling. To take matters into our own hands is to bring heartache and trials into our lives (as Eve did metaphorically into hers).

The Repercussions of the Fall

Genesis 3:16	Moses 4:22
Unto the woman he said, I will greatly multiply thy sorrow and thy conception; in sorrow thou shalt bring forth children; and thy desire shall be to thy husband, and he shall rule over thee.	Unto the woman, I, the Lord God, said: I will greatly multiply thy sorrow and thy conception. In sorrow thou shalt bring forth children, and thy desire shall be to thy husband, and he shall rule over thee.

He shall rule over thee. Metaphorically speaking, Eve was deceived, but Adam was not. Thus, the transgression of Eve established (at the beginning of her mortal probation) her need to be saved by her husband—who could see through the adversary's sophistry. Thus, the "husband" that the woman (or Church) should desire is Christ; and He shall rule over His bride (the Church).[19] This position is rightfully His because He is perfect and cannot be deceived.

Banishment from God's Presence

Genesis 3:22–23	Moses 4:28–29
And the Lord God . . . sent [them] forth from the garden of Eden.	And I, the Lord God . . . will send [them] forth from the Garden of Eden.

Sent forth together. As Eve's act introduced this telestial, mortal probation, she would be sent forth to be tried and tested. However, she would not be expected to brave the lone and dreary world alone. God would send with her a help, Adam—he being physically stronger than she—that he might serve as a protector and provider. So also

God has not sent us (the Church) to walk the danger-strewn path of mortality alone. He has sent us a companion in Christ. His strengths far exceed ours. He will serve as our protector and provider throughout this daunting existence, so long as we keep His Spirit with us.

CONCLUSION

In the story of Adam and Eve we find distinct hints of Christ's covenant relationship with His Church. The tale's figurative description of Eve's choice to hearken to the devil, and Adam's resistance to any form of disobedience, strongly mirror the weakness of the mortals who comprise the Lord's Church and the strength of the Messiah who seeks to redeem us.

The two charts below summarize the notion that Eve often symbolizes the bride of Christ, or the Church, and Adam frequently represents Christ and His appointed prophets.

Eve as a Symbol For the Bride	The Church or Bride of Christ
Eve came from Adam, and was different from him in her physical origin (Genesis 2:21–24).	The Church comes form Christ, and its members are different in their physical makeup when compared to their Savior.
Adam and Eve were married by God for time and all eternity while in Eden—the first temple.	The Church becomes Christ's eternal bride by entering into a covenant relationship with Him in the holy temple.
In the scriptural accounts of the Fall, Eve receives the commandments from Adam, who gets them from the Father and then conveys them to her (Genesis 2:16–17).	The Church gets the commandments through prophets, who get them from God and Christ (see Hebrews 1:1–2).
Eve is Adam's helpmeet or partner in Eden (Genesis 2:18).	The members of the Church are Christ's helpers, serving as saviors on Mt. Zion (Obadiah 1:21).
Adam and Eve are commanded by God to be one (see Genesis 2:24).	Christ and His Church are to be one (Doctrine and Covenants 35:2).

Eve fell, and thus Adam had to enter mortality to rescue her from her choice (2 Nephi 2:25).	The Church is made up of fallen souls who need Christ to enter into mortality to rescue them from their choices.
Eve partook of sin, and then gave to Adam (Genesis 3:6).	The members of the Church commit sins, and then Christ takes upon Him all sins through Atonement (Alma 7:13; 2 Corinthians 5:21).
Adam rules over Eve (Genesis 3:16).	Christ rules and reigns over the Church (Revelation 11:15).
Adam is Eve's companion in this life of trails and tests—serving as her helper, provider, and protector (Genesis 3:23).	Christ is our companion through the tests and trails of mortality—helping, providing for, and protecting us (John 14:18).

Adam As a Type for Christ	Christ
Adam was physically the first man created by God the Father (Moses 3:7).	Christ was the firstborn spirit of God the Father (Colossians 1:15).
Adam was created in the Father's image (Genesis 1:27).	Christ was created in the Father's image (Hebrews 1:3).
Adam was foreordained (Abraham 3:22–23).	Christ was foreordained (Abraham 3:22–23).
Adam was the head of the human family (Doctrine and Covenants 107:55).	Christ is the spiritual head of the family of God (Ephesians 4:15).
Adam was a sinless man who chose for the benefit of others, to take upon himself sin, and in so doing died (2 Nephi 2:25).[20]	Christ is a sinless man who chose, for the benefit of others, to take upon Himself sins, and in so doing died (Mosiah 26:23).
Adam provided all mankind with a chance at mortal birth and thus eternal life (2 Nephi 2:25).	Christ provides all mankind with the chance of spiritual rebirth and eternal life (1 John 5:1, 4).
Adam ruled on earth in its paradisiacal, Edenic splendor (Genesis 1:26, 28).	Christ will rule on the earth when it returns to its paradisiacal splendor during the Millennium (Article of Faith 10).

Michael is the "first Adam" (1 Corinthians 15:45).	Christ is the "last Adam" (1 Corinthians 15:45).
Adam's premortal name, Michael, means "who is like unto God."[21]	Christ, the premortal Jehovah, is "like unto God" (Abraham 3:24).
According to ancient legend, while Adam was making a sacrifice he was smitten in his side, causing blood and water to flow out.[22]	While Jesus was making His sacrifice on our behalf, He was smitten in His side, causing water and blood to flow out (John 19:34).

NOTES

1. See Isaiah 54:1–6; Jeremiah 31:32; Ezekiel 16:8; Hosea 2; Romans 7:1–6; 2 Corinthians 11:2; Ephesians 5:21–33; Revelation 19:7; 21:2, 9. See also Gaskill (2003), 79, 191–97, 321.

2. Elder McConkie spoke of Adam as being "a similitude of Christ." See B. McConkie (1981), 449. Elder McConkie's comment comes in the context of the Apostle Paul's declaration that Christ is the "second Adam."

3. See Parry (1994), 126; Campbell (2003), 56; Book of Jubilees 3:19; Jamieson, Fausset, and Brown (n. d.), 18.

4. See chapter 2, note 39.

5. Ambrose, "Paradise" 12, in Oden (2001), 76. See also Ginzberg (1967–1969), 3:85; Campbell (2003), 61.

6. Wilson (1999), 139.

7. Rockwood (1992), 17–18.

8. See, for example, Oden (2001), 67, 71; Quodvultdeus, "Book of Promises and Predictions of God" 1:3, in Oden (2001), 71; Augustine, "City of God" 22:17, in Oden (2001), 70; Jerome, "Homilies" 66, in Oden (2001), 70; Ambrose, "Letters to Laymen" 85, in Oden (2001), 71.

9. See Sailhamer (1976–1992), 2:47.

10. "As Eve was bone of the bones of her husband and flesh of his flesh, we also are members of Christ's body, bones of his bones and flesh of his flesh." Ambrose, "Letters to Laymen" 85, in Oden (2001), 71.

11. Rockwood (1992), 16–17; Ginzberg (1967–1969), 1:66. "The creation of the woman from the man's rib signifies that the woman is one with the man, as Christ is one with the church. Her creation also symbolizes the creation of the church. The union of the man and woman . . . symbolizes [the church's] . . . union with Christ." Oden (2001), 67. Augustine wrote:

"Even in the beginning, when woman was made from a rib in the side of the sleeping man, that had not less purpose than to symbolize prophetically the union of Christ and his church. . . . With Eve . . . 'he built the rib into a woman.' . . . So too St. Paul speaks of 'building up the body of Christ,' which is his church. . . . This was to prefigure the oneness of Christ and the church." Augustine, "City of God" 22:17, in Oden (2001), 70.

12. See Oden (2001), 71.

13. Augustine, "City of God" 22:17, in Oden (2001), 70.

14. See Habershon (1974), 43–44. "We have heard about the first Adam [and how he was injured in his side in order to produce Eve]; let us come now to the second Adam and see how the church is made from his side. The side of the Lord Savior as he hung on the cross is pierced with a lance." Jerome, "Homilies" 66, in Oden (2001), 70. "The taking of Eve from Adam's side also bears a resemblance to the relationship between the church and the Son of God, who permitted himself to become weak that others of his body (the Church) might have strength." Keller (1990), 177. See Calvin (1964), 1:97.

15. Quodvultdeus, "Book of Promises and Predictions of God" 1:3, in Oden (2001), 71.

16. Ambrose, "Paradise" 10:48, in Oden (2001), 68.

17. "While Eve is described as 'enticed' . . . , Adam acts decisively out of obedience to God . . . (1 Timothy 2:14)." Of course, this represents us, not them. King (1995), s. v. Moses 4:18–19.

18. Ephrem the Syrian, "Commentary on Genesis" 2.20.3, in Oden (2001), 78.

19. See Victorinus, "Commentary on the Apocalypse of the Blessed John," in Roberts and Donaldson (1994), 7:345–46.

20. Stephen E. Robinson wrote: "The first Adam parallels the state of the second Adam, Christ. For in their respective gardens, Eden and Gethsemane, each had the ability to die if they so chose, but neither was under the necessity of dying." See Robinson (1990), 139. Ada Habershon wrote that Adam's life ended in death, whereas Christ's death brought forth life. See Habershon (1974), 123. Thus, both the Fall and the Atonement were brought about through agency and as a result of love for God, and love for us.

21. LDS Bible Dictionary (1979), 732; Cornwall and Smith (1998) 180.

22. Nibley renders one passage of "The Combat of Adam and Eve against Satan" as follows: "So Adam continued to make this sacrifice for the rest of his days. And God caused his word to be preached to Adam. On the fiftieth day [while] Adam [was] offering sacrifice as was his custom,

Satan appeared in the form of a man and smote him in the side with a sharp stone even as Adam raised his arms in prayer. Eve tried to help him as blood and water flowed on the altar. 'God sent his word and revived Adam saying: Finish thy sacrifice, which is most pleasing to me. For even so will I be wounded and blood and water will come from my side; that will be the true sacrifice, placed on the altar as a perfect offering. . . . And so God healed Adam.'" J. P. Migne, translator, in *Troisième et Dernière Encyclopédie Théologique* (Paris: P. J. Migne, 1856) 23:329–30, cited in Nibley (1986), 171–72. See also Ginzberg (1967–1969), 1:71, 89, 166, 285; 5:93, n. 55, 116, n. 108, 139, n. 20, 190, n. 56.

FOUR

The Creation and Its Relationship to the Fall

NARRATIVE, OR THE telling of stories, has long been part of ritual. From antiquity down to the present, certain stories have been told and retold as a means of teaching people about their own history and their personal relationship with God. Chief among those sacred "stories of instruction" has been the Creation and the Fall. From ancient times, and almost cross-culturally, these stories have been used, told, and retold in an effort to teach man about who he is, where he has come from, and how he finds himself in his fallen and ofttimes miserable state.[1]

That being said, for years I've puzzled about the presence of the story of the Creation in our Temple rituals. The reason the story of the Fall is told therein seems quite obvious. But the purpose of sharing the Creation narrative eluded me for many years. Was this simply being articulated in an effort to inform patrons that God was the source of creation? Was the primary message about returning and reporting? Was this story included in the Holy Endowment so as to inform participants that there was a beginning to all things—and that God was the ultimate source of that beginning? Or was one of a number of other messages intended?[2]

The other thing that, for some time, puzzled me about the Creation account was its consistent juxtaposition to the story of the Fall. Each time the story of the Creation is conveyed in scripture or the Temple, it is immediately followed up with a presentation of the story of Adam and Eve. It seems clear that these two chronicles are related, and that, as divinely given "stories of instruction," God intends us to see a connection between them. They are undeniably parallel stories; "two peas in a pod," *per se*. This far into our study, the reader should have a clearer understanding as to the message of the Fall and why the Lord uses it as a teaching device—particularly in the Holy Endowment. However, the question still remains, what is the point of the Creation account, and how is that narrative intimately tied to the story of the Fall of man?

The key to understanding the Creation is the same as the key to understanding the Fall. Just as we must consider ourselves as if we were Adam and Eve, so also we must consider ourselves as the central act and purpose of the creation. As one text notes, "the stories with which the Bible begins"—namely the Creation and the Fall—are "symbols of truths learned in history." The Bible presents events of the past and applies them to mankind in general. Thus the Creation is my story and my creation; the Fall is my story and my fall.[3] One who participates in a rite or ordinance in which the story of the Creation or the Fall is told must ask himself or herself: What is this narrative telling me about my own creation or my own fall? How does this story highlight the good and/or evil I have done in my own life, or in the world? and What divine or sacred knowledge does this narrative seek to reveal to me?

In the Creation story all things were created "good" by God. Indeed, in the scriptural account again and again God refers to His creations as "good" or "very good"—as the *King James Version* puts it. One commentator interpreted that to mean "wonderful!" or "perfect!"[4] However, all that which was originally created as "good" has been corrupted by you and me. Thus, the placement of the Creation story in juxtaposition to the story of the Fall teaches us how God made all things perfect and how man took those perfect things and made them imperfect through his disobedience.[5]

The story of the Creation celebrates God's power to change each fallen individual—to bring all back to life, and specifically back to a life of faithfulness and obedience (something each of us falls short of). Similarly, just as the Creation story talks of God separating the light from the darkness, we see how God can do the same in our own lives.[6] And just as the Creation story speaks of God giving life to all of His creations, we see in this narrative how God can give life to those who accept Him and embrace His ways. Like the Creation story, which teaches us that God made men and women after His own image, we understand that each of us are not only children of God, but have the potential (as all children do) to become as our Father is. Each of these symbolic messages are tied up in the reality that God must re-create or resurrect us into something greater than we, of ourselves, can become.[7] One commentator wrote that the practice of depicting or discussing the story of the Creation over and over again in rituals, ordinances, or rites ". . . reflects the belief that the act of creation is not simply what happened once in history but something eternally accomplished by God's creative word. In fact, one could argue that [the Creation story] really recounts what God intended in creation, not what really resulted, and that . . . [the] creation happens among us through Christ."[8] In other words, in the Temple it is appropriate to begin the Endowment with the Creation story because the story is about our creation more than it is about the earth's creation. "The account of the creation of this earth becomes a part of each individual's personal story about his or her place in the universe and kingdom of God."[9] Just as the Fall of Adam and Eve is really the story of our personal fall, so also the creation account is actually a metaphorical retelling of our creation and our placement in the divine plan.[10] The story of the Creation is a story of God re-creating you and I from fallen humans to "new creations" in Christ (2 Corinthians 5:17).[11]

Consider, therefore, the Creation from the previously mentioned "bird's eye view." Note how the creative process completely transformed the matter that would become the earth—and how this "transformation" well mirrors the conversion God is trying to bring to pass in each of our lives.

For example, "in the beginning"—before it took up its orbit around the "light"—the earth was said to be empty, dark, desolate and useless. As one commentator noted, "this seems a pretty good description of man's state so long as he insists on living for himself, on his own terms, refusing to hearken to the light of Christ."[12]

However, the scriptural account informs us that the Holy Spirit "moved upon" this darkened orb, and the earth was then found "in proximity with the light."[13] So it is in our own lives. As we allow the Spirit to influence us, we find ourselves more and more in proximity to He who is "the Light of the world" (John 8:12). Again, we read:

> In application to ourselves, we might consider this to be a representation of the nourishing influence of the Spirit in our lives. Under the influence of this light and within the protective canopy of this air or spirit, the earth began to come to life. Isn't this exactly what happens to us when we are nourished by the Spirit and bathed by the light? We, too, come to life, as it were, and begin to bring forth good fruit.[14]

Curiously, the Creation account tells us that under the counsel or direction of the "Light" the earth "brought forth abundantly" (Genesis 1:20–21 & 8:17). It became a source of life; which nourished and strengthened "everything in its presence—fish, fowls, insects, [and] animals."[15] We too, under the influence of the "Light," become a source of nourishing life for those around us—spouses, children, those whom we serve in our callings, etc. Association with the "Light," and obedience to the "Light," seem to be the key.

As we stay in the orbit, as it were, of the light of Christ, the Spirit, and the Lord's representatives on earth, and as we observe and follow that light, do we not bring forth more abundantly? Do we not sustain and nourish all that is around us? Do we not ultimately receive the image of God in our countenances?[16]

The creation, organization, and utilization of the earth—as described in the Creation accounts—mirrors our own creation. We begin as chaotic, disorganized matter, which God organizes and brings out of chaos so that we can be utilized to sustain and support all God places within our stewardship.

Over and over again the various Creation accounts—Temple and scriptural—state of the earth that it was obedient to God's commands. "The key to each stage of progression [during the creation] was obedience. This is as true of man's progression as it was for the earth's."[17] God was able to take desolate, useless earth and give it life, beauty, purpose, and productivity because it was willing to be obedient to His commands. Such can be the case with us, if we are willing to allow Him to change us; to mold and shape us; to stretch and use us.

As attested to by commentator after commentator, the story of the Creation is particularly valuable for what it can teach us about ourselves: our origin, our divine nature, and what God has done *for* us and wishes to do *to* us. For those of us who are willing, it reminds us that God is constantly trying to make us into something usable, better and new—just as He did to the unorganized matter from which He composed this earth. Thus, at the beginning of the Creation story we are informed that *all* things are in chaos without God and that it is God who brings order to chaos, or who tames the chaos—in the world and in our lives.[18] As one commentator wrote: "The lives of many people are chaotic (cf. Mark 1:32–34). . . . The [Genesis] text claims that even the chaos of our historical life can be claimed by God for his grand purposes."[19] Just as God calmed the chaos of the disorganized waters during the creative process, He can calm the chaos that swirls in our own lives—spiritually, temporally, and in every other way—if we but let Him.[20] Elder Howard W. Hunter of the Twelve, after recounting the miracle of Jesus raising the daughter of Jairus from the dead, said this: "Whatever Jesus lays his hands upon lives. If Jesus lays his hands upon a marriage, it lives. If he is allowed to lay his hands on the family, it lives."[21] The Creation teaches us that God seeks to bring order to the chaos in our lives—and He does that by inviting us to come unto Christ and be perfected in Him (Moroni 10:32). He seeks to place His hands upon our heads, upon our lives! Thus, the juxtaposing of the Creation and the Fall in the Temple and scripture reminds us that we who have introduced evil through our choice to fall must now turn to Christ that we might be made "new creations" through Him (2 Corinthians 5:17), banishing evil forever from our lives.[22] This is the process depicted in the temple—a "good" and perfect creation by a loving God; a corruption of and falling away from that state of goodness and perfection by *every* man and woman; and the covenants of the Holy Temple that serve to get each back to a state wherein he or she is worthy and authorized to return to God's presence—once again deemed "good" by the great Creator!

NOTES

1. See Julien Ries, "The Fall," in Mircea Eliade, editor, *The Encyclopedia of Religion*, 16 volumes (New York: Macmillian, 1987), 5:256–267.

2. Among its many symbolic messages, the story of the Creation teaches us much about God, Christ, and the purpose of the mortal experience. It offers teachings about environmentalism, aesthetics, stewardship and accountability, the power and influence of God's brooding Spirit, and even about the types of employment God deems moral and acceptable. [See Alonzo L. Gaskill, *Sacred Symbols: Finding Meaning in Rites, Rituals & Ordinances* (Springville, UT: Cedar Fort, 2011), 95–104.] When utilized in a liturgical context, the story of the Creation should typically be viewed on a general level—from a bird's eye view, *per se*. Fixation on the minute details of that narrative, specifically when it is found juxtaposed to the story of the Fall, can cause the observer to miss the point of the story and, therefore, the Lord's intended application.

3. See Paul Ricoeur, *The Symbolism of Evil* (Boston, MA: Beacon Press, 1967), 242, note 4.

4. See Leland Ryken, James C. Wilhoit, and Tremper Longman, III, editors, *Dictionary of Biblical Imagery* (Downers Grove, IL: Inter Varsity Press, 1998), 180. Curiously, this "stands in marked contrast to later Greek and other philosophical and theological perspectives, which view the material realm as intrinsically evil and morally suspect." [Ryken, Wilhoit, and Longman (1998), 180.] God sees good in the material creation; uses the material creation; is the source of the material creation; and only expresses concern in the material creation when it is misused.

5. While Jesus' Atonement is the answer to the woes *we have brought upon ourselves*, nevertheless, the message of the Fall is sure—We have done this! We are Adam and Eve! This is our story! And all that God created "good" we have distorted, disrupted, damaged, or corrupted.

6. The main activity on day one of the Creation was the dividing of the light from darkness. As we have suggested, this is not a reference to a distinction between day and night or a creation of the sun and the moon. [See James L. Kugel, *Traditions of the Bible: A Guide to the Bible as It Was at the Start of the Common Era* (Cambridge, MA: Harvard University Press, 1998), 47.] According to the Genesis account, that happened on day four of the Creation. Indeed, as Basil the Great wrote: "The condition in the world before the creation of light was not night but darkness." [Basil the Great, "Hexaemeraon," 2.8, in Andrew Louth, editor, *Ancient Christian Commentary on Scripture: Genesis 1–11* (Downers Grove, IL: InterVarsity

Press, 2001), 7.] In other words, God had yet to create day and night on the first day; but light and dark most certainly *did* exist! So what is the division of light from darkness that took place at the very beginning of the creation? It appears to be a dividing of the divine light (Doctrine and Covenants 88:6–11) from the demonic dark (1 Nephi 12:17). It appears to be a reference to the separation that took place between those who followed Lucifer and those who followed God and Christ. That introductory miracle during the Creation highlights what Jesus is trying to do *to*—and *for*—each of us. [See Louis Ginzberg, *The Legends of the Jews*, seven volumes (Philadelphia: The Jewish Publication Society of America, 1967–1969), 1:8–9 & 12–13; Ambrose, "Hexaemeron" 1.9 & 4:1, in Louth (2001), 7 & 17; John Chrysostom, "Homilies on Genesis" 6.14, in Louth (2001), 16.]

7. See James A. Wallace, Robert P. Waznak, and Guerric DeBona, *Lift Up Your Hearts—Homilies for the "A" Cycle* (New York: Paulist Press, 2004), 102–106. This same text notes: "The resurrection of Christ is not just about the glorious event of the past but about seemingly impossible transformations that occur in the present because of Christ's power and the Holy Spirit." See Wallace, Waznak, and DeBona (2004), 94.

8. Kevin W. Irwin, "The Sacramentality of Creation and the Role of Creation in Liturgy and Sacraments," in Kevin W. Irwin and Edmund D. Pellegrino, editors, *Preserving the Creation: Environmental Theology and Ethics* (Washington, DC: Georgetown University Press, 1992), 79.

9. Andrew C. Skinner, *Temple Worship: 20 Truths That Will Bless your Life* (Salt Lake City, UT: Deseret Book, 2007), 196.

10. LDS author James Ferrell wrote: "For most of my life, I thought the Creation story was just about the formation of an earth. I wasn't so sure that it mattered much today. But then I noticed something amazing: The Creation story was about me. I'm quite serious. The Creation is not merely the story of a heavenly body. It is also, metaphorically, the story of the creation of heavenly beings—me, you, all of us. So when we study the creative progression of the earth, we're actually also learning about our own mortal and eternal progression. When we see that, the Creation matters. Today." James L. Ferrell, *The Hidden Christ: Beneath the Surface of the Old Testament* (Salt Lake City, UT: Deseret Book, 2009), 9.

11. See Ryken, Wilhoit, and Longman (1998), 181–182. "In Pauline language, the passage from the 'old man' to the 'new man' [2 Corinthians 5:17] . . . expresses the incorporation of the individual in the reality signified by the 'types' of the first and the second Adam; the inner mutation—'putting on the new man'—is the shadow cast on the place of experience

by a transformation that cannot be wholly experienced subjectively, nor observed from outside, but can only be signified symbolically as a participation in the 'types' of the first and second Adam. It is in this sense that St. Paul says that the individual is 'transformed [μεταμορφοῦσθαι—metamorphosed] into the same image [εἰκών] (2 Corinthians 3:18), 'conformed [σύμμορφος] to the same image [εἰκών]' of the Son (Romans 8:29), and that he 'bears the image of the heavenly' after having 'borne the image of the earthly' (1 Corinthians 15:49)." Ricoeur (1967), 274–275.

12. See Ferrell (2009), 13.

13. See Ferrell (2009), 13.

14. Ferrell (2009), 13.

15. Ferrell (2009), 14.

16. Ferrell (2009), 14.

17. Ferrell (2009), 16.

18. See Ryken, Wilhoit, and Longman (1998), 179–180.

19. Walter Brueggermann, *Genesis: A Bible Commentary for Teaching and Preaching* (Atlanta, GA: John Knox Press, 1973), 29.

20. In Mosaic symbolism water was often a symbol for chaos. Lucifer has been referred to as the "chief" of "the waters" and as "the Angel of the Sea." [See Ginzberg (1967–1969), 1:18.] Thus, in the Creation story water is frequently used as a symbol of the adversary—shifting, unstable, chaotic, etc. The fact that the earth was covered with water (at the beginning of the Creation account) is traditionally interpreted as a symbol for its "chaotic" and "disorganized" state—and potentially for his influence prior to God's intervention through the Creation. [See, for example, Clifford and Murphy, "Genesis," in Brown, Fitzmyer, and Murphy (1990), 10–11, 541 & 545.]

21. Howard W. Hunter, "Reading the Scriptures," *Ensign*, November 1979, 65.

22. Ricoeur (1967), 240. See also 243.

FIVE

Textual Insights into the Doctrine of the Fall

A

LTHOUGH A MAIN focus of this text has been how you and I can better see the story of the Fall as our story—our fall—nevertheless, no book on this subject would be complete without an examination of the doctrines related to, and stemming from, the Fall of Adam and Eve. This chapter is a survey of those doctrines.

THE CREATION OF ADAM AND EVE

Genesis 1:27	Moses 2:27	Abraham 4:27
So God created man in his own image, in the image of God created he him; male and female created he them.	And I, God, created man in mine own image, in the image of mine Only Begotten created I him; male and female created I them (See also Moses 6:9).	So the Gods went down to organize man in their own image, in the image of the Gods to form they him, male and female to form they them.

God created man in His own image. Adam and Eve, the first of the human family, were created in the image of God the Father and "his wife-partner,"[1] God the Mother.[2] As one commentator noted, "Reason indeed precludes the idea that a father could beget children without a mother to bear them."[3] President Gordon B. Hinckley stated, "Logic and reason would certainly suggest that if we have a Father in Heaven, we have a Mother in Heaven. That doctrine rests well with me."[4] Adam and Eve were literally the parents of all humanity. Thus we, like them, are God's offspring and were made in the image of the divine.[5] Daniel H. Ludlow wrote, "The terms 'in our image' and 'after our likeness' indicate that God had bodily parts just as man does."[6] Indeed, the Prophet Joseph noted:

> God himself was once as we are now, and is an exalted man, and sits enthroned in yonder heavens! That is the great secret. If the veil were rent today, and the great God . . . [were] to make himself visible,—I say, if you were to see him today, you would see him like a man in form—like yourselves in all the person, image, and very form as a man; for Adam was created in the very fashion, image and likeness of God, and received instruction from, and walked, talked and conversed with him, as one man talks and communes with another.[7]

Elder Milton R. Hunter of the Seventy argued that it is by reason of our being the "offspring of the Gods" that humans inherit "intelligence, reasoning powers, memory, and other mental faculties which endow them with power to have dominion over all living things and an extensive dominion over the elements."[8] We are like no other creature God has created.

Genesis 2:7–8	Moses 3:7–8	Abraham 5:7–8
And the Lord God formed man of the dust of the ground and breathed into his nostrils the breath of life; and man became a living soul. And the Lord God planted a garden eastward in Eden; and there he put the man whom he had formed.	And I, the Lord God, formed man from the dust of the ground, and breathed Into his nostrils the breath of life; and man became a living soul, the first flesh upon the earth, the first man also; nevertheless, all things were before created; but spiritually were they created and made according to my word. And I, the Lord God, planted a garden eastward in Eden, and there I put the man whom I had formed.	And the Gods formed man from the dust of the ground, and took his spirit (that is, the man's spirit), and put it into him; and breathed into his nostrils the breath of life, and man became a living soul. And the Gods planted a garden, eastward In Eden, and there they put the man, whose spirit they had put into the body which they had formed.

Dust of the ground. The language used here is metaphorical. Adam was *not* literally made of dust. As President Brigham Young remarked, "When you tell me that father Adam was made . . . from the earth, you tell me what I deem an idle tale." The idea that Adam was "fashioned the same as we make adobes" is a "baby story" and if he had been made in such a manner he would be nothing but a brick in the resurrection. "He was made . . . as you and I are made, and no person was ever made upon any other principle."[9]

Although Adam's physical body was created only after this earth had been organized, his spirit had been in existence in an organized capacity for millions, if not billions, of years prior to the creation.[10] Indeed, even the matter from which Adam's body was made existed prior to his being physically organized. "Matter or element is self-existent and eternal in nature, creation being merely the organization and reorganization of that substance which 'was not created or made, neither indeed can be' (Doctrine and Covenants 93:29)."[11] In an official statement from the First Presidency and Council of the Twelve, we read: "The Creator is an Organizer. God created the earth as an organized sphere; but He certainly did not create, in the sense of bringing into primal existence, the ultimate elements of the materials of which the earth consists, for 'the elements are eternal' (Doctrine and Covenants 93:33). So also life is eternal, and not created; but life, or the vital force, may be infused into organized matter."[12]

Eastward in Eden. It has been common practice throughout history for churches, temples, cemeteries, and so on to be oriented toward the east—the direction anciently symbolic of the presence of God.[13] In some religious traditions, such as early Christianity, it was also common practice to pray facing the east. In the fourth-century AD, Basil the Great wrote, "For this reason we all look to the east in our prayers, but few know that this is because we are seeking the ancient fatherland, which God planted in Eden, toward the east."[14] Eden was symbolically in the presence of God—or, in other words, Adam and Eve had access to God while in Eden. It was the first of the earthly temples.[15]

The Garden of Eden is more than a place; it is also a way of life and a state of [the] soul. Because God himself planted the Garden of Eden (Genesis 2:8), there is something prescriptive as well as descriptive in the image of [Eden]. . . . The very simplicity of life in the garden is part of its difference from the complexities of civilization, as signaled partly by the unashamed nakedness of Adam and Eve. . . . If the Garden of Eden is an image of divine provision, it is paradoxically also a place of human labor. . . . In addition to its status as an image of nature and relaxation, therefore, the garden is also an image of human industry, work and striving. . . . God is ever providing a place as well as promising new and more perfect places, even as humankind is enjoined to collaborate in obedience to the unfolding divine purpose. . . . When Adam and Eve are expelled from the garden, they lose a spiritual status based on unfettered communion with God.[16]

Early in this dispensation, a number of the Brethren taught that Eden was originally located in what today is known as Independence, Missouri.[17] President Brigham Young stated: "In the beginning, after this earth was prepared for man, the Lord commenced his work upon what is now called the American continent, where the Garden of Eden was."[18] President Heber C. Kimball was even more specific when he announced: "The spot chosen for the garden of Eden was Jackson County, in the State of Missouri, where Independence now stands; it was occupied in the morn of creation by Adam . . . who came . . . for the express purpose of peopling this earth."[19] Even the Prophet Joseph is said to have declared that Eden was "on the American continent—even in Jackson County, Mo."[20]

One text notes that God's love for His children is told "in the things which He puts around them to make them pure and happy."[21] Eden, which means "pleasantness" or "delight," was a symbol of that love—as are the kingdoms of glory, which await us in the resurrection.

Breathed into his nostrils the breath of life. As the Abrahamic account makes clear, the "breath of life" is metaphorical language for the spirit of man.[22] President Joseph F. Smith noted that in this idea that God "breathed the breath of life into Adam and Eve" we find support for the doctrine of a premortal life. Each of God's children lived as spirits, in His presence, before we were ever sent to this earth to inhabit mortal tabernacles. That which the Father places in Adam—namely his spirit—existed long before the mortal man was created.[23]

The idea that God "planted" the garden, "breathed" air into Adam's nostrils, then "walked" in Eden in the "cool of the day" serves to establish God as an anthropomorphic being, rather than a shapeless, formless deity that is everywhere and yet nowhere.[24]

First flesh. This statement has confused some, as (according to all four accounts of the Creation[25]) Adam was clearly created *after* the animals.[26] However, it is traditionally understood that the intent of the phrase "first flesh" is not to suggest that Adam was the first of God's creations upon this earth. Rather, it suggests that Adam (i.e., "mankind"[27]) was the first to partake of mortality. In other words, because of their transgression, Adam and Eve became the "first flesh" or the first mortals. Their Fall subsequently brought mortality to all of God's other creations also. Thus, the term *flesh* here would be synonymous with the term *mortal*.[28]

There may also be found in this term some suggestion about the preeminent nature of man over beast, as it relates to God's plan.

Spiritually were they created. All of God's creations—man, the animals, the plants, even this earth—were created spiritually before they were created physically (see Moses 3:5).[29] In what perhaps is an artificial breakdown, we might say that all things go through three stages of creation. First of all there is the spirit creation, wherein you and I became the spirit offspring of God. Second there is the physical creation, wherein Adam and Eve were placed upon this earth with physical bodies. You and I, as their descendants, have been born with physical bodies in their likeness—albeit their bodies were immortal and ours are mortal. Finally, there will be the resurrected creation, in which all of God's creations will receive resurrected, glorified, immortal bodies commensurate to whichever kingdom of glory they have inherited.

God put the man in the garden. A number of the General Authorities have indicated that Adam and Eve were not created upon this earth, but rather were placed here after their creation. Indeed, all that the Father made was created elsewhere—both spiritually and physically—and then transplanted to the earth on which they would dwell.[30] President Joseph Fielding Smith wrote, "When the time came for this earth to be peopled, the Lord, our God, transplanted upon it from some other earth, the life which is found here."[31] It appears that, prior to the Fall, "the whole earth [was] enveloped in the glory of God."[32] When Adam and Eve partook of the "forbidden" fruit, the earth physically fell into its current orbit.[33] At the beginning of the Millennium it will be placed back into its terrestrial orbit, once again becoming paradisiacal in nature. Then, at the conclusion of the Millennium, this earth will be moved into orbit with the other celestialized orbs.[34]

On a related note, in Moses 1:33–35 we are informed that our earth is not the only populated sphere participating in this plan of salvation. We read:

> Worlds without number have I created; and I also created them for mine own purpose; . . . And the first man of all men have I called Adam, which is many. But only an account of this earth, and the inhabitants thereof, give I unto you. For behold, there are many worlds that have passed away by the word of my power. And there are many that now stand, and innumerable are they unto man; but all things are numbered unto me, for they are mine and I know them.

Thus, we know that this earth is but one of many participating in the plan of salvation.[35] "Adam is the first man of all the men . . . who were created for *this* earth [but] *not* necessarily the first man that God had created for any of His worlds. . . . The Lord had peopled other worlds before He placed Adam and Eve on this one."[36] The Fall that took place upon this earth was also but one of many. Each individual earth—"worlds without end"—has had an Adam and Eve whose divine calling was to provoke that earth's Fall or, in other words, to introduce mortality on their earth. Thus, *Adam* and *Eve* are not primarily names, but rather titles pertaining to their specific calling to introduce mortality and thereby instigate the plan of God.[37] As one author observed: "*Adam* and *Eve* appear to be general titles which have been used numerous times by the Creator to signify the first parents of a world. Adam, then, did not name Eve. He was calling her by her title, previously conferred by God. In the book of Moses, Moses calls the woman Eve even before Adam does."[38]

Genesis 2:9	Moses 3:9	Abraham 5:9
And out of the ground made the Lord God to grow every tree that I pleasant to the sight, and good for food; the tree of life also in the midst of the garden, and the tree of knowledge of good and evil.	And out of the ground made I, the Lord God, to grow every tree, naturally, that is pleasant to the sight of man; and man could behold it. And it became also a living soul. For it was spiritual in the day that I created it; for it remaineth in the sphere in which I, God, created it, yea, even all things which I prepared for the use of man; and man saw that it was good for food. And I, the Lord God, planted the tree of life also in the midst of the garden, and also the tree of knowledge of good and evil.	And out of the ground made the Gods to grow every tree that is pleasant to the sight and good for food; the tree of life, also, in the midst of the garden, and the tree of knowledge of good and evil.

God made all that is pleasant and good. All that is good was created by God, specifically for our pleasure and use. And all that is evil or bad in the earth is a direct result of Lucifer's premortal rebellion and the subsequent Fall of mankind. These things have been designed by the father of lies for our destruction and downfall. When the millennial day dawns, Satan will be bound and his works removed, and God's children will once again enjoy all that is pleasant and good.[39]

Every tree. The Lord's reference to "every tree" here appears to encompass not simply trees, but all of the vegetation God had caused to grow in Eden. It is a generic term, much like the name-title *Adam*, which referred not to one man but to mankind in general.[40]

It became a living soul. One commentator noted that the "it" here is not simply man, but "all of the earth's vegetation"—and by extension, every living thing that God prepared for the use of man.[41] Whereas much of the Christian world supposes that only man possesses a spirit, The Church of Jesus Christ of Latter-day Saints holds that "not only has man a spirit, and is thereby a living soul, but likewise the beasts of the field, the fowl of the air, and the fish of the sea have spirits, and hence are living souls."[42] Indeed, even this earth has a spirit and is a living entity.[43]

The tree of life. Christ is the tree of life (see 1 Nephi 11:21), who is central to God's work.[44] He is depicted at the center of the Garden because He is at the center of the plan of salvation—including all of its ordinances and teachings. Robert L. Millet wrote:

> Jesus Christ is the central figure in the doctrine of The Church of Jesus Christ of Latter-day Saints. The Prophet Joseph Smith explained that "the fundamental principles of our religion are the testimony of the Apostles and Prophets, concerning Jesus Christ, that He died, was buried, and rose again the third day, and ascended into heaven; and all other things which pertain to our religion are only appendages to it" (TPJS, 121). Latter-day Saints believe that complete salvation is possible only through the life, death, resurrection, doctrines, and ordinances of Jesus Christ and in no other way.[45]

The tree of knowledge of good and evil. The pairing of these opposites, "good" and "evil," is what is known as a *merism*—that is, "a literary figure by which totality is expressed by the first and last in a series or by opposites."[46] It is a Hebrew idiom meaning "all things."[47] Thus, the fruit of the tree of knowledge of good and evil represents the totality of the mortal experience: agency, trials, faith, knowledge, and experience.[48] Minus the knowledge (i.e., experience) of good and evil, the plan would be void and mankind would be incapable of the growth requisite for exaltation.[49] This is not to imply that we need to sin in order to become like God. Rather, we need the opportunity and enticement of sin, that we can overcome it and master the flesh, thereby becoming like God.

The First Commandment

Genesis 1:28	Moses 2:28	Abraham 4:28
And God blessed them, and God said unto them Be fruitful, and multiply, and replenish the earth, and subdue it: and have dominion over the fish of the sea, and over the fowl of the air, and over every living thing that moveth upon the earth.	And I, God, blessed them, and said unto them: Be fruitful, and multiply, and replenish the earth, and subdue it, and have dominion over the fish of the sea, and over the fowl of the air, and over every living thing that moveth upon the earth.	And the Gods said: We will bless them. And the Gods said: We will cause them to be fruitful and multiply, and replenish the earth, and subdue it, and to have dominion over the fish of the sea, and over the fowl of the air, and over every living thing that moveth upon the earth.

Multiply and replenish the earth. First of all, the Old English word *replenish* means "to fill." This is not a repopulation of the earth, but rather a first time filling of it. Second, the primary purpose of this command was to make it possible for each of God's spirit children to leave their premortal abode, come to earth, take a body, and gain the experience necessary to become as God is.[50] Hence we know that God had introduced this commandment prior to Eden, as it was foundational to the plan and the discussion that went on in the Grand Council before the world was.[51]

Elder Russell M. Nelson noted that God explained to Adam and Eve that they needed to be fruitful and multiply and that the only way that they could do so was by partaking of the tree of knowledge of good and evil. According to Elder Nelson, had Adam and Eve not partaken of this "forbidden" fruit, the plan of God would have been frustrated.[52] Thus, they did exactly what God desired of them. President Joseph Fielding Smith indicated that to say that the two commandments given in Eden were contradictory is not to understand "the facts" surrounding the Fall.[53]

Genesis 2:10	Moses 3:10	Abraham 5:10
And a river went out of Eden to water the garden; and from thence It was parted, and became into four heads.	And I, the Lord God, caused a river to go out of Eden to water the garden; and from thence it was parted, and became into four heads.	There was a river running out of Eden, to water the garden, and from thence it was parted and became into four heads.

A river parting into four heads. As noted previously, in Hebrew culture the number four meant "geographic fulness" or "totality."[54] Here we are told that the river that flows forth from Eden parts into four different directions.[55] Thus, a number of different ideas may be implied.

Perhaps the number four in this episode was to imply that all of the earth, prior to the Fall, was in a paradisiacal condition. Joseph Fielding McConkie wrote:

> Some have argued that the paradisiacal glory of which we speak was confined to the Garden of Eden while evolutionary processes were taking place through the rest of the earth. The great difficulty with this idea is that it confines the effects of the Atonement to forty acres (or whatever size the Garden of Eden was). The plain testimony of scripture is that the entire earth and all created things were affected by the Fall and thus recipients of the blessings of the Atonement.[56]

The water flowing forth in four directions is mirrored by John's vision of the river flowing out from under the throne of God in the Heavenly Jerusalem (see Revelation 22:1–2; see also Zechariah 14:8); and it implies that it is the Spirit and its revelations that come from Eden (and the temple), flowing to all the world (see John 7:37–39).[57] If this parallel is intended, then it is possible that the number four here has reference to the Garden of Eden as the first temple.[58]

Finally, perhaps the use of the number four in this episode is a symbol for the idea that chaos (via the Fall) went forth from Eden unto all the world.[59] Moses certainly uses water as a representation of chaos.[60]

A river running out of Eden. Since the Garden of Eden was said to be the location of the Tigris and Euphrates rivers, and today rivers by those names are found in Iraq and Armenia, some have assumed that the Garden of Eden was located in that region of the world—in all probability somewhere in the Mesopotamia Valley or in western Iran.[61] Although it is true that one of Eden's four rivers was called "Euphrates" (Genesis 2:14), and another "Hiddekel" (Genesis 2:14) or "Tigris," nevertheless, it must be remembered that when the great deluge took place in the days of Noah any formerly existing rivers would have been entirely submerged and thus almost certainly wiped out or eroded away. Hence, the two rivers currently called the Tigris and Euphrates are not the same rivers referred to in the Genesis account.

In addition, according to the Genesis account, one of the four rivers ("Gihon") is said to have been in Ethiopia (Genesis 2:13), which happens to be on the African continent.[62] Yet the modern day Tigris and Euphrates are on the Asian continent. Hence, because the Tigris and Euphrates are not on the same continent as the river Gihon, the four ancient rivers cannot be the same as the modern rivers by the same names.[63] Clearly, sometime after the flood of Noah's day, the rivers currently called the Tigris and Euphrates were simply named after the biblical rivers, just as the modern day Jordan River in Utah was named after the biblical river in which Jesus was baptized.[64]

THE SECOND COMMANDMENT

Genesis 2:16–17	Moses 3:16–17	Abraham 5:12–13
And the Lord God commanded the man, saying, Of every tree of the garden thou mayest freely eat: But of the tree of the knowledge of good and evil, thou shalt not eat of it: for In the day that thou eatest thereof thou shalt surely die.	And I, the Lord God, commanded the man, saying: Of every tree of the garden thou mayest freely eat, But of the tree of the knowledge of good evil, thou shalt not eat of it, nevertheless, thou mayest choose for thyself, of It is given unto thee; but, remember that I forbid, for in the day thou eatest thereof thou shalt surely die.	And the Gods commanded the man, saying: Of every tree of the garden thou mayest freely eat, But of the tree of knowledge of good and evil, thou shalt not eat of it; for In the time that thou eatest thereof, thou shalt surely die. Now I, Abraham, saw that it was after the Lord's time, which was after the time of Kolob; for as yet the Gods had not appointed unto Adam his reckoning.

Thou mayest freely eat. Prior to partaking of the fruit of the tree of knowledge of good and evil, Adam could not die. Thus, when he ate of the other fruits, he did so not to sustain his life, but for enjoyment or pleasure.[65]

The tree of knowledge of good and evil. The question has been posed: Did Adam and Eve really eat something? And if so, what was it? Some, even within the Church, have assumed that there was literally a "forbidden" fruit,[66] nevertheless, that may not actually be the case. Elder Bruce R. McConkie stated that the "forbidden" fruit was nothing more nor less than compliance with whatever laws were in force so that their bodies would change from immortal and paradisiacal to mortal.[67] Similarly, Elder Dallin H. Oaks indicated that the "forbidden" fruit was simply a figurative expression for something God had technically labeled as forbidden so that Adam and Eve would have a device by which they could provoke the Fall and thereby instigate the plan for all of God's children.[68] One LDS scholar noted:

If we were to reason that it was [literally] the fruit itself that brought about this change in the bodies of Adam and Eve, we would then have to suppose that our first parents fed some of the fruit to all the other living things upon the whole earth. Had they not done so, "all things which were created must have remained in the same state in which they were after they were created; and they must have remained forever, and had no end" (2 Nephi 2:22; see also Moses 3:9). Every plant and animal, including all sea life and the fowls of the air, would have been required to eat some of this fruit (and must also have been precluded from partaking of it either by design or accident before this point of time).[69]

So, it appears that partaking of the fruit was simply an act officially forbidden by God whereby Adam and Eve could intentionally instigate the will of God through technically disobeying or transgressing a law.

Thou mayest choose for thyself. According to a traditional reading of the text, God announces to Adam and Eve that it is permissible for them to partake of the vast majority of the trees and vegetation found in Eden. However, one tree is strictly forbidden—namely the tree of knowledge of good and evil. Notice that this dictate not to partake is different from any other commandment found in holy writ. Nowhere else does God use the wording "thou mayest choose for thyself." Indeed, nothing akin to that appears after the giving of any of the commandments. One commentator wisely noted: "The Lord did not say, 'Thou shalt not commit adultery' or 'Thou shalt not kill' and then say, 'Nevertheless thou mayest choose for thyself, for it is given unto thee.'"[70] True, we have agency to choose. But God, with this sole exception, does not give us commandments and then suggest to us that disobedience is an option.

Thus, the perception that God's decree regarding the fruit of the tree of knowledge of good and evil was a standard prohibition is in error. God was obviously not issuing a commandment akin to those found in the Ten Commandments. Of course, modern prophets have clarified why this pronouncement is different from other commandments of God. As we have already noted, the Prophet Joseph stated: "Adam did not commit sin in eating the fruits, *for God had decreed that he should eat and fall.*"[71] Father wanted Adam to partake.

Contrary to popular interpretation, it was God's will that they do so. Thus, according to modern revelation, in the verse under consideration God is not giving a prohibition, but rather an option.

As discussed earlier, all too frequently the two commandments (Genesis 1:28; 2:16–17) or directives that God gave Adam and Eve are seen as contradictory commandments. However, this is not the case. It is not in God's nature to give contradictory commands. Nor is it in accordance with His plan to give His children two or more commandments that require that at least one be broken in order that the others might be kept. To suggest this of God is to entirely misunderstand both His nature and the nature of His plan. How could God give a commandment and then punish His children when they are obedient to it? Yet this is often the way the Fall is interpreted.

Many assume that God commanded Adam and Eve to do two different things—one of the two commandments being impossible to keep if the other was kept. Although we have already discussed in detail the fallacy behind the claim that God placed Adam and Eve in such a paradoxical state,[72] permit here a brief reminder of President Joseph Fielding Smith's explanation as to why there is no contradiction between the instruction to have children and also not to partake of the fruit of the tree of knowledge of good and evil. On several occasions he stated: "The Lord said to Adam, here is the tree of knowledge of good and evil. If you want to stay here then you cannot eat of that fruit. If you want to stay here then I forbid you to eat it. But you may act for yourself and you may eat of it if you want to. And if you eat it you will die."[73] Thus, there is no contradiction—no paradox. And because the Lord was giving Adam and Eve options rather than commands, He is described as employing the phrase, "thou mayest choose for thyself, for it is given unto thee."

As is well known, Adam and Eve did not yet have blood in their veins during their stay in Eden. Thus, they were incapable of having children.[74] As President Smith noted, God was simply informing Adam and Eve that if they wanted to have children they would need to partake of the fruit of the tree of knowledge of good and evil, that blood might enter their veins, and they would then have the procreative ability required. Ellis Rasmussen, former dean of Brigham Young University's College of Religious Education, wrote,

"It is reasonable that on earth as in the premortal Council in Heaven (Abraham 3:25–28; TG, 'Agency') humankind was free to choose to live either in 'a state of probation' or 'in a state of innocence, having no joy, for they knew no misery; doing no good, for they knew no sin' (2 Nephi 2:23, 21–22)."[75] Here Father in Heaven was introducing Adam and Eve to those options and reminding them that they could choose for themselves, because they had been divinely endowed with the gift of agency.[76]

Remember that I forbid it. For a detailed discussion of this phrase, see chapters one and two.

Thou shalt surely die. The Hebrew reads more along the lines of, "In the day you eat of it you will be condemned to die," rather than "in the day you eat you will die."[77] A knowledge of evil presupposes spiritual death. The more intimate the knowledge, the more lengthy the separation from God (or the length of death). Yet, such an experience is necessary if we are to be tested, tried, and stretched. As Augustine said, "I do not think that a man would deserve great praise if he had been able to live a good life for the simple reason that nobody tempted him to live a bad one."[78]

In these two trees is represented the reality of opposites: "pleasure and pain, good and evil, virtue and vice."[79] Thus, father Lehi stated: "And to bring about his eternal purposes . . . it must needs be that there was an opposition; even the forbidden fruit in opposition to the tree of life; the one being sweet and the other bitter" (2 Nephi 2:15). In early Christian writings we find comments such as these: "The tree [of knowledge of good and evil] brought ruin to Adam; [whereas] the tree [of life] shall bring you into paradise."[80] And "The Tree of Life stood in the middle of paradise like a trophy. The Tree of Knowledge stood as a contest . . . of competition and struggle."[81]

Augustine wrote: "If . . . it be asked what death God threatened man with . . . , whether . . . bodily or spiritual . . . , we answer: It was all!"[82] Once he partook of the fruit, Adam was expelled from Eden, bringing to pass his "spiritual death" that very day. Adam then lived a total of 930 years, which would be just shy of one day in God's time (see 2 Peter 3:8; Abraham 3:4). Hence, by the reckoning of God, Adam died physically in the very "day" that he partook.[83]

Genesis 2:19–20	Moses 3:19–20	Abraham 5:20–21
And out of the ground the Lord God formed every beast of the field, and every fowl of the air; and brought them unto Adam to see what he would call them: and whatsoever Adam called every living creature, that was the name thereof. And Adam gave names to all cattle, and to the fowl of the air, and to every beast of the field; but for Adam there was not found an help meet for him.	And out of the ground I, the Lord God, formed every beast of the field, and every fowl of the air; and commanded that they should come unto Adam, to see what he would call them; and they were also living souls; for I, God, breathed into them the breath of life, and commanded that whatsoever Adam called every living creature, that should be the name thereof. And Adam gave names to all cattle, and to the fowl of the air, and to every beast of the field; but as for Adam, there was not found an help meet for him.	And out of the ground the Gods formed every beast of the field, and every fowl of the air, and brought them unto Adam to see what he would call them; and whatsoever Adam called every living creature, that should be the name thereof. And Adam gave names to all cattle, to the fowl of the air, to every beast of the field; and for Adam, there was found an help meet for him.

God formed each beast and fowl. Exactly how the animals were formed is never explicitly stated. President Brigham Young did indicate that the concept that Adam and Eve were made from the dust was a metaphor and should not be taken literally.[84] However, it is unclear as to whether it should be extrapolated that animals were created in the same way that humans were.[85] It is curious to note that, although God speaks of both as being created from the dust, only with man is it stated that God "breathed into his nostrils the breath of life" (Genesis 2:7; Moses 3:7; Abraham 5:7). This may suggest a slight difference in their mode of creation.[86] Regardless, all of God's creations are said to be "living souls."[87]

Adam gave names to every beast. From the account of the naming of the animals we learn a number of things about Adam, his intellect, and his nature.[88]

First of all, Adam was no "caveman." He was an intelligent, intellectually developed human being[89] with reasoning skills and a fully developed language.[90] According to one early Christian commentator, Adam's naming of the animals is said to have taken place "in order that God might make known the wisdom of Adam."[91] Regarding Adam's intellectual gifts, President Joseph Fielding Smith stated:

> The first man placed upon this earth was an intelligent being, created in the image of God, possessed of wisdom and knowledge, with power to communicate his thoughts in a language, both oral and written, which was superior to anything to be found on the earth today. This may sound very sweeping and dogmatic to those who hold to the other view, but it is not any more so than their statements to the contrary. Moreover, I do not say it of myself, but merely repeat what the Lord has said; and surely the Creator, above all others, ought to know![92]

We may also draw from this verse that at this time in the earth's history neither Adam, nor the animals that he was commanded to name, were predators. There was a peace, harmony, and camaraderie that existed between all. "They were neither afraid of him nor were they afraid of each other. A species of predatory animals would pass by with a species of animal that is preyed upon following safely right behind."[93] Such will be the case again when this earth returns to its Edenic or paradisiacal splendor during the Millennium.

A third point evident in this verse is that assigning Adam to name the animals shows that, at least in part, they were made for him.[94] They were given by God to Adam for his use and preservation. In Doctrine and Covenants 49:19 we read: "For, behold, the beasts of the field and the fowls of the air, and that which cometh of the earth, is ordained for the use of man for food and for raiment, and that he might have in abundance." And in Doctrine and Covenants 59:18 the Lord adds: "Yea, all things which come of the earth, in the season thereof, are made for the benefit and the use of man, both to please the eye and to gladden the heart." Thus, the command to name the animals implies Adam's dominion over them.[95] However, although God gave Adam (or mankind) dominion over the animals, with that stewardship comes responsibility and accountability. In other words, God-given dominion is not a right for excess or abuse.

Over the years since the Restoration, the Brethren have been quite clear on this matter.[96]

But for Adam there was not found an help meet. It is in the process of naming the animals that Adam is said to gain his awareness that, unlike them, he is alone. There is no partner for Adam as there is for each of God's other creations.[97] One commentator wrote:

> That [Moses] intends the account of the naming of the animals to be read as part of the story of the creation of the woman is made certain in verse 20, where at the conclusion of the man's naming the animals the author remarks: "but for Adam, he did not find a partner like himself." The clear implication is that the author sees in the man's naming the animals also his search for a suitable partner. In recounting that no suitable partner had been found, the author has assured the reader that the man was not like the other creatures.[98]

As in our aforementioned passage (i.e., Genesis 2:18; Moses 3:18; Abraham 5:14), here the importance of marriage between a man and woman is highlighted. Adam is seen longing for a mate to make him whole. This longing is God-given. And as with Adam, so also with us: God presents other companionships as an example of what He expects of us.[99]

Genesis 2:18	Moses 3:18	Abraham 5:14
And the Lord God said, It is not good that man should be alone; I will make him an help meet for him.	And I, the Lord God, said unto mine Only Begotten, that It was not good that the man should be alone; wherefore, I will make an help meet for him.	And the Gods said: Let us make an help meet for the man, for it is not good that the man should be alone, therefore we will form an help meet for him.

It is not good that man should be alone. The plan of salvation, the great plan of happiness, predates this earth and its creation. It is eternal. It is the same yesterday, today, and forever. It is "one eternal round." It cannot be improved upon, as it is perfect. And we must therefore suppose that each time the plan is introduced to spirits awaiting an opportunity at mortality, it is the same. No one is saved on alternate principles. No one is given a different set of rules or commandments that they are to obey in order to enjoy exaltation in the celestial kingdom of God. And marriage—eternal marriage—is part of that unchanging requirement.

There is more expressed in this verse than a simple concern for man's loneliness.[100] Without the companionship of husband and wife, the plan could never have been initiated.[101] And without the sons of Adam marrying the daughters of Eve, the plan would grind to an immediate halt. The requisite oneness of man and woman, the eternal nature of marriages solemnized in holy temples, the divinely sanctioned and commanded act of procreation—all these are eternal requirements.

The avoidance of marriage for selfish reasons, or the painful struggle of same-gender attraction, do not negate the reality that "it is not good for man [or woman] to be alone." For this reason the Father has given us the sacred and eternal new and everlasting covenant of marriage. Without it no man or woman can become as God is. No alternate version or man-made imitation of that covenant will do.[102] Of this verse, Daniel H. Ludlow wrote: "The first marriage on this earth (of Adam and Eve) was obviously meant to be eternal because there was no death of any kind on the earth at that time."[103] In "The Family: A Proclamation to the World" we read: "Marriage between a man and a woman is ordained of God . . . [and] is essential to His eternal plan."[104] The Prophet Joseph declared:

> Except a man and his wife enter into an everlasting covenant and be married for eternity, while in this probation, by the power and authority of the Holy Priesthood, they will cease to increase when they die; that is, they will not have any children after the resurrection. But those who are married by the power and authority of the priesthood in this life, and continue without committing the sin against the Holy Ghost, will continue to increase and have children in the celestial glory.[105]

Similarly, in Doctrine and Covenants 131 we are informed: "In the celestial glory there are three heavens or degrees; And in order to obtain the highest, a man must enter into . . . the new and everlasting covenant of marriage" (Doctrine and Covenants 131:1–2).

Continuing this theme that it is not good for man to be alone, several of the next few verses deal with the covenant relationship of marriage.

Help meet. For a detailed discussion of the term *help meet*, see chapter two.

Genesis 2:21–24	Moses 3:21–24	Abraham 5:15–18
And the Lord God caused a deep sleep to fall upon Adam, and he slept: and he took one of his ribs, and closed up the flesh instead thereof; And the rib, which the Lord God had taken from man, made he a woman, and brought her unto the man. And Adam said, This is now bone of my bones, and flesh of my flesh: she shall be called Woman, because she was taken out of Man. Therefore shall a man leave his father and his mother, and shall cleave unto his wife: and they shall be one flesh.	And I, the Lord God, caused a deep sleep to fall upon Adam; and he slept, and I took one of his ribs and closed up the flesh in the stead thereof; And the rib which I, the Lord God, had taken form man, made I a woman, and brought her unto the man. And Adam said: This I know now is bone of my bones, and flesh of my flesh; she shall be called Woman, because she was taken out of man. Therefore shall a man leave his father and his mother, and shall cleave unto his wife; and they shall be one flesh.	And the Gods caused a deep sleep to fall upon Adam; and he slept, and they took one of his ribs, and closed up the flesh in the stead thereof; And of the rib which the Gods had taken from man, formed they a woman, and brought her unto the man. And Adam said: This as bone of my bones, and flesh of my flesh; now she shall be called Woman, because she was taken out of man; Therefore shall a man leave his father and his mother, and shall cleave unto his wife, and they shall be one flesh.

Deep sleep. As noted above, this deep sleep has been taken, among other things, as a representation of Adam's resignation to God's will and his willingness to abide the Father's divine wisdom.[106] There is no struggle or fight against God. This applies to our day-to-day struggles to be obedient. But it also applies to our covenant obligation to marry. Elder Bruce R. McConkie once stated:

> In my judgment there is no more important single act that any Latter-day Saint ever does in this world than marry the right person in

the right place by the right authority. The right person is someone for whom the natural and wholesome and normal affection that should exist does exist. It is the person who is living so that he or she can go to the temple of God and make the covenants that we there make. The right place is the temple, and the right authority is the sealing power which Elijah restored.[107]

The deep sleep or submissiveness referred to here precludes the temptation of some to choose something other than the new and everlasting covenant of marriage. It precludes same-gender marriages (regardless of what name they might be called), common-law marriages, or civil marriages that (by choice) are never solemnized in a holy temple.

From the rib of Adam God made Eve. The rib is a metaphor[108] that, among other things, suggests the oneness of Adam and Eve—a oneness that each eternal marriage is to emulate. Elder Milton R. Hunter wrote, "The story of the creation of Eve . . . is symbolical of marriage."[109] It highlights the divine command that "man leave his father and his mother" and "cleave unto his wife: and they shall be one flesh." Marriage is by divine decree the most important of human relationships.[110] It is only surpassed by our relationship with God. The temple sealing ceremony substantiates this. Adam and Eve were to become one, as all husbands and wives are commanded to become one. One commentator noted that the story of the uniting of Adam and Eve teaches that marriage is to be an exclusive relationship (i.e., a man leaves . . .), which is a permanent (i.e., . . . and cleaves) God-sealed bond (i.e., be one flesh).[111] One Jewish commentator noted that the command for man and woman to be one is, in part, fulfilled in the having of offspring. "The child is created by both parents, and there in the child, their flesh is united into one."[112] One Latter-day Saint author wrote:

> The phrase [bone of my bones, and flesh of my flesh] refers to a mutual covenant the two parties have made with each other. Bone in Hebrew symbolizes power, and flesh weakness. "Bone of my bones and flesh of my flesh" thus becomes a ritual pledge to be bound in the best of circumstances (power) as well as the worst (weakness). The man's use of this phrase here implies a covenant similar to a marriage agreement and is, in fact, reminiscent of the phrase "for better or for worse" used in marriage vows.[113]

She shall be called Woman. Previously Adam had named all of the animals, selecting their designations based on "some characteristic seen by Adam in [each] creature as [they] passed before him."[114] Here, as he had with all of God's other creations, the great patriarch of the human family gives Eve a name—*woman*. He also selects this designation because of her characteristics. She is to be called "woman" because she came out of "man." In Hebrew "man" is *Ish*, and "woman" is *Ishshah* (or sheman). Eve is like Adam, whereas none of the animals were.

They were both naked. Surprisingly, a number of commentators have seen in this phrase evidence that, prior to the Fall, "the weather was perfectly temperate, and therefore they had no need of clothing."[115] Although the nakedness is likely intended metaphorically, there is support for the notion that Eden's atmospheric conditions were ideal. Indeed, Elder McConkie suggested that when the millennial day dawns, such a condition will return to the earth. He wrote: "When the Millennium comes and the earth returns to its original paradisiacal state, once again the seasons as we know them will cease and . . . seed time and harvest will go on concurrently at all times. The whole earth at all times will be a garden as it was in the days of Eden."[116]

The nakedness of Adam and Eve also suggests that they dwelt in a state of perfect righteousness. They had no cause for shame.[117] There was no concern for modesty because there were no corrupt thoughts or desires.[118] Things telestial did not exist, just as they will not exist when the Millennium begins. As one text puts it: "They were not weighed down by bodily needs as they cleaved to each other."[119] In Eden the things of this world had little draw upon them. To a great extent it is this earth's telestial state that makes the world's offerings so attractive to fallen mankind.[120]

The Temptation of Adam and Eve

Genesis 3:1–5	Moses 4:5–11	2 Nephi 2:17–18
Now the serpent was more subtil than any beast of the field which the Lord God had made. And he said unto the woman, Yeah, hath God said, Ye Shall not eat of every tree of the garden? And the woman said unto the serpent, We may eat of the fruit of the trees of the garden: But of the fruit of the tree which is in the midst of the garden God hath said, Ye shall not eat of it, neither shall ye touch it, lest ye die. And the serpent said unto the woman, Ye shall not surely die: For God doth know that in the day ye eat thereof, then your eyes shall be opened, and ye shall be as gods, knowing good and evil.	And now the serpent was more subtle than any beast of the field which I, the Lord God, had made. And Satan put it into the heart of the serpent, (for he had drawn away many after him,) and he sought also to beguile Eve, for he knew not the mind of God, wherefore he sought to destroy the world. And he said unto the woman: Yeah, hath God said—Ye shall not eat of every tree of the garden? (And he spake by the mouth of the serpent.) And the woman said unto he serpent: We may eat of the fruit of the trees of the garden; But of the fruit of the tree which thou beholdest in the midst of the garden, God hath said—Ye shall not eat of it, neither shall ye touch it, lest ye die. And the serpent said unto the woman: Ye shall not surely die; For God doth know that in the day ye eat thereof, then your eyes shall be opened, and y shall be as gods, knowing good and evil.	And I, Lehi, according tot the things which I have read, must needs suppose that an angel of God, according to that which is written, had fallen from heaven; wherefore, he became a devil, having sought that which was evil before God. And because he had fallen from heaven, and had become miserable forever, he sought also the misery of all mankind. Wherefore, he said unto Eve, yea, even that old serpent, who is the devil, who is the father of all lies, wherefore he said: Partake of the forbidden fruit, and ye shall not die, but ye shall be as God knowing good and evil.

Adam is approached first. Although the scriptural accounts in Genesis and Moses have Eve being tempted first, in the holy temple we are instructed that the adversary first approached Adam, but upon being rebuffed he turned his attention to Eve. One Latter-day Saint author observed:

> The text does not say that the two are separated at the time of the temptation but actually suggests the opposite. The serpent addresses the woman with the plural Hebrew you form and she replies with the plural we and us: "And he [the serpent] said unto the woman, Yea, hath God said, Ye [plural Hebrew] shall not eat of every tree of the garden? And the woman said unto the serpent, We may eat of the fruit of the trees of the garden: But of the fruit of the tree which is in the midst of the garden, God hath said, Ye [Hebrew plural] shall not eat of it, neither shall ye touch it, lest ye [Hebrew plural] die. And the serpent said unto the woman, Ye [Hebrew plural] shall not surely die." When she partook of the fruit she then gave some to "her man" [*King James Version* husband] who was "with her." . . . The text does not say that the serpent first tempted the man alone and, after he refused, went to the woman; it says only that he tempted the woman, who then gave the fruit to "her man and he did eat."[121]

The fact that the Genesis account differs from the temple account does not necessarily suggest that one is correct and the other incorrect. Indeed, this may simply be evidence that each account has a different symbolic message to convey to different audiences.

Satan put it into the heart of the serpent. This statement has been interpreted variously. In the Genesis account the serpent is said to be subtle or crafty, and therefore he approaches Eve to deceive her. In the Moses account, on the other hand, Lucifer tricks the serpent into doing his bidding. However, in 2 Nephi, father Lehi informs us that the serpent *is* the devil (see also Revelation 12:9; 20:2; Mosiah 16:3; Doctrine and Covenants 76:28). Hence, it is unclear as to whether we should understand that the serpent Satan approached Adam and Eve during their stay in Eden.

Because of a somewhat commonly held belief that animals were able to speak prior to the Fall, some commentators—both LDS and non-LDS—have suggested that the serpent did the tempting on behalf of the devil.[122] Indeed, legends concerning animals becoming dumb at the time of the Fall are widespread.[123] In support of this view, note that Moses 4, Genesis 3, and 2 Nephi 2 all speak of the dialogue between the serpent and Eve. Additionally, when the repercussions for the Fall are delivered (see Genesis 3:14–15; Moses 4:20–21), there appears to be one punishment for the serpent (i.e., to go about on his belly eating the dust of the earth) and another for the devil (i.e., to have his head crushed by Christ, the "seed" of the woman).[124] Furthermore, a number of scriptures certainly refer to speaking animals (see, for example, Numbers 22:28; 2 Peter 2:16; Revelation 4:6–9).[125]

On the flip side of the argument, the Hebrew word translated as "serpent" in the Genesis account is related to the Hebrew word for "luminous" or "shining." Thus, some have suggested that the Genesis account should not read "serpent" but rather "angel of light."[126] In addition, it is believed that prior to the Fall the serpent was a symbol or type for Christ—hence its use in Numbers 21:8, Alma 33:19–20, and Helaman 8:13–15.[127] Thus, associating the serpent with the devil would simply suggest that in Eden, Lucifer was seeking to usurp the role of Christ by appearing to Adam and Eve as an angel of light (see 2 Nephi 9:9).

In the end, it is uncertain which of these interpretations Moses and Lehi intend for us to understand. It is quite possible that both were in the authors' minds when their respective texts were written.

He had drawn many away after him. There is no doubt that Lucifer drew many away after him during the debate in the premortal world. And certainly he has had significant success here upon the earth. As C. S. Lewis put it, Satan is not just *the* devil, but "the leader or dictator of devils"[128] (see also 2 Nephi 9:37). He is but the head of a vast army of deceived spirits seeking to destroy the work of God. It is common for Latter-day Saints to speak of one-third of the hosts of heaven following Lucifer after his rebellion in the premortal world. However, the language of scripture is not one-third, but rather a "third part" (see Revelation 12:4; Doctrine and Covenants 29:36–38). Anciently the concept of a third part was a symbolic device that implied limited power or influence.[129] It suggested that bounds had been set and that God is in control. When this concept is utilized toward a particular individual or event, the suggestion is that they have a limited degree of power or influence.[130] The distinction between one-third and a third part may seem subtle, yet it is real. The fraction, one-third, implies 33 percent. The phrase "third part" implies a numerically undetermined segment of the population who stand as a symbol for the fact that Satan's power over the premortal spirits was limited. Thus, the numerology in the passage implies that we have no knowledge of the fraction or percentage of Father's children that followed the adversary. All we know is that Satan had a limited influence over those in the presence of God, and he has none over those who, through their personal righteousness, bind him.

He sought the misery of all mankind. Even with all of his power and the minions that follow him and do his bidding, Satan is not happy. He likely knows his time is limited and that he cannot succeed in his attempts to destroy God's work. Elder Gerald Lund of the Seventy once penned the following commentary on this clause:

> These verses point out that Satan is the epitome of the saying, "Misery loves company." His very goal for us is misery. . . . I once heard a man say that there are two doors to sin—the front door is pride and the back door is low self-esteem. Many times people sin not because they really want to or because they are rebellious, but because they are so discouraged, so filled with hopelessness, or so desirous of meeting their basic needs that they go after them in unwise ways. Someone once noted that the majority of sins committed by people are an inadequate or misguided attempt to meet our basic needs. Most sins are not committed by evil people, just misguided people. How many instances of adultery, particularly on the part of women, are motivated more by a desire to be loved and accepted than for physical passion? We are seeking to meet those basic needs and Satan knows that; so he drives it and hammers on it.[131]

Lucifer knows that he is destined to be miserable for eternity. His great desire is to cause you and me to be miserable enough in mortality that we will sin, thereby placing ourselves in his power and, if we do not repent, ensuring our eternal misery in the world to come.

He knew not the mind of God. The prophet Moses informs us that it was because Satan "knew not the mind of God" that he sought to destroy the world. One commentator wrote: "It may seem odd that one who presumably had retained his memory of the councils in heaven would not know that he could neither destroy the world nor thwart God's plan by enticing Adam and Eve to fall."[132] Indeed, whatever else it may mean, the statement that Satan "knew not the mind of God" appears first and foremost to highlight the fact that Lucifer's goals, aspirations, and desires were not those of the Father. Thus, in 1 Corinthians 2:16 the Apostle Paul informs us "For who hath known the mind of the Lord, that he may instruct him? But we have the mind of Christ." Of this verse, Elder Bruce R. McConkie wrote, "Christ acts and speaks by the power of the Spirit. Those saints who walk in the light as he is in the light, who keep his commandments, who actually enjoy the presentment or gift given them following baptism, thereby have his mind. They think what he thinks, know what he knows, say what he would say, and do what he would do in every situation—all by revelation from the Spirit."[133]

Thus, clearly Satan "knew not the mind of God" in that he was not one with the Father and the Son. His will was, and is, the antithesis of Their will.

Beyond this, what exactly Lucifer comprehended of the plan and God's intent is unclear. The fact that he was present for at least part of the Grand Council suggests that he had some understanding of the plan and the purpose of mortality—if not an entire understanding. However, in light of the scriptural declaration that he "knew not the mind of God," it does not seem prudent to dismiss the possibility that Satan was ignorant of *some* portion of the Father's will and plan.[134] It is quite possible that certain portions of the plan were not introduced until after Lucifer was cast out and that those aspects of the Father's work were kept hidden from the adversary of all mankind.[135] We simply do not know. Doctrine and Covenants 10 definitely suggests some degree of naiveté on his part: "Satan stirreth them up, that he may lead their souls to destruction. And thus he has laid a cunning plan, *thinking* to destroy the work of God" (Doctrine and Covenants 10:22–23; emphasis added).

In the end the adversary's work does more to move the plan forward than it does to hinder God's work. Irenaeus wisely noted: "The serpent . . . did not profit when persuading man to sin."[136] Elder James E. Talmage wrote: "Satan . . . furthered the purposes of the

Creator by tempting Eve; yet his design was to thwart the Lord's plan. . . . His diabolical effort, far from being the initiatory step toward destruction, contributed to the plan of man's eternal progression."[137] As noted previously, this language is clearly figurative, in that Eve was not deceived. But as it relates to each of us, Lucifer provides the opposition vital to a functional plan of salvation.

Neither shall ye touch it. According to Eve, the Father warned our first parents that they should not only avoid eating the forbidden fruit, but that they should also avoid even touching it (Moses 4:9). Do not flirt with temptation! Elder Neal A. Maxwell wrote:

> We are . . . to avoid even the appearance of evil. Going to "Lucifer's Lounge" is not only risky for us, but may also mislead, divert, or discourage another weaker colleague. It is up to us to use our agency to make certain that we are not tempted above that which we are able to bear. . . . A good example would be the fulltime missionaries who are sent out in diverse circumstances in order to be a light and to carry the gospel message to others. They are given (and follow for the most part) rather strict rules in terms of circumstances they are to avoid and circumstances they are to depart from. The fulltime disciple ought to follow similar rules rather than assume that he will be blessed regardless of his choice of circumstances. In coping with temptation we can usually interrupt the temptation by a change of thought, scenery, or circumstance. Almost always we can reduce the temptation. Alcoholics on the road to reform don't hang around bars. Temptation does not have a crowbar with which to force its way into our consciousness; we decide whether or not we will give place to a thought or impulse.[138]

We are certainly promised that we will never be tempted above that which we can withstand (see 1 Corinthians 10:13). However, as is well known, we have no such promise if we consciously place ourselves in temptation's way (see Doctrine and Covenants 82:10). If we choose to handle the very "fruit" God has commanded us to avoid, we will *almost assuredly* find the temptation for just a small taste beyond our capacity to withstand.

Ye shall not surely die. This declaration has almost universally been understood to be Satan's great lie to Eve. They *did* die upon partaking of the fruit. They died both spiritually *and* physically!

However, as we noted above, the Hebrew rendered "ye shall not surely die" is more accurately translated "In dying ye shall not die, but shall be as the gods."[139] Thus, although traditionally we assume that Satan lied to Adam and Eve here, it appears (from the Hebrew) that he was actually quite accurate in what he told them.[140] In physically dying you will not die (i.e., permanently die), but will become as the gods (living eternally and potentially becoming as they are). "True to form, Satan had taken a truth and applied it in such a way as to achieve his unrighteous purposes."[141]

Ye shall be as gods. In very general terms we might argue that there is a tri-fold purpose to mortality. First of all we have come here to gain a physical, mortal body that could eventually be resurrected, making each of the faithful physically like God. Second, we needed experiential knowledge that could only be had by living with a veil between ourselves and God, thus requiring that every man or woman learn to walk by faith and master this physical body. Third, we needed to participate in the saving and exalting ordinances of the fulness of the gospel of Jesus Christ. Only via these three (and their appendages) could Adam and Eve (or you and I) ever become as God is. Thus, Satan accurately declared to Eve that by partaking of the fruit she could become "as gods."[142]

The experiential knowledge referred to could not be gained in the premortal world nor in Eden. There we could gain intellectual knowledge—facts, as it were. But minus a veil of forgetting, opposition, the enticements of darkness, and adversity, we could only intellectually know the plan. We could not be enlarged and changed by it. As Church Patriarch Eldred G. Smith stated:

> God gives us darkness to see into the distance. He gives us light to see close up. The stars shine in the daylight as much as they do at night, yet we need the darkness in which to see the stars. . . . This life is full of contrasts. We have pleasure and pain, good and evil, virtue and vice. . . . So, this life is a testing period that man may learn obedience by his own experience. Through modern revelation the Lord tells us, " . . . it must needs be that the devil should tempt the children of men, or they could not be agents unto themselves; for if they never should have bitter they could not know the sweet" (Doctrine and Covenants 29:39).[143]

Mortality was and is the only road to godhood—and from the inception of the plan, the divinization of mankind was the goal of God.

Genesis 3:6–7	Moses 4:12–13
And when the woman saw that the tree was good for food, and that it was pleasant to the eyes, and a tree to be desired to make one wise, she took of the fruit thereof, and did eat, and gave also unto her husband with her; and he did eat. And the eyes of them both were opened, and they knew that they were naked; and they sewed fig leaves together, and made themselves aprons.	And when the woman saw that the tree was good for food, and that it became pleasant to the eyes, and a tree to be desired to make her wise, she took of the fruit thereof, and did eat, and also gave unto her husband with her, and he did eat. And the eyes of them both were opened, and they knew that they had been naked. And they sewed fig-leaves together and made themselves aprons.

Eve saw that the tree was good. This comment can be taken in two ways. A literal reading of the passage could suggest that Eve saw that the tree was "good and tempting," and thus, being deceived by the devil, she desired to eat of it. However, if we take into consideration the instructions Adam and Eve surely were given in the premortal world, and presumably again in Eden, we will recall that it was the Lord's will that they partake of the fruit of the tree of knowledge of good and evil.[144] In this context the passage is better read as Eve "saw that the tree was good for bringing to pass God's will." Hence, Elder Dallin H. Oaks, along with *many* others, has declared that Eve partook of the fruit, not because she was deceived, but "in order to initiate the conditions of mortality."[145] This "fruit" would make her "wise" in the sense that through her act she would gain experiential knowledge and thereby become as God is.

She gave unto her husband. Lucifer seeks our destruction because he desires "that all men might be miserable like unto himself" (2 Nephi 2:27). However, this is not Eve's motivation here. She does not give of the fruit to Adam because she wishes him harm, desires that he feel guilty, or wants him to suffer repercussions as she will suffer repercussions for having partaken. Eve ate to fulfill God's will, and she offered the fruit to Adam for that same purpose—to fulfill their foreordained calling and purpose in Eden. It will be recalled that in the process of their verbal interchange Adam acknowledged that it was God's will that they partake, that mankind might be born (see 2 Nephi 2:25). "Eve partook of the fruit, as she had been foreordained to do, and Adam partook after her, to the hallelujah shouts of the hundreds of generations of spirits."[146] Adam, like Eve, knew that this needed to happen.

Their eyes were opened. In a way it might be more accurate to say that Adam and Eve's eyes were closed because they partook of the fruit. By this we mean that, whereas they were able to freely converse with God, Christ, and the angels prior to their Fall, now they would have a veil drawn between them, their spiritual eyes would be shut, and they would be required to walk by faith. They were closed off from the presence of God.

Of course the way in which the phrase "their eyes were opened" is meant here is that Adam and Eve could now learn by experience and faith; they could experience a totally new condition, which would be an eye opener to them. As discussed above, our first parents were not literally deceived. Rather, the story seeks to depict through Adam and Eve the reality that you and I often are beguiled into sinning and then frequently find ourselves wondering how we could have been so foolish. The opening of the eyes of Adam and Eve here stands as a symbol for the reality that, because of the Fall, an experiential knowledge of good and evil can be had, as can the growth that comes from such a knowledge.[147] Augustine also noted that "it was not in order to see outward things that 'their eyes were opened,' because they could see such things already. It was in order that they might see the difference between the good they had lost and the evil into which they had fallen. This is why the tree is called the tree of knowledge of good and evil. . . . It takes the experience of the pains of sickness to open our eyes to the pleasantness of health."[148]

They knew that they were naked. It is significant that initially their nakedness was not a negative thing (see Genesis 2:25; Moses 3:25; Abraham 5:19). However, now it is clearly depicted as pejorative. There is a subtle difference in the Hebrew that has not been carried over into the English translation.

There is a difference in meaning between *arôm* ("naked") in [Genesis] 2:25 and *êrm* ("naked") in [Genesis] 3:7. Whereas both terms are infrequently used in the Pentateuch, *êrm* is distinguished by its use in Deuteronomy 28:48, where it depicts the state of Israel's exiles who have been punished for their failure to trust and obey God's word: "Because you did not serve the Lord your God joyfully and gladly in the time of prosperity, therefore in hunger and thirst, in nakedness [*beêrm*] and dire poverty, you will serve the enemies the Lord sends against you." In distinguishing the first state of man's nakedness (*arôm*) from the second (*êrm*), the author has introduced a subtle yet perceptible clue to the story's meaning. The effect of the Fall was not simply that the man and woman come to know they were "naked" (*arôm*). The effect is rather that they come to know that they were "naked" (*êrm*) in the sense of being "under God's judgement," as in Deuteronomy 28:48 (cf. Ezekiel 16:39; 23:29).[149]

Here their nakedness suggests their guilt (i.e., they had officially transgressed the law of God). But it also suggests that, because they had transgressed, they had forfeited God's Spirit—which would leave them naked or void of that important gift.

Of course, God was not disappointed or angry with Adam and Eve's choice, as they had done exactly what they had been sent to do. As we've noted, the metaphor being depicted is about you and me—mankind in general. When we sin we stand naked before God. We lose His Spirit. And if we fail to sincerely repent, we will be required to stand before the judgment bar of the Great Jehovah with no viable excuse to cover our guilt. Not coincidentally, the Hebrew word for Atonement (from which we draw our English word) means literally "to cover." Christ's sacrificial atonement covers our sins, our guilt, our nakedness.

They sewed fig leaves together and made aprons. Fig leaves have a number of different connotations—some related to Adam and Eve and others to you and me.[150] In this section we will discuss what symbolic messages they send regarding our first parents. In chapter two of this work we examined fig leaves as a symbol for you and me.

Anciently, both aprons and figs symbolized fertility and reproduction.[151] One scholarly source noted: "In ancient Semitic custom, young children ran about with a loose shirt or cloak. As they reached sexual maturity, they began to wear an 'apron' or loincloth; . . .

wearing [an apron] represented adulthood."[152] Of course, the symbols of fertility and reproduction are important because it wasn't until the Fall that Adam and Eve were able to "multiply and replenish the earth" as they had been commanded (Moses 5:11). Thus, appropriately, upon placing themselves in a position to "be fruitful and multiply," Adam and Eve donned what became the symbols of their newly received power.

Elder James E. Talmage associated figs with the covenant people.[153] Thus, when Adam and Eve chose to be obedient to the will of the Father by provoking the Fall, they became the first of His covenant people. Hence their donning of fig leaves became a symbol of the covenant. Related to this is the fact that anciently aprons also served as symbols for "priesthood"[154] and "work."[155] It is likely for this reason that the high priest who served in the Mosaic tabernacle was required to wear an apron or *ephod* (see Exodus 28).[156] He was engaged in the work of the Lord, a work that required that he be in possession of priesthood power. Adam and Eve were sent forth from Eden to work. But first God had equipped them by ordaining Adam to the holy priesthood and initiating both Adam and Eve into certain sacred ordinances. Of the Mosaic priest's apron and its relationship to the aprons of Adam and Eve, one source informs us:

> Adam and Eve, while in the garden, possessed two items of clothing that apparently held ritual meaning: the apron (Genesis 3:7) and the garment of skins (see Genesis 3:21). . . . No doubt [the apron] held some sort of ceremonial significance for the first couple. . . . It is quite likely that these vestments, belonging to Adam and Eve and obtained while in the garden, served as archetypes for later sacral vestments belonging to the Israelite temple system.[157]

Finally, the early Christians saw the fig-leaf aprons as symbols of repentance. Irenaeus put it this way: "For [Adam] showed his repentance in making a girdle, covering himself with fig leaves, when there were many other trees that would have irritated his body less. He, however, in awe of God, made a clothing that matched his disobedience. . . . [But] God in his mercy . . . clothed them with tunics of skin instead of fig leaves."[158] Thus this act by Adam and Eve suggests that their hearts were right, that they were not rebellious. The fig leaves foreshadow their works of obedience, as recorded in the Book of Moses:

> And Adam and Eve . . . [offered] the firstlings of their flocks, for an offering unto the Lord. And Adam was obedient unto the commandments of the Lord.
>
> And after many days an angel of the Lord appeared unto Adam, saying: Why dost thou offer sacrifices unto the Lord? And Adam said unto him: I know not, save the Lord commanded me.
>
> And then the angel spake, saying: This thing is a similitude of the sacrifice of the Only Begotten of the Father, which is full of grace and truth.
>
> Wherefore, thou shalt do all that thou doest in the name of the Son, and thou shalt repent and call upon God in the name of the Son forevermore. (Moses 5:4–8)

In Eden they sought to comply with the Father's will, and once they entered mortality that spirit of compliance continued with them. One LDS source states that "by sewing fig leaves together and making aprons for themselves, Adam and Eve covered their nakedness (Moses 4:13). In so covering themselves with leaves, they became trees, as it were." Trees that are green represent "righteous men" and women.[159] Thus one prominent message of the fig leaves is the righteousness of Adam and Eve, which stands in juxtaposition to the traditional assumption that they were the first sinners.

Genesis 3:8	Moses 4:14
And they heard the voice of the Lord God walking in the garden in the cool of the day: and Adam and his wife hid themselves from the presence of the Lord God amongst the trees of the garden.	And they heard the voice of the Lord God, as they were walking in the garden, in the cool of the day; and Adam and his wife went to hide themselves from the presence of the Lord God amongst the trees of the garden.

In the cool of the day. This phrase, "in the cool of the day," if it does refer to evening,[160] may also imply that Adam and Eve were in Eden for some time before they partook of the fruit.[161] President Joseph Fielding Smith noted that we can "safely conclude" this.[162] LDS commentators Reynolds and Sjodahl suggested that Adam and

Eve must have been there long enough to learn a written language and be fully equipped "mentally and otherwise" for what they would experience outside of Eden.[163]

Why would they have remained in Eden for such an extended period of time—particularly if their primary purpose for being there was to provoke the Fall? We can only conjecture. Perhaps God utilized this time to teach them the horticultural and agronomic skills that would be necessary for them to survive in the "lone and dreary world" once they exited Eden.

When Adam and Eve began their careers outside the Garden of Eden, it was with a high degree of culture. Adam knew how to take care of trees and cultivate the soil. He knew the different animals, for he had named them according to their characteristics. He could observe some of the heavenly constellations, which, like a celestial timepiece, indicated not only day and night, but also seasons, particular days and years, and, we might add, cycles.[164]

Or perhaps it had something to do with the assignments God gave Adam to both "dress"[165] the garden (Genesis 2:15) and also to name the animals. One commentator mused: "The amount of time involved and the organizational difficulties associated with having each living creature come to Adam one by one for a name . . . causes wonderment."[166]

THE REPERCUSSIONS OF THE FALL

Genesis 3:9–13	Moses 4:15–19
And the Lord God called unto Adam, and said unto him, Where art thou? And he said, I heard thy voice in the garden, and I was afraid, because I was naked; and I hid myself. And he said, Who told thee that thou wast naked? Hast thou eaten of the tree, whereof I commanded thee that thou shouldest not eat? And the man said, The woman whom thou gavest to be with me, she gave me of the tree, and I did eat. And the Lord God said unto the woman, What is this that thou hast done? And the woman said, The serpent beguiled me, and I did eat.	And I, the Lord God, called unto Adam, and said unto him: Where goest thou? And he said: I heard thy voice in the garden, and I was afraid, because I beheld that I was naked, and I hid myself. And I, the Lord God, said unto Adam: Who told thee thou wast naked? Hast thou eaten of the tree whereof I commanded thee that thou shouldst not eat, if so thou shouldst surely die? And the Man said: The woman thou gavest me, and commandest that she should remain with me, she gave me of the fruit of the tree and I did eat. And I, the Lord God, said unto the woman: What is this thing which thou hast done? And the woman said: The serpent beguiled me, and I did eat.

Where art thou? The question asked by God is rhetorical. He knows where they are. As Elder Neal A. Maxwell has noted: "The Father . . . knows the past, present and future, since all their dimensions are continually before Him" (see Doctrine and Covenants 38:2; 130:7).[167]

The real meaning behind the question is found in the Moses account, where the Lord asks not, "Where are you?" but rather "Where are you going?" In other words, the Lord's query is about what decision Adam and Eve have made and not about their physical location. Our first parents are called upon to give an accounting of their actions, just as all will be on the judgment day. No sinful act will go unnoticed (see Psalm 69:5; Isaiah 3:9; Doctrine and Covenants 58:60)—nor will any sacrifice or act of obedience and faith.

Genesis 3:14–15	Moses 4:20–21
And the Lord God said unto the serpent, Because thou hast done this, thou art cursed above all cattle, and above every beast of the field; upon thy belly shalt thou go, and dust shalt thou eat all the days of thy life: And I will put enmity between thee and the woman, and between thy seed and her seed; it shall bruise thy head, and thou shalt bruise his heel.	And I, the Lord God, said unto the serpent: Because thou hast done this thou shalt be cursed above all cattle, and above every beast of the field; upon thy belly shalt thou go, and dust shalt thou eat all the days of thy life; And I will put enmity between thee and the woman, between thy seed and her seed; and he shall bruise thy head, and thou shalt bruise his heel.

Because thou hast done this. It is not punishments or cursings but, rather, consequences that God doles out upon the woman and man.[168] Lucifer, on the other hand, appears to experience a punishment. One Latter-day Saint scholar wrote, "Eve has been blamed for woes ranging from the origin of sin to the presumed inferiority of the female sex. . . . Yet, if it were possible to eradicate all our culturally induced prejudices about Eve and examine the original Hebrew text of the whole Eden account, we would find a story that actually says very little of what it has throughout the centuries been credited with saying."[169]

On thy belly . . . enmity between thee and the woman. There appears to be a "twofold sentence, one on Satan and the other on the agent he employed"—namely, the serpent.[170] As noted above, it is unclear whether we are to take literally the notion that the devil spoke through the snake. This passage would seem to suggest that he did. What we can say with certainty is that everyone involved— Adam, Eve, Lucifer, the animals (represented by the snake), and the earth (represented by the fruit)—was affected by the Fall. Repercussions came upon all.[171]

If there really was a curse placed upon the serpent for its having followed Satan in the Garden, that curse is traditionally believed to have been the physiological loss of its legs. Sources ancient and modern highlight the possibility that snakes once walked about on legs "like a chicken."[172]

On thy belly shalt thou go. One commentator noted that

Satan's crime was that he tempted Eve to eat that which she should not; and his punishment was that he was required to eat that which he would not (i.e., dust!).[173] It has been noted that the "crawling in the dust, and taking dust into [his] mouth with [his] food . . . are marks of [his] degradation."[174] Elsewhere it has been suggested that God's punishment upon Satan, as represented in the curse of the serpent, is that, instead of being more clever than all the beasts, he would be more cursed than them all.[175] In other words, just as the serpent was cursed to be near the bottom of the animal kingdom, Lucifer is cursed to be at the bottom of the spirits God created.

I will put enmity between thee and the woman. The enmity mentioned is not, as some commentators have erroneously assumed, a reference to mankind's natural aversion to snakes—and vice versa.[176] The Lord is informing us here that enmity (hatred or disdain) will exist between Christ and Lucifer. According to the Hebrew, Lucifer will have power to bruise Christ's heel (through the Atonement), but Christ will have power to crush Satan's head (through that same Atonement).[177] Certainly throughout the history of this earth Satan will have power to cause Christ pain and sorrow because of the dominion he will obtain over many. However, in the end victory will be Christ's when He once and for all puts "all enemies under his feet" (see Doctrine and Covenants 49:6; 58:22; 76:61; 1 Corinthians 15:25).[178] Since anciently the head was a representation of the seat of one's life, the severed head was frequently employed in scripture as a representation of the "decisive defeat of the enemy."[179] Thus, we are told that Christ will crush Satan's head (see Genesis 3:15; Moses 4:21), symbolizing His eventual "utter defeat" over the adversary of all mankind.[180]

There is a significant set of parallels present in the Fall. Christ embodies and suffers each of the penalties of Adam and Eve's actions. For example, Eve would have pain in her travail; and Christ would have "travail of his soul" (Isaiah 53:11). Eve would be in subjection to Adam; and Christ would subject Himself to the Father (1 Corinthians 15:28). The ground would be cursed for Adam's sake; and Christ would become "a curse" for our sake (Galatians 3:13). Thorns would cause Adam to suffer; and thorns would cause Christ to suffer (Matthew 27:29). Sweat would be a result of Adam's sin; Christ would sweat "as it were great drops of blood" because of the sins of Adam and his posterity (Luke 22:44). Because of their transgression, sorrow entered the world; Isaiah informs us that Christ would become, for us, "a man of sorrows, and acquainted with grief" (Isaiah 53:3). Adam and Eve brought death into the world; Christ died to remove it (see Helaman 14:16–17).[181]

Although not specifically stated in the verse, the reference to the devil's enmity toward the seed of the woman highlights the reality that Lucifer will go about tempting and afflicting God's children. Indeed, the great adversary of God and all mankind serves a purpose. Heavenly Father would never entice us to make bad choices, as that would be contrary to His nature. Thus, the devil serves as the source of that necessary opposition.[182] President Brigham Young once stated:

> I wish to tell you a truth; it is God's truth; it is eternal truth: neither you nor I would ever be prepared to be crowned in the celestial kingdom of our Father and our God, without devils in this world. Do you know that the Saints never could be prepared to receive the glory that is in reserve for them, without devils to help them to get it? . . . Refer to the Book of Mormon, and you will find that Nephi and others taught that we actually need evil, in order to make this a state of probation. We must know the evil in order to know the good. There must needs be an opposition in all things.[183]

Significantly, Adam—then known as mighty Michael—headed the force that cast Lucifer out of the premortal world.[184] Here we see that he also caused Satan's removal from Eden. Finally, near the conclusion of the Millennium, it will once again be Adam who will defeat the devil and his hosts, casting them permanently from this earth into outer darkness (see Doctrine and Covenants 88:112–15).

Genesis 3:16	Moses 4:22
Unto the woman he said, I will greatly multiply thy sorrow and thy conception; in sorrow thou shalt bring forth children; and thy desire shall be to thy husband, and he shall rule over thee.	Unto the woman, I, the Lord God, said: I will greatly multiply thy sorrow and thy conception. In sorrow thou shalt bring forth children, and thy desire shall be to thy husband, and he shall rule over thee.

I will greatly multiply. According to the LDS version of the King James Bible, the Hebrew for this clause would more accurately be rendered something akin to "God will greatly multiply thy discomfort and size during conception."[185] In other words, she will give birth to mortal offspring, which will require an uncomfortable increase in her size. Ellis T. Rasmussen wrote:

> Sorrow is used in Genesis 3:16 and 17 to translate the Hebrew *etzev*, which connotes "toil, pain, travail." Doubtless the burdens and pain of pregnancy and childbirth were thereby anticipated (Genesis 3:16b). This is a great revelation to women. Eve and her daughters can become cocreators with God by preparing bodies for his spirit children to occupy on earth and later in eternity. Mothering would entail inconvenience, suffering, travail, and sorrow; these the Lord foretold as natural consequences and not as a curse.[186]

Eve's calling to be the "mother of all living" would be painful in the pregnancy, delivery, and nurturing of her offspring. However, it would also allow her to serve as a partner with God (and her husband) in the creation of life. Through the Fall, Eve had been endowed with one of God's greatest gifts to mortals—the power of creation. But it would require sacrifice.

In sorrow thou shalt bring forth children. President Spencer W. Kimball indicated that he felt that this would better be worded as in "distress,"[187] "pain," or "waiting"[188] you will bring forth children. He wrote: "I think there is a great gladness in most Latter-day Saint homes when there is to be a child [born] there."[189] Thus, again the emphasis is on the physical discomfort, but not on the regret.

Thy desire shall be unto thy husband. We examined the possible meaning of this phrase in chapter two of this work.

Thy husband shall rule over thee. Both within and without the Church this clause is traditionally interpreted to mean that in Eden man and woman were equal. They certainly had their individual roles. However, the societal ordering of men and women, which would later develop after their Fall, apparently did not exist in paradise.[190] Before the Fall, Adam and Eve were one. Similarly, we could extrapolate from this passage that in the highest degree of the celestial kingdom men and women will once again be perfectly one.

Rodney Turner has described the consequences of the Fall in the following manner.[191]

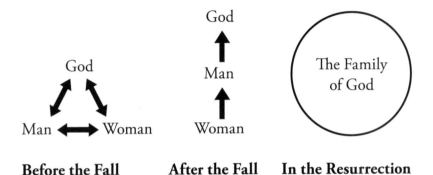

In the eternities men and women will continue to have their individual roles. But it is the righteous and faithful performance of those roles that will make their companionship whole.

President Spencer W. Kimball stated that he preferred to substitute the word *preside* for the word *rule*.[192] In other words, God's intent in this post-Fall world in which we live is that men preside in righteousness over their homes, counseling with their wives in all things. President Kimball added: "The wife follows the husband as he follows Christ. No woman has ever been asked by the Church authorities to follow her husband into an evil pit. She is to follow him as he follows and obeys the Savior of the world, but in deciding this, she should be sure she is fair."[193] President J. Reuben Clark Jr. noted that Eve's calling to begin the creating of mortal bodies was "as eternally important in its place as the priesthood itself."[194] Tragically, in many families and in many cultures, Genesis 3:16 has been seen as authorization for unrighteous dominion on the part of men.

Genesis 3:17–19	Moses 4:23–25
And unto Adam he said, Because thou hast hearkened unto the voice of thy wife, and hast eaten of the tree, of which I commanded thee, saying, Thou shalt not eat of it: cursed is the ground for thy sake; in sorrow shalt thou eat of it all the days of thy life; Thorns also and thistles shall it bring forth to thee;	And unto Adam, I, the Lord God, said: Because thou hast hearkened unto the voice of thy wife, and hast eaten of the fruit of the tree of which I commanded thee, saying—Thou shalt not eat of it, cursed shall be the ground for thy sake; in sorrow shalt thou eat of it all the days of thy life. Thorns also, and thistles shall it bring forth to thee, and thou shalt eat the herb of the field. By the sweat of thy face shalt thou eat bread until thou shalt return unto the ground—for thou shalt surely die—for out of it wast thou taken: for dust thou wast, and unto dust shalt thou return.

Because thou hast hearkened unto thy wife. Note that the temple depiction of the Fall does not contain the clause "because thou hast hearkened unto the voice of thy wife." The restored gospel teaches us that Eve's counsel to Adam was exactly what it should have been.

Cursed shall be the ground for thy sake. The very language of this clause establishes that this is not a punishment, but rather a help to Adam.[195] God seeks to serve the man rather than punish him for doing exactly what he had been sent to Eden to do. C. S. Lewis wrote: "The travail of all creation . . . at its most intense, may be necessary in the process of turning finite creatures (with free wills) into—well, Gods."[196]

This cursing of the ground also suggests that the Fall caused a physical change to the world in which Adam and Eve dwelt. What initially was paradisiacal—and spontaneous in its growth of the good things of the earth—would, in its post-Fall nature, not yield naturally. Rather, the earth now would have to be worked if man was to benefit from it. Curiously, one commentator noted:

> Even the land, which, along with the serpent, was the only thing actually cursed in the Hebrew text, seems to have been redeemed as

part of the restoration of the gospel by Joseph Smith, according to a revelation he recorded in 1831: "And, as I, the Lord, in the beginning cursed the land, even so in the last days have I blessed it, in its time, for the use of my saints, that they may partake the fatness thereof" (Doctrine and Covenants 61:17).[197]

Advancements in science—agronomy, horticulture, and so on—have placed us in an enviable position. The daunting realities that Adam and Eve faced when first cast out of Eden are nearly incomprehensible.

Hugh Nibley offered an interesting insight into the relationship between the repercussions brought upon Eve and those levied upon Adam. He wrote:

> Now a curse was placed on Eve, and it looked as if she would have to pay a high price for taking the initiative in the search for knowledge. To our surprise the curse was placed on Adam also. For Eve, God "will greatly multiply thy sorrow and thy conception. In sorrow shalt thou bring forth children." (Genesis 3:16.) The key is the word for sorrow, *atsav*, meaning to labor, to toil, to sweat, to do something very hard. To *multiply* does not mean to add or increase but to repeat over and over again; the word in the Septuagint is *plethynomai*, as in the multiplying of words in the repetitious prayers of the ancients. Both the conception and the labor of Eve will be multiple; she will have many children. Then the Lord says to Adam, "In *sorrow* shalt thou eat of it all the days of thy life" (that is, the bread that his labor must bring forth from the earth). The identical word is used in both cases; the root meaning is to work hard at cutting or digging; both the man and the woman must sorrow and both must labor. (The Septuagint word is *lype*, meaning bodily or mental strain, discomfort, or affliction.) It means not to be sorry, but to have a hard time. If Eve must labor to bring forth, so too must Adam labor (Genesis 3:17; Moses 4:23) to quicken the earth so it shall bring forth. Both of them bring forth life with sweat and tears, and Adam is not the favored party.[198]

Again, as with Adam's call to farm without tools or store-bought seeds, the daunting task of having children in Eve's day (without modern medicine and doctors) seems overwhelming. Yet, as with the science of farming, so also with medicine—God has advanced our knowledge so that the toil and difficulty of women have been greatly reduced.

Thorns and thistles. Although we discussed this in more detail in chapter two, one early Christian insight seems appropriate here. In the early third century, one Latin father suggested that this curse upon the land was designed to remind Adam (and his posterity) of Christ. He noted that Christ willingly bore a crown of "thorns and thistles" on our behalf as "a symbol of the sins that the soil of the flesh brought forth" and that "the power of the cross removed."[199]

Dust thou art, and unto dust shalt thou return. There is a play on words here. The Hebrew word for man is derived from the Hebrew word for ground or dust.[200] One commentator noted: "Adam is shaped from the dust of the ground. This relation to the earth is subtly reinforced for the Hebrew ear in the assonance of *dm* 'human' and *admâ* 'ground' (Genesis 2:7). It is then sealed in the tragic epitaph, 'dust thou art, and unto dust shalt thou return' (Genesis 3:19 KJV)."[201]

Genesis 3:20	Moses 4:26
And Adam called his wife's name Eve; because she was the mother of all living.	And Adam called his wife's name Eve, because she was the mother of all living; for thus have I, the Lord God, called the first of all women, which are many.

The mother of all living. Eve's name (*hawwah*) is derived from the Hebrew word for life, *hayyim*.[202] Curiously, in Sumerian the same cuneiform character or symbol is used to write both the word "life" and the word "rib." This seems significant in light of Eve's name and metaphorical origin.[203]

By partaking of the fruit first, Eve became the "mother of all living," in that she opened the door to all who seek both mortal and eternal life.[204] She opened the door to mortal life by giving birth to the first humans—and all of us are direct descendants of her. She opened the door to eternal life because through her posterity would be born the Messiah. We read: "Adam called his wife's name Life, because she was to be the mother of all human beings, and because she was to be the mother of HIM who was to give life to a world dead in trespass, and dead in sins."[205]

In the scriptural accounts Adam does not name Eve until after they have fallen, implying that prior to that point she was *not* physically capable of becoming a mother, as blood had not yet entered her veins.[206] It is only after the Fall that Eve truly became the "mother of all living."[207]

While in Gethsemane, the burden of the sins of all mankind bore down upon Christ with unfathomable intensity. During that incomprehensibly wrenching few hours[208] Jesus suffered in ways inconceivable, and with the result, as Elder Bruce R. McConkie wrote, that: "We know that he lay prostrate upon the ground as the pains and agonies of an infinite burden caused him to tremble, and would that he might not drink the bitter cup."[209] Luke records: "And being in an agony, he prayed more earnestly; and he sweat as it were great drops of blood falling down to the ground" (JST, Luke 22:44). King Benjamin taught his people: "And lo, he shall suffer temptations, and pain of body, hunger, thirst, and fatigue, even more than man can suffer, except it be unto death; for behold, blood cometh from every pore, so great shall be his anguish for the wickedness and the abominations of his people" (Mosiah 3:7). Is it possible that one of the reasons blood must be shed in order for an atonement to be made[210] is that blood is a symbol for the fallen or mortal nature of man? As Adam and Eve only possessed blood by virtue of the Fall,[211] and mankind after their redemption shall no longer have blood, so also in an effort to atone for the sins of all mankind—ridding the world of sin and death upon conditions of repentance—Jesus had the blood literally pressed out of Him. In this context, perhaps blood is not a multiplicity of different shadows but one complete symbol of the cycle of mortality, sins, and redemption. In order to find efficacy in the Atonement, we must—in the image of Christ—somehow find the strength to press the mortal and fallen out of our nature and being, or we will not be exalted.

BANISHMENT FROM GOD'S PRESENCE

Genesis 3:21	Moses 4:27
Unto Adam also and to his wife did the Lord God make coats of skins, and clothed them.	Unto Adam, and also unto his wife, did I, the Lord God, make coats of skins, and clothed them.

Coats of skins. The very first death to take place upon this earth was that of a lamb.[212] It stood as a symbol—a foreshadowing or type—of the death of the Messiah, the Lamb of God, which would destroy Satan and his work and would reconcile man to God.[213] One early Christian commentator rhetorically asked: "Why would beasts have been killed in their presence? Perhaps this happened so that by the animal's flesh Adam and Eve might nourish their own bodies and that with the skins they might cover their nakedness, but also that by the death of the animals Adam and Eve might see the death of their own bodies."[214]

At least in part, these skins represent the glory possessed by God, Christ, and all exalted beings. Early Jewish sources strongly support this interpretation of the symbolic connotations of the sacred priestly garments. For example, while in the Garden of Eden and prior to their Fall, Adam and Eve are said to have worn "garments of light" akin to the glory and light that radiated from the Father.[215] When they partook of the fruit of the tree of knowledge of good and evil, God stripped them of those garments of light and made coats of skins for them as a replacement.[216] "God killed certain animals in order to furnish Adam and Eve with clothes."[217] They "received their garments [of skin] from God after the fall . . . and [Adam's] descendants wore them as priestly garments at the time of the offering of the sacrifices. Furthermore they . . . [are said to have had] supernatural qualities."[218]

On a related note (and as we noted above), in the book of Hebrews we are told that the veil of the temple represents the flesh of Christ (see Hebrews 10:19–22). This being the case, when one ceremonially acts out his or her ascent back to God, at the final stages of the endowment, it is Christ who stands between the patron and the Father. Christ is, of course, our mediator or go-between (see 1 Timothy 2:5; 2 Nephi 2:27). Since it is Christ who is the Mediator through whom we communicate with our Father (both at the veil and in prayer)—and through whom we gain access to the celestial kingdom—then it is also Christ who is symbolized by the clothing we receive at the conclusion of the temple initiatory ceremonies.[219] This clothing represents the crucified flesh of Christ and should be received with a covenant and reminder to always live in accordance with what that newly procured covering represents. This should give new meaning to the idea of taking upon oneself the name (see 2 Nephi 31:13; Mosiah 5:8) or image (see Alma 5:19; 1 John 3:1–3) of Christ.

Thus, the coats of skins made for Adam and Eve represent the flesh of Christ and the purity and glory that He and His Father possess through their supernal righteousness. And just as Adam and Eve received these earthly tokens of the heavenly reality until they could return and reclaim the light they had lost through the Fall, we too wear a temporary covering symbolic of the reward that awaits the faithful.[220] One commentary on this passage states: "God made them coats of skins, large, and strong, and durable, and fit for them; such is the righteousness of Christ. Therefore *clothe yourselves with the Lord Jesus Christ.*"[221] As noted above, the Hebrew translated "to cover" is actually the same as the Hebrew word from which we get our English word *Atonement.* Thus, God's covering Adam and Eve here suggests that He will provide an atonement for them.[222]

As we highlighted in chapter two, this passage also suggests the loving kindness and care of the Father. As a result of their transgression, Adam and Eve have been sent out into the lone and dreary world. However, the Father has still ensured that their needs are met.[223] He gave them the knowledge necessary (either in Eden or after their Fall) to create shelter, clothing, grow food, hunt animals, cook, tend to medical needs, have a Church organization, know how to function within the priesthood, and so forth.

Genesis 3:22–24	Moses 4:28–31
And the Lord God said, Behold, the man is become as one of us, to know good and evil: and now, lest he put forth his hand, and take also of the tree of life, and eat, and live forever: Therefore the Lord God sent him forth from the garden of Eden, to till the ground from whence he was taken. So he drove out the man; and he placed at the east of the garden of Eden Cherubims, and a flaming sword which turned every way, to keep the way of the tree of life.	And I, the Lord God, said unto mine Only Begotten: Behold, the man is become as one of us to know good and evil; and now lest he put forth his hand and partake also of the tree of life, and eat and live forever, Therefore I, the Lord God, will send him forth from the Garden of Eden, to till the ground from whence he was taken; For as I, the Lord God, liveth, even so my words cannot return void, for as they go forth out of my mouth they must be fulfilled. So I drove out the man, and I placed at the east of the Garden of Eden, cherubim and a flaming sword, which turned every way to keep the way of the tree of life.

The man is become as one of us. Such was the design of the plan of salvation. Neither Adam and Eve, nor you and I, could ever become like God without this mortal probation. An experiential knowledge of good and evil was requisite for all. There was no other way to prepare for and eventually gain our exaltation. To become eternally like God each of us needs to become mortal (like God was before us), thereby acquiring a knowledge of good and evil requisite for all those who seek omniscience.

Regarding the phrase, "The man has become like one of us," one commentator noted that this obviously presupposes a plurality of gods, or *elohim*, that cannot be explained away.[224] Adam and Eve had begun the process of becoming like the gods. And because of their Fall, you and I may do the same.[225]

He drove them eastward. As noted previously, the use *east* of in relation to the Fall of Adam and Eve is significant. Most of Christendom believes that the driving of the first of the human race eastward is evidence of God's displeasure with them. As we cited earlier, Elder Talmage noted: "It has become a common practice with mankind to heap reproaches on the progenitors of the family, and to picture the supposedly blessed state in which we would be living but for the fall; whereas our first parents are entitled to our deepest gratitude for their legacy to posterity—the means of winning title to glory, exaltation, and eternal lives."[226] The presence of the eastward direction in the text is designed to ensure that the student of scripture will perceive the Fall as the positive and divinely foreordained event that it was. As one text records:

> Eastward in Eden the Lord planted a garden—containing both the tree of life and the tree of knowledge of good and evil—where he placed Adam and Eve (see Genesis 2:8). As a result of the Fall, they were expelled to the east from the garden, and the Lord placed cherubim and a flaming sword to prevent their reentering the garden in their fallen state to partake of the tree of life. In biblical Hebrew, one oriented oneself by facing east. Thus, the movement into mortality, away from God's presence, was a movement forward—to the east.[227]

If something moves eastward it is symbolically moving "toward God." Indeed, anciently, east was the direction that represented God.[228] In the Genesis Rabbah we read: "Under all circumstances the east provides refuge."[229] Thus the Fall of man was not a tragedy wherein our first parents apostatized or fell from grace. On the contrary, it was a movement toward God in the truest sense. As B. H. Roberts put it, the Fall was the "beginning of the rise of man."[230]

Cherubim and a flaming sword. After partaking of the "forbidden" fruit, Adam and Eve were officially in a sinful or fallen state. They were at odds with God's Spirit and were incapable of remaining in His presence. The placement of the cherubs was to prevent Adam and Eve from immediately partaking of the tree of life, for such an act would ensure their damnation. It is for this reason that Alma states:

> What does the scripture mean, which saith that God placed cherubim and a flaming sword on the east of the garden of Eden, lest our first parents should enter and partake of the fruit of the tree of life, and live forever? . . . There was a space granted unto man in which he might repent; therefore this life became a probationary state; a time to prepare to meet God; a time to prepare for that endless state which has been spoken of by us, which is after the resurrection of the dead. (Alma 12:21, 24)

If they were to be exalted, they needed first to repent, enter into covenants, and have the probationary state to prove themselves faithful to those same covenants.[231] God gave the consequence of death so that sin would cease when this probationary state is over, thereby ensuring that man would not live eternally as a sinner, but rather eternally with God.[232] Hence, Alma wrote: "And now behold, if it were possible that our first parents could have gone forth and partaken of the tree of life they would have been forever miserable, having no preparatory state; and thus the plan of redemption would have been frustrated, and the word of God would have been void, taking none effect" (Alma 12:26; see also Alma 42:5).

One commentator suggested that the guarding of Eden may also be a sign of God's omniscience and Adam and Eve's naiveté. In other words, although they willingly did the Father's will by partaking of the fruit, and no doubt felt excited at beginning their foreordained callings, nevertheless, they would shortly be shocked at how much harder than expected mortality would prove to be. Thus, ensuring that they could not change their minds and seek refuge, the way back was "closed and guarded."[233] In reality, the mortal experience is what they needed—as it is the need of each of us—even though in the midst of trials all wish they could retract back into Eden. "Adam and Eve discovered repentance—the Rabbis tell us—and thereby [in that way] they came nearer to God *outside* of Eden than when Eden."[234]

My words cannot return void. The dictates, pronouncements, and will of God shall be fulfilled. As the Prophet Joseph stated:

> The Standard of Truth has been erected; no unhallowed hand can stop the work from progressing. Persecutions may rage, mobs may combine, armies may assemble, calumny may defame, but the truth of God will go forth boldly, nobly, and independent, till it has penetrated every continent, visited every clime, swept every country, and sounded in every ear, till the purposes of God shall be accomplished, and the Great Jehovah shall say the work is done.[235]

CONCLUSION

As is well known among the Latter-day Saints, rather than an act of disobedience, rebelliousness, or sin, the Fall of Adam and Eve was an act of faith and faithfulness and a blessing to all of God's creations. It is as foundational to the great plan of happiness as is the Creation or the Atonement. Without the Fall the plan would have been frustrated and mortality would have come to none of God's creations.

Thus, from a doctrinal perspective, as presented in this chapter, the results of the Fall of Adam and Eve include the following:

- Adam and Eve could have children (see Moses 5:11; 6:48; 2 Nephi 2:23, 25).

- All would experience physical death (see Moses 4:25; 6:48; 2 Nephi 9:6).

- Misery and woe would be the lot of mankind throughout mortality (see Moses 6:48; Genesis 3:16–17).

- Sin becomes common to the mortal experience (Moses 6:49, 55; 2 Nephi 2:22–25).

- Spiritual death comes upon all (see Alma 42:9).

- The ground is cursed and we must work (see Moses 4:23–25; Genesis 3:17–19).

- We can learn to recognize good from evil (Moses 4:28; 6:55–56; 2 Nephi 2:23; Genesis 3:22).

- We can have joy in mortality (Moses 5:10; 2 Nephi 2:23, 25).

- We can know the joy of our redemption (see Moses 5:11).

- We can obtain eternal life (see Moses 5:11).

Notes

1. See Kimball (1998), 25.

2. Although forgotten by most, nearly every culture and religion in antiquity had a belief in both a Mother in Heaven and a Father in Heaven. The Indians of Mesoamerica believed that they had been born to heavenly parents in a celestial world prior to their coming into mortality. The Canaanites believed in a mother goddess called Ashtoreth. The Hittites centered their worship on the great "Earth-Mother," their chief goddess, later revered in both Crete and Greece. The Egyptian mother-goddess was Isis, although they also had other female deities. The Mother Goddess of

Western Asia went by many names: Aphrodite, Astarte, Artemis, Diana, Venus, and so on. The Eastern Orthodox speak of the Theotokos and the Catholics of Mary as the "Mother of God." One Catholic theologian wrote: "Scholarly opinion is virtually unanimous in [acknowledging a] Semitic mother goddess at Yahweh's side in Jewish worship." [Johnson (1994), 92–93.] Elsewhere we read: "While nearly all world religions have had female divinities and feminine symbolism, the god of Western Judeo-Christian culture and scripture has been almost unremittingly masculine. Still, the idea of a Heavenly Mother or a female counterpart to the male father-god is not unknown in Christianity. Recently discovered Gnostic texts from the first century after Christ reveal doctrinal teachings about a divine mother as well as father." [Wilcox (1992), 64. See also Pagels (1976), 293–303.] In addition, note the following LDS sources that refer to a mother-goddess in other religious traditions: Hunter (1959),137, 155; Nibley (1988–1990), 1:468; Parry, Parry, and Peterson (1998), 23; Petersen (1978), 27; Turner (1990), 204.

3. Rasmussen (1993), 7.

4. Hinckley (1997), 257.

5. See Clark (1965–1975), 4:203, 206; 5:244. It will be noted that the Moses 2:27 account indicates that we were all created, not just after the image of our Heavenly Father and Mother, but also after the image of God's Only Begotten. Elder Milton R. Hunter wrote: "They were created first as spirit beings in the image of their Heavenly Parents and later as mortals in a similar likeness. Thus the males were created in the image and likeness of God the Eternal Father while the females were formed in the image and likeness of God their Eternal Mother. In other words, all the men and women who have ever lived on this earth or who ever shall live here are literally sons and daughters of Heavenly Parents. . . . Since Jesus Christ was the oldest son of our Eternal Parents in the spirit world, all the human family were patterned after their oldest brother, and He and they in the image and likeness of their Parents." Hunter (1951), 104, 106.

6. Ludlow (1981), 105.

7. Smith (1976), 345.

8. See Hunter (1951), 104, 106.

9. Young, in *Journal of Discourses* 2:6; 3:319; 7:285. Elder Parley P. Pratt noted that Moses wished to reveal to mankind the true origin of Adam and Eve, but they could not receive it. So, according to Elder Pratt, Moses veiled the truth by saying "Man [was] moulded [sic] from the earth, as a brick!" and "Woman [was] manufactured from a rib!" See Pratt (1978),

30. Similarly, the First Presidency (Joseph F. Smith, Anthon H. Lund, and Charles W. Penrose) wrote that Adam "was not fashioned from earth life and adobe but begotten by his Father in Heaven." Cited in Peterson (1987), 130. See also Young, in *Journal of Discourses*, 4:218; 11:122; Joseph F. Smith, remarks made on December 7, 1913, cited in *Deseret Evening News*, December 27, 1913, section 3, page 7.

10. *Times and Seasons* (1844), 758. See also B. McConkie (1980–1981), 1:32–33, n. 7.

11. B. McConkie, *Mormon Doctrine* (1979), 589, s. v. "pre-existence."

12. "The Father and The Son: A Doctrinal Exposition by The First Presidency and The Twelve," June 30, 1916, in Clark (1965–75), 5:26.

13. See Cirlot (1962), 245; Holzapfel and Seely (1994), 17; Gaskill (2003), 150–56.

14. Basil the Great, "On the Holy Spirit" 27:66, in Oden (2001), 54.

15. Parry (1994), 126; Campbell (2003), 56; Book of Jubilees 3:19; Jamieson, Fausset, and Brown (n. d.), 18.

16. Ryken, Wilhoit, and Longman (1998), 315–16.

17. Joseph Smith is said to have taught it (see Brooks [1960, 1965], 1:114), as did Brigham Young (see *Journal of Discourses*, 8:195), Wilford Woodruff (see Brooks [1960, 1965], 1:114–15), Heber C. Kimball (see *Journal of Discourses*, 10:235), George Q. Cannon (see *Journal of Discourses*, 11:337), Joseph Fielding Smith (see [1998], 3:74), Bruce R. McConkie (see Mormon Doctrine [1979], 303), and others (see Hunter [1951], 109; Brewster [1988], 201–2; Whitney [1973], 207, n. 2; Widtsoe [1960], 127).

18. Young, in *Journal of Discourses*, 8:195.

19. Kimball, in *Journal of Discourses*, 10:235.

20. See Rich (1913), 1:101–2.

21. Reynolds and Sjodahl (1980), 124.

22. Such is the case in Rabbinic sources also. See, for example, Neusner (1985), 158.

23. See Joseph F. Smith, John R. Winder, and Anthon H. Lund, in Clark (1965–1975), 4:205. See also Clark (1965–1975), 5:26; Ludlow (1981), 109; Rasmussen (1993), 10.

24. Vawter (1977), 68.

25. In other words, Genesis, Moses, Abraham, and the temple.

26. Hyrum Andrus disagrees with the four aforementioned canonized accounts. He holds that Adam was created before any of the animals. He has written: "Though others have expressed a different view of the meaning of this statement, it is the writer's opinion that the context of the Lord's declaration (see Moses 3:6–7) indicates that He is clearly speaking of the placement of life upon the earth after the earth had been formed and sanctified and before the fall of Adam. In speaking of the placement of life upon the earth, God declared that man was the 'first flesh upon the earth.' Man must therefore have arrived upon the earth before the animals, etc. were then formed and brought 'unto Adam to see what he would call them.' Here again it appears that man was on earth when the animals arrived. But because man was the first flesh upon the earth it does not follow that he resided here for a time in a desolate state. A garden was first planted, and then man was placed there as a lone figure until woman and the animals were formed." See Andrus (1967), 171–72. It is worth noting that Andrus bases his interpretation on a single verse in the Book of Moses, which he himself suggests may not be "the most accurate account." See Andrus (1967), 137–38.

27. "The Hebrew word *adm* means man in the generic sense—human rather than male. While these verses [Genesis 2:7; see also Moses 3:7 and Abraham 5:7] represent the creation of an actual, historical man, they also represent the creation of the woman and the whole human family." Jackson (2001), 83.

28. See Smith (1954), 328; B. McConkie (1985), 84; Matthews, *A Bible! A Bible!* (1990), 172; J. McConkie (1998), 164–65.

29. See also Hunter (1951), 104; Reynolds and Sjodahl (1980), 123; Smith (1998), 1:75; B. McConkie, Mormon Doctrine (1979), 170, 210.

30. See, for example, Young, in *Journal of Discourses*, 3:319; Smith (1925), 113; Smith (1998), 1:74, 139–40; Pratt (1978), 29–30. Roberts (1966), 268–69. The Genesis Rabbah states that "the trees were . . . transplanted . . . into the garden of Eden." Neusner (1985), 161.

31. Smith (1998), 1:139–40. Elsewhere he noted that God transplanted "them from another earth as we are taught in the scriptures." See Smith (1954), 276–77.

32. Andrus (1967), 193. "Some scriptures depict Eden as a distinct place on earth from which Adam and Eve were driven at the Fall (e.g., Moses 4:29, 31; 5:4). But because their fall brought about the fall of all the earth (2 Nephi 2:22), it seems best to consider the whole world, and not only part of it, as being in an Edenic condition." Jackson (2001), 88.

33. Richard Cowan wrote: "At the time of Adam's fall, the earth itself—which originally was in a celestial condition, having been created spiritually in heaven (see Moses 3:5)—fell into . . . its present telestial condition." Cowan (1996), 74–75. Hyrum Andrus wrote: "According to the scripture, sometime after Adam was placed in the garden the earth's reckoning of time was changed significantly from the same time schedule as that of Kolob to that which it now possesses, and it is implied that that change occurred at the fall [see Abraham 5:13]. To change the reckoning of time on a given sphere requires that there be a change in its revolutions, as its schedule of time is determined by the speed of its revolutions. If, as implied, the earth's reckoning of time was changed significantly, vital alterations would have had to be made concerning its place in the cosmos, which may have necessitated a removal of the earth from near Kolob to this solar system. Nowhere in our solar system do planets have a reckoning of time approaching that of Kolob." Andrus (1967), 200–201.

34. Young, in *Journal of Discourses*, 17:143; Smith (1998), 1:75; Smith (1976), 181; Ehat and Cook (1980), 60, 84; Times and Seasons (1843), 672. See also Young, in *Journal of Discourses*, 7:163; 8:8; 9:317; Andrus (1967), 200.

35. See Hunter (1951), 97; Andrus (1967), 107–8.

36. Hunter (1951), 97.

37. Rockwood (1992), 28; Bailey (1992), 1:16–17; Salisbury (1976), 66; King (1995), s. v. Moses 4:26.

38. Rockwood (1992), 28.

39. Even the corruption and decay of the earth result not from God's actions but rather from our choices. God created an earth void of death. We introduced death. God created an earth void of sin. We introduced sin. All things were initially created in a paradisiacal state. It was Lucifer's premortal fall, and Adam and Eve's Fall from Eden, that have introduced all opposition, decay, and sin into the world.

40. King (1995), s. v. Moses 3:9.

41. See King (1995), s. v. Moses 3:9. See also Smith (1998), 1:63.

42. Smith (1998), 1:63. See also Doctrine and Covenants 77:2; Smith (1993), 2:48–51; Packard (1992), 1:42; B. McConkie, Mormon Doctrine (1979), 38; Jones (2003), 73, 90.

43. See Whitney (1999), 1:14. See also McConkie, Mormon Doctrine (1979), 210–11; Mouritsen (1977), 49; Jensen (1992), 3:1404–05; Bell (1992), 30.

44. Millet (1997), 39; Holland (1997), 160; Miller (1993), 94–96; McConkie and Millet (1987–1992), 1:56; Jerome, "Homilies" I, in Oden (2001), 55.

45. Millet (1992), 2:724. See also Bradford and Dahl (1992), 1:394.

46. Clifford and Murphy (1990), 12. See also Vawter (1977), 71.

47. Hertz (1962), 10.

48. Hertz noted that if you take literally the notion that Adam and Eve had no understanding of "good and evil" until they ate of that fruit—which God commanded them not to partake of—then they certainly could not be held accountable for their actions, as they would have no moral compass with which to make decisions about right and wrong—"a view which contradicts the spirit of Scripture." Hertz (1962), 10.

49. The seventh-century Arab monastic and theologian John of Damascus wrote: "The tree of knowledge of good and evil is the power of discernment." John of Damascus, "Orthodox Faith" 2:11, in Oden (2001), 62.

50. Hunter (1951), 112.

51. Elder Orson Pratt argued that the command to "multiply and replenish" was given on the sixth day. However, he reasoned that, since in his opinion Adam and Eve were not given their physical or terrestrial bodies until the seventh day, "the command must have been given while they were in the spirit world" prior to their entrance into Eden. See Pratt (2002), 84. See also Andrus (1967), 191, n. 27; Smith (1925), 29; Pratt, in *Journal of Discourses*, 21:200–201; Pratt (1880), 22; Budge (1999), 4:415. This idea appears to run counter to all four of the authorized creation accounts. However, it will be noted that the temple account of the creation also varies slightly from the other three accounts when it delineates what was accomplished during each of the "creative periods." Elder Pratt and Hyrum Andrus find their support for the idea that Adam was placed upon the earth on the morning of the seventh day in Doctrine and Covenants 77:12, which states: "We are to understand that as God made the world in six days, and on the seventh day he finished his work, and sanctified it, and also formed man out of the dust of the earth." Of the seeming contradiction between the standard creation accounts and the Doctrine and Covenants, Dr. Richard Cowan has written: "After giving an account of the six days of creation and of the Lord's resting on the seventh, this scripture reminds us that there were not yet living creatures on earth because they had only been created spiritually in heaven. At that point God 'formed man from the dust of the ground' (Moses 3:5–7). That physical creation is probably the one spoken of by the Lord in Doctrine and Covenants 77:12. Note that the wording there is more like the description of the physical creation in Moses 3:7 than it is like the account of the earlier spiritual creation in Moses 2:27." Cowan (1996), 94.

52. Nelson (1993), 34.

53. See Smith (1993), 2:211.

54. Gaskill (2003), 119. See also Draper (1991), 24, 77, 94; Neusner (1985), 173.

55. The language is a bit puzzling, as this river is said to flow "out" of Eden but then "into" the Garden to water it. See Rasmussen (1993), 11. Some see this as meaning that four different rivers converged in Eden. However, others understand it to be suggesting that one river flows out of Eden into four different directions. Keil and Delitzsch suggest the following: "The stream took its rise in Eden, flowed through the garden to water it, and on leaving the garden was divided into four heads or beginnings of rivers, that is, into four arms of separate streams." See Keil and Delitzsch (n. d.), 81. See also Wenham (1987), 64–65.

56. J. McConkie (1998), 161.

57. Johnston (1990), 63.

58. Parry (1994), 133. One scholar noted, "If the Garden of Eden is an image of divine provision, it is paradoxically also a place of human labor." Ryken, Wilhoit, and Longman (1998), 316. Such is the case with the temple also.

59. In a similar vein, in Revelation 14:20 John employs the number 1,600, a multiple of 4. "Symbolically, the number is the square of four, denoting geographical completeness, multiplied by the square of ten, the number denoting all of a part. Taken together, the number suggests that God's judgment actually involves all John's world, not just those who are around Jerusalem, and that all those who belong to that portion outside the protecting power of God will be directly affected." Draper (1991), 164.

60. Kselman and Barre (1990), 541. Fitzmyer notes that "it can denote the abode of the dead (see Psalm 107:26; Romans 10:7) or the final prison of Satan and the demons (Revelations 20:3). It is used often in the LXX [as] the symbol of chaos and disorder." Fitzmyer (1970), 739, n. 31. Mann (1986), 278–79, indicates that the sea represents the "place of final punishment for demons." Edwin Firmage indicated that the sea was a symbol for the "repository of impurity." Firmage (1992), 6:1132. See also Williamson (1983), 104; Clarke (n. d.), 5:420; Freyne (1992), 2:900; Morris (1999), 171; Liefeld (1976–1992), 8:913.

61. See, for example, Sailhamer (1992), 99; Clarke (n. d.), 1:43–44; Hunter (1951), 107.

62. Of course this author does not assume that the Ethiopia mentioned in Genesis is likely the same Ethiopia of modern-day Africa. But, in an effort to be consistent, if some assume that the biblical Euphrates (Genesis

2:14) and Tigris (Genesis 2:14) are the same as the modern rivers by those names, we should also assume that the biblical Ethiopia is the same as the modern country by that name. In so doing, it becomes evident that this theory is flawed.

63. Admittedly, one might argue that ancient Ethiopia is not the same as modern Ethiopia, and thus the two rivers could have been on the same continent. However, this argument still serves to show that we are entirely unable to utilize the biblical names as a means of determining the location of the Garden of Eden.

64. See Rasmussen (1993), 11; Ludlow (1981), 109. Elder Milton R. Hunter conjectured that the four rivers of Eden could be identified in modern North America. He wrote: "Where then in the world are there four rivers that flow together, making one? The Mississippi River and its tributaries fit well with the description given in Genesis and in the Book of Moses. Among the principal rivers that flow together in the upper Mississippi Valley are the Mississippi, Missouri, Ohio, and Illinois." Hunter (1951), 134–35. See also Peterson (1987), 134–35. While this appears to support the teaching that the Garden of Eden was in Missouri (see commentary on Genesis 2:7–8, Moses 3:8, and Abraham 5:8 above), once again this ignores the fact that, if the entire face of the earth was flooded in the days of Noah, any rivers from the days of Adam and Eve would likely have been erased. Indeed, even a lengthy regional flood would be sufficient to destroy the shape and location of these ancient rivers.

65. Nachmanides (1971–1976), 1:76.

66. See, for example, Doxey (1973), 59; Talmage (1981), 28–29, n. 3; Rockwood (1992), 24; Snow, in *Journal of Discourses*, 19:271–72.

67. See B. McConkie, "Christ and the Creation" (1982), 15. "Adam and Eve's partaking of the fruit was figurative." Parker (2003), 85.

68. See Oaks (1993), 73.

69. J. McConkie, "The Mystery of Eden" (1990), 28.

70. Parker (2003), 87.

71. Ehat and Cook (1980), 63, emphasis added.

72. See chapter two: "You and I As Adam and Eve."

73. Smith (1982), 124. See also Smith (1993), 4:81; King (1995), s. v. Moses 3:16–17.

74. Smith (1993), 1:181; Snow, *Journal of Discourses*, 19:272–73; Rich, in *Journal of Discourses*, 19:371–72; B. McConkie, *The Millennial Messiah* (1982), 643–44.

75. Rasmussen (1993), 12.

76. Judd King calls this "the earliest example of God's teaching his children the principle of agency." See King (1995), s. v. Moses 3:17. In actuality it seems that the events associated with the Grand Council in Heaven would have taught this principle before the Fall. And it would be hard to imagine that the principle and its surrounding doctrine were not taught even before that, simply in light of the fact that we were endowed with that gift during our time in the premortal world. See Smith (1998), 1:66; Warner (1992), 1:26.

77. Nachmanides (1971–1976), 1:74; Vawter (1962), 17.

78. Augustine, "On the Literal Interpretation of Genesis," 11.4.6, in Oden (2001), 80.

79. Smith (1958), 23.

80. Cyril of Alexandria, "Catechetical Lectures," 13:31, in Oden (2001), 62.

81. Severian of Gabala, "On the Creation of the World," 6:1, in Oden (2001), 61.

82. Augustine, "City of God," 13:12, in Hutchins (1982), 18:365.

83. Irenaeus, "Against Heresies," 5:23, in Roberts and Donaldson (1994), 1:551–52; Jubilees 4:30, in Charlesworth (1983, 1985), 2:63–64.

84. See Young, in *Journal of Discourses* 2:6; 3:319; 7:285.

85. Elder Orson Pratt made some curious comments regarding the creation of animals and humans. See, for example, *Journal of Discourses*, 18:289; 19:314.

86. Kent P. Jackson wrote: "God was more directly involved in the creation of humans than in the creation of other things. Notice the carefully chosen language for the origin of plants and animals: 'Let the earth bring forth grass. . . . And the earth brought forth grass' (Moses 2:11–12). 'Let the waters bring forth abundantly the moving creature . . . which the waters brought forth abundantly' (Moses 2:20–21). And 'Let the earth bring forth the living creature' (Moses 2:24). Plants and animals were created when God commanded the earth and the sea to bring them forth. But the process of human creation is depicted in strikingly different terms; 'Let us make man. . . . And I, God, created man' (Moses 2:26–27). . . . Whatever the process for creating humans may have been, the scriptures are clear in differentiating between that process and the process by which other life was made." Jackson (2001), 81–82.

87. See Doctrine and Covenants 77:2; Smith (1998), 1:63; Smith (1993), 2:48–51; Packard (1992), 1:32; B. McConkie, *Mormon Doctrine* (1979), 38,

210–11; Jones (2003), 73, 90; Whitney (1999), 1:14; Mouritsen (1977), 49; Jensen (1992), 3:1404–05; Bell (1992), 30.

88. Of Genesis 2:19, Ellis Rasmussen wrote: "The common noun adam in Hebrew is a collective noun meaning 'man,' 'human,' or 'mankind'; as a common noun, it is used with 'the'; but it may be used as a proper noun, Adam, without 'the,' and it appears as such for the first time in this verse. For its use as a collective noun, see Genesis 5:2." Rasmussen (1993), 13.

89. If Adam, while in Eden, was intellectually as a child, he would not have had the ability to name each of the animals. Clarke (n. d.), 1:45. See also 1:50.

90. Adam's language is known as the Adamic tongue (Moses 6:5–6, 57; 7:13; Ether 1:33–37; 3:22–24; 12:24). Scripture indicates that this pure language will be restored, likely during the Millennium (see Zephaniah 3:9).

91. Ephrem the Syrian, "Commentary on Genesis" 2.9.3, in Oden (2001), 65.

92. Smith (1998), 1:95.

93. Ephrem the Syrian, "Commentary on Genesis" 2.9.3, in Oden (2001), 65.

94. See Clifford and Murphy (1990), 12.

95. Hertz (1962), 9. Anciently, to give one a name, or to know one's name, placed the individual with that knowledge in power over the thing or person named. See Gaskill (2003), 219–20.

96. See Jones (2003). See also Doctrine and Covenants 89:12–13.

97. Nachmanides (1971–1976), 1:77–79; Jamieson, Fausset, and Brown (n. d.), 18. "Events seem to be in topical rather than chronological sequence in this chapter: the bringing of the female spiritual being into a body of earthly materials is related in one scripture before the naming of certain creatures (Abraham 5:14–19), whereas it is mentioned before but completed afterward, according to other scriptures (e.g., Genesis 2:18, 21–22; Moses 3:18, 21–22)." Rasmussen (1993), 12. See also Neusner (1985), 183; Clarke (n. d.), 1:45; Pagels (1989), xix, xxi; Reynolds and Sjodahl (1980), 129.

98. Sailhamer (1992), 102. See also Sailhamer (1976–1992), 2:47.

99. Adam saw the companionship had by each of the animals, and he is said to have longed for that same blessing in his own life. You and I, in like manner, see couples in successful temple marriages, and we long for the same blessing in our own lives.

100. See King (1995), s. v. Moses 3:18.

101. Reynolds and Sjodahl wrote: "Being alone . . . Adam could not fill the measure of his creation." (1980), 128.

102. Of course, through the mercy and love of our Father and our Savior, those who never have the opportunity to marry in mortality will not be denied the blessings of the new and everlasting covenant of marriage in the eternities. It is only those who reject this covenant, or are found unworthy of it, that will lose these blessings.

103. Ludlow (1981), 111. See also Peterson (1987), 137.

104. First Presidency (1995), 102.

105. Smith (1976), 300.

106. Church (1992), 7.

107. B. McConkie (1955), 13.

108. See Reynolds and Sjodahl (1980), 129.

109. Hunter (1951), 145. President Spencer W. Kimball made a similar comment. See (1976), 71; Peterson (1987), 138; King (1995), s. v. Moses 3:20–23.

110. See, for example, Evans (1955), 113–14; Christensen (1996), 28–29; Barlow (1982), 70; Barlow (1986), 53. "The Rabbinic term for marriage is . . . 'the sanctities,' . . . the purpose of marriage being to preserve and sanctify that which has been made in the image of God." See Hertz (1962), 10.

111. Kidner (1967), 66.

112. Nachmanides (1971–1976), 1:80.

113. Rockwood (1992), 17–18. See also Campbell (2003), 53.

114. Reynolds and Sjodahl (1980), 129.

115. See, for example, Clarke (n. d.), 1:46; King (1995), s. v. Moses 4:27.

116. McConkie, *The Millennial Messiah* (1982), 413.

117. Reynolds and Sjodahl (1980), 131; Rasmussen (1993), 13.

118. See King (1995), s. v. Moses 3:25.

119. Oden (2001), 67.

120. This is not to suggest that mankind will go about naked during the Millennium. Additionally, because the term naked is traditionally seen as a metaphor for innocence or guilt, it is not certain whether Adam and Eve really were nude during their stay in Eden. To focus on whether or not they wore actual clothing prior to their Fall is to miss the point of the intentionally metaphorical language.

121. Rockwood (1992), 19.

122. See, for example, Reynolds and Sjodahl (1965), 145; Skousen (1974), 51–52; Smith (1976), 291–92; Smith (1954), 194–95; Ehat and Cook

(1980), 188–89; Fitzmyer (1990), 1402; 2 Enoch 58:6 in Charlesworth (1983, 1985), 1:184; Jubilees 3:28 in Charlesworth (1983, 1985), 2:60; Whiston (1981), 26; Oden (2001), 74; John of Damascus, "Orthodox Faith" 2:10, in Oden (2001), 75.

123. Jubilees 3:28 states: "On that day [i.e., the day of the Fall] the mouth of all the beasts and cattle and birds and whatever walked or moved was stopped from speaking because all of them used to speak with one another with one speech and one language." See Charlesworth (1983, 1985), 2:60. See also "Life of Adam and Eve," Latin version, 38:1, in Charlesworth (1983, 1985), 2:274. Ginzberg (1967–1969), 5:101, n. 83, and 1:71, suggests that the animals knew the language of Adam while in Eden. See also Vawter (1977), 78; Hamilton (1982), 46; Hertz (1962), 10; Pfeiffer and Harrison (1962), 7; Peake (1919), 140; Dummelow (1936), 9; Clarke (n. d.), 1:48–49, 51.

124. Judd King made an interesting observation regarding the statement that "Satan put it into the heart of the serpent." He noted that to take this phrase literally would have some curious implications for the agency of animals. The scriptures do not typically depict animals as the agents of the devil. Nor do we traditionally see them as the mouthpiece of Satan. So a literal reading of this clause would suggest that the serpent (at least during his time in Eden) had agency, could hear and speak, had reasoning skills, and could bear responsibility for his own actions. After all, we are told that the snake allowed Satan into his heart (Moses 4:6), and that he was a "subtle" or "sneaky" creature (Moses 4:5). This implies a choice was made by the serpent. We are told that the reptile engaged in a discussion with Eve (see Moses 4:7–11), and that via that discussion he was able to deceive the woman (see Moses 4:19). This implies intellectual gifts or analytical skills, on top of the ability to speak. For this deception the snake was said to be punished (see Moses 4:20), which implies accountability. See King (1995), s. v. Moses 4:5–21. It is a very curious approach to the passage, although hardly something one could safely declare as a doctrine of the Church. Indeed, in the opinion of this author, King's observation shows why the reader should perceive the serpent's participation in Eden as a symbol rather than a reality.

125. Reason would have it that, if these animals were able to speak in Eden, surely they will be able to speak again, possibly as soon as the Millennium, but if not then, presumably in the next life. See Revelation 4:9; 5:11–12; 19:4; Smith (1976), 291; Smith (1948), 2:69; Ehat and Cook (1980), 184, 185, 186.

126. See, for example, Hamilton (1982), 42. See also "Revelation of Moses," in

Roberts and Donaldson (1994), 8:566. Ginzberg records: "Satan assumed the appearance of an angel." Ginzberg (1967–1969), 1:95; "Life of Adam and Eve," Latin version, 9:1 and Greek version, 17:1–2, 15, in Charlesworth (1983, 1985), 2:260, 261, 277; Jamieson, Fausset, and Brown (n. d.), 19; Clarke (n. d.), 1:48.

127. See Skinner (2000), 359–84; Wilson (1999), 363. The serpent is also seen as a symbol of the resurrection or immortality. See Vawter (1977), 78.

128. Lewis (1961), vii; cited in Jensen (1998), 109.

129. See Draper (1991), 95–96; Parry and Parry (1998), 110–11; Johnson (1976–1992), 12:492, 515; Ford (1975), 132–133, 190; Morris (1999), 120, 154.

130. See Draper (1991), 108; Parry and Parry (1998), 110.

131. Lund (1999), 378.

132. Jackson (2001), 91.

133. B. McConkie (1987–1988), 2:322. See also *Lectures on Faith*, 5:2.

134. Regarding the ignorance of Lucifer, one commentator wrote: "Apparently he did not know the divine plan of redemption as we know it (2 Ne. 9:5–10). For his own purposes, therefore, Satan sought to persuade the ancestors of the family of humankind to do a deed that would separate them from the presence of God in spiritual death and later separate their spirits from their bodies in physical death; then they would be like his unembodied spirit followers and subject to him (2 Ne. 9:8)." Rasmussen (1993), 14. Elder John A. Widtsoe wrote that Lucifer appears to have "forgotten, or did not know, that by [Adam and Eve's] very 'disobedience' the purposes of the Lord with respect to his spirit children would be accomplished." Widtsoe (1960), 195. See also Ladle (2004), 49.

135. One commentator suggested: "By questioning Eve the serpent ascertained the mystery of the tree." Oden (2001), 74. Ephrem the Syrian wrote: "The serpent cunningly learned, through questioning Eve, the character of paradise, what it was and how it was ordered. When the accursed one learned . . . that the Tree of Knowledge, clothed with an injunction [or commandment of prohibition], served as the veil for the sanctuary, he realized that its fruit was the key . . . that would . . . cause them great remorse." Ephrem the Syrian, "Hymns on Paradise" 3:4–5, in Oden (2001), 74.

136. Irenaeus, "Against Heresies" 3.23.8, in Roberts and Donaldson (1994), 1:458.

137. Talmage (1981), 63. Again, from Ellis Rasmussen we read: "Their choice did not relegate them and their descendants to a hopeless predicament.

It initiated a program, already planned, whereby humankind could work toward eternal life." Rasmussen (1993), 14.

138. Maxwell (1976), 67–68.

139. See Genesis footnote 3:4a in the LDS edition of the *King James Version* of the Bible. See also Irenaeus, "Against Heresies" 5:23, in Roberts and Donaldson (1994), 1:551; Clark (n. d.), 1:44, 54; Pagels (1989), 67.

140. Widtsoe (1998), 107; Young, in *Journal of Discourses*, 15:126.

141. Andrus (1967), 187–88.

142. One commentator suggested that the devil's declaration to Eve was deceptive, in that Eve might have assumed that Satan meant all she had to do was partake of the fruit and she would instantly become a god. See Rasmussen (1993), 14. However, as noted above, Adam and Eve understood clearly the plan, their role, the repercussions of partaking of the fruit, and the need for the mortal experience. So regardless of what Lucifer intended Eve to understand by his words, she partook not because she thought she had found some shortcut to godhood.

143. Smith (1958), 23. See discussion in chapter one, note 62.

144. Ehat and Cook (1980), 63; Young, in *Journal of Discourses* 2:302, 10:312; Widtsoe (1998), 103; Woodruff, in *Journal of Discourses* 23:126; Pratt (2000), 88; Whitney (1921), 93; Roberts (1996), 344–45; Talmage (1975), 70; Widtsoe (1960), 192; Widtsoe (1937), 51–52; Clark (1997), 27; Smith (1993), 2:213–15, 4:80; Smith (1998), 1:109–10, 115; Packer (1996), 49–50; B. McConkie (1978), 221; B. McConkie, "Eve and the Fall" (1979), 68; B. McConkie (1985), 82; Oaks (1993), 73; Hafen (1990), 9; Holland (1997), 202–4; First Presidency (1995), 102, paragraph 3; LDS Bible Dictionary (1979), 670, s. v. "Fall of Adam"; Matthews, "The Fall of Man" (1990), 38–41, 62, 67, 77–78; Millet (1990), 191; Millet (1997), 11–12; J. McConkie, "The Mystery of Eden" (1990), 32–35; Rasmussen (1993), 14; Jackson (1994), 14; Parker (2003), 79, 88–89, n. 3; Turner (1972), 206; Peterson (1992), 213; Ludlow (1981), 114; Rockwood (1992), 6, 21, 24; Adams (1990), 99; Campbell (2003), 6, 8, 13–14, 23, 27, 29–31, 81, 89, 101, 112–14, 166; Ladle (2004), 47; Bennion (1988), 96–97; Bailey (1998), 23. See also Oden (2001), 100; Lewis (1993), 440; Ryken, Wilhoit, and Longman (1998), 247. See also Vawter (1977), 79.

145. Oaks (1993), 72–73.

146. Campbell (2003), 114.

147. Judd King wrote: "These words describe figuratively what the 'knowing good from evil' experience would be." King (1995), s. v. Moses 3:19–20.

148. Augustine, "City of God" 14:17, in Oden (2001), 81.

149. Sailhamer (1976–1992), 2:49. See also Sailhamer (1992), 103.

150. S. Michael Wilcox noted that some symbols, including those employed in the temple, have multiple meanings. Wilcox (1995), 25.

151. Julien (1996), 23–24; Cooper (1995), 14; McConkie and Parry (1990), 49; Bayley (1990–1993), 2:248; Meyers (1992), 1:319.

152. Meyers (1992), 1:319.

153. See Talmage (1981), 443. See also Cooper (1995), 66.

154. Conner (1992), 141; Unger (1966), 317.

155. Julien (1996), 23–24; Cooper (1995), 14. The symbol of "work" also seems applicable to Adam and Eve, in that their choice to eat of the fruit was a choice to give up ease for a life of sacrifice and work.

156. Although there is not absolute agreement in the scholarly community, an ephod is traditionally believed to have been an apron. See McKenzie (1965), 241; Myers (1987), 342; Brown (1999), 85–86.

157. Parry (1994), 145.

158. Irenaeus, "Against Heresies" 3.23.5, in Roberts and Donaldson (1994), 1:457. See also Oden (2001), 82; Ginzberg (1967–1969), 5:89, n. 70.

159. McConkie and Parry (1990), 15, 103–4.

160. It is traditionally understood that the cool of the day is the time around sundown, when the fresh evening breezes would bring welcome relief from the region's oppressive daytime heat. See Speiser (1962), 24; Jamieson, Fausset, and Brown (n. d.), 19; Hertz (1962), 11; Pfeiffer and Harrison (1962), 7; Peake (1919), 140; Dummelow (1936), 9; Clarke (n. d.), 1:52. Judd King made an interesting observation. If this is taken literally, then "the phrase suggest[s] a variety of temperature[s] in the garden. If there was a 'cool' part of the day, likely there was a part that was not 'cool.'" King (1995), s. v. Moses 4:14.

161. Ginzberg (1967–1969), 5:106, n. 97.

162. Smith (1949), 67.

163. See Reynolds and Sjodahl (1955–1961), 6:86–87. Similarly, in the pseudepigraphical 2 Enoch we are informed that Adam and Eve remained in Eden some 5 1/2 hours. [See 2 Enoch 32:1, in Charlesworth (1983, 1986), 1:154.] Those who take literally the notion that a thousand years in man's time is but one day in God's (see Psalm 90:4; 2 Peter 3:8; Abraham 3:4) tend to see in this a suggestion that Adam and Eve may have been in Eden for some 229 years (by man's reckoning), at

which point they partook of the "forbidden fruit." Similarly, the Talmud states that Adam and Eve were residents of the Garden for twelve hours. (See Sanhedrin 38b.) One Latter-day Saint commentator conjectured: "A revelation seems to imply that Adam was placed upon the earth at the beginning of the seventh day. See Doctrine and Covenants 77:12. If the seventh day was indeed a day of the Lord's time, and there is no reason to assume that it was not, Adam and Eve were evidently in the garden for the major portion of that period before the fall," since God approaches them regarding their transgression "in the cool of the day," or in other words, at evening. Andrus (1967), 191, n. 27. The reader should note that, although a number of commentators believe that Adam was placed in Eden on "Sunday" morning, this is not the way Moses, Abraham, and Genesis depict the event. Each of those texts suggest that Adam was placed in Eden on "Saturday" (rather than "Sunday," as suggested by Doctrine and Covenants 77:12).

164. Reynolds and Sjodahl (1980), 143–44.

165. To "dress" means to work, labor, or serve.

166. King (1995), s. v. Moses 3:19–20.

167. Maxwell (1999), 47.

168. Vawter (1977), 84–85; Rasmussen (1993), 17; Rockwood (1992), 20; Campbell (2003), 102.

169. Rockwood (1992), 3.

170. Clarke (n. d.), 1:52–53.

171. One commentator wrote: "The animal kingdom provides the temptation (serpent), the plant kingdom the mode for the fall (fruit and tree), and the humans the agents of the deed." Rockwood (1992), 19.

172. See, for example, Quincy (1883), 84; Cowdery (1835), 236; Peterson (1995), 196–97; King (1995), s. v. Moses 4:20; Reynolds and Sjodahl (1965), 139; Andrus (1967), 204–5; Nyman (1985), 92. Any copy of the Egyptian Book of the Dead will depict the serpent walking on two legs. See, for example, Faulkner (1994), plate 27; Budge (1995), 46, 623, and pictures on p. xiv; Budge (1995), 58. There is also some scientific support for the notion that snakes once had legs. Paleontologists have found fossil evidence that a serpent dubbed *Pachyrhachis problematicus* walked on two legs. See Wilford (1997), A16.

173. See Church (1992), 10.

174. Dummelow (1936), 10.

175. Ephrem the Syrian, "Commentary on Genesis" 2.29.2, in Oden (2001),

89. One LDS scholar wrote: "Satan was informed through symbolic terms that he would not have the privilege of earth life that even cattle and beasts have." Rasmussen (1993), 16.

176. See, for example, Vawter (1977), 82.

177. Occasionally commentators see this as saying that Satan will bruise the heel of Adam's posterity (i.e., you and me), but Christ will crush the head of Satan. See, for example, Talmage (1981), 43; King (1995), s. v. Moses 4:21.

178. Andrus (1967), 189; Irenaeus, "Against Heresies" 3.23.1, 7, in Roberts and Donaldson (1994), 1:456, 147; Ginzberg (1967–1969), 1:95.

179. Ryken, Wilhoit, and Longman (1998), 362. See also Unger (1966), 461.

180. Wilson (1999), 214. According to Martin Luther, "by not being more definite, God mocked Satan, thereby causing him to fear the seed of all women." See Keller (1990), 173–74. See also Pelikan (1958), 1:195–96.

181. Church (1992), 12.

182. Lund (1989), 102.

183. Young, in *Journal of Discourses,* 4:373. See also 4:372–73.

184. M. McConkie (1998), 205; B. McConkie, "Eve and the Fall" (1979), 67; Petersen (1976), 8–10.

185. See Genesis 3:16 footnote 16b in the LDS edition of the *King James Version* of the Bible.

186. Rasmussen (1993), 17.

187. Kimball (1976), 72.

188. Regarding his use of *pain* or *waiting,* see Ludlow (1981), 113.

189. Kimball (1976), 72.

190. Reynolds and Sjodahl (1965), 140; Rockwood (1992), 11–12, 21; Clifford and Murphy (1990), 12; Clarke (n. d.), 1:53, 56; John Chrysostom, "Homilies on Genesis" 17:36, in Oden (2001), 93; Vawter (1977), 84–85.

191. Turner (1972), 310.

192. Kimball (1998), 316.

193. Kimball (1976), 70.

194. Clark (1997), 29.

195. Romney (1976), 168.

196. Lewis (1993), 440.

197. Rockwood (1992), 25.

198. Nibley (1986), 89–90. See also Rasmussen (1993), 18.

199. Tertullian, "On the Crown," 14:3, in Oden (2001), 95.

200. Jackson (2001), 83; Rasmussen (1993), 18; Vawter (1977), 66.

201. Ryken, Wilhoit, and Longman (1998), 9.

202. Sweet (1995), 15; Hamilton (1982), 52; Jackson (2001), 85.

203. See Vawter (1977), 75.

204. Clement of Alexandria, "Stromateis," 3.64.1, in Oden (2001), 98.

205. Clarke (n. d.), 1:55. See also Jackson (2001), 85.

206. Smith (1993), 1:181; Snow, in *Journal of Discourses*, 19:272–73; Rich, in *Journal of Discourses*, 19:371–72; B. McConkie, *The Millennial Messiah* (1982), 643–44. It has been said that, prior to the Fall, all living creatures had spirit in their veins. See Snow, ibid.; Smith (1998), 1:76–77; Smith (1976), 199–200; Widtsoe (1998), 374.

207. Indeed, because of their lack of blood (while in Eden), they were not susceptible to sickness, disease, or death. See Smith (1998), 1:77. One commentator suggested that, above and beyond the receipt of blood, something else opened Adam and Eve up to sickness and death: "Adam's transgression resulted in a withdrawal of the powers of divine life or glory which had prevailed upon the earth since the time it was created and sanctified. The withdrawal of these divine powers, in turn, opened the way for the forces of death, which had been introduced into the bodies of Adam and Even by the forbidden fruit. . . . Consequently, it is said that the fall brought death, for, had the divine powers of life and glory not been withdrawn, the forces of death might not have gained ascendancy in the earth. Joseph Smith taught that in God's presence, 'all corruption is devoured by the fire.'" Andrus (1967), 202–3. Being in God's light and glory gives life. If that light withdraws, immediate spiritual death and eventual physical death are the sure result.

208. McConkie (1980–1981), 4:124.

209. B. McConkie (1985), xiii.

210. Durham (1987), 116; Taylor (1882),149.

211. The Hebrew root from which the name *Adam* comes means literally "to show blood." See Brown, Driver, and Briggs (1999), 10.

212. Parry (1994), 142–43.

213. See Clarke (n. d.), 1:55.

214. Ephrem the Syrian, "Commentary on Genesis" 2.33.1, in Oden (2001), 98.

215. Ginzberg (1967–1969), 1:74–75, 79; 5:97, n. 69; 5:103–4, n. 93. See also Tvedtnes (1994), 651–52; "Life of Adam and Eve," in Charlesworth (1983, 1985), 2:281, n. 20a; Neusner (1985), 227.

216. See discussion in chapter two, note 164.

217. Ginzberg (1967–1969), 5:104, n. 93. See also J. McConkie (1985), 202; Tvedtnes (1994), 649–50.

218. Ginzberg (1967–1969), 5:103, n. 93.

219. See discussion in chapter two, note 165.

220. The temple, its ordinances, and its clothing are but earthly vehicles to get us back to the celestial kingdom or presence of God. One non-LDS commentator indicated that certain articles of temple clothing symbolized "being shielded or protected." Todeschi (1995), 27. Once we return to the Father, many of these earthly vehicles will likely be done away with or will be replaced by the heavenly things that they represented (see Revelation 21:22). Perhaps this explains why Joseph stated of Moroni, when he appeared on September 21, 1823: "I could discover that he had no other clothing on but this robe, as it was open, so that I could see into his bosom" (JS—H 1:31). Joseph describes Moroni as wearing a garment of white that was "lighter than at noonday" (JS—H 1:30). But there is no mention of the earthly "coat of skins" that fallen men are required by covenant to wear. In the Nag Hammadi's "Dialogue of the Savior," Judas and Matthew are recorded as having said to Christ, "We want to understand the sort of garments we are to be clothed with when we depart the decay of the flesh." To this the Lord replied, "Not with these transitory garments are you to clothe yourselves." Jesus added, "You will clothe yourselves in light and enter the bridal chamber." See the "Dialogue of the Savior" 138:50, 143:84, 85, in Robinson (1988), 252–54.

221. Church (1992), 12, emphasis in original.

222. Hamilton (1982), 48.

223. See Reynolds and Sjodahl (1965), 142; Hertz (1962), 12, 13; Vawter (1977), 87; Kidner (1967), 72.

224. Vawter (1977), 87.

225. "When Adam fell, the Lord said, 'Behold, the man is become as one of us'; and so he was driven away from the tree of life. But Christ's prayer in John [17:21] is 'that they also may be one in us'; and in Revelation [22:14] man is welcomed back to the tree of life, and Christ's prayer is answered." Habershon (1974), 55.

226. Talmage (1975), 70.

227. Holzapfel and Seely (1994), 17.

228. Cirlot (1962), 245.

229. Neusner (1985), 236. See also Cooper (1995), 59; Drinkard (1992), 2:248; McConkie and Parry (1990), 44; Ryken et al. (1998), 225.

230. Roberts (1996), 344. Elder Orson F. Whitney taught that the Fall placed mankind "upon progression's highway." Whitney (1921), 93.

231. As one early Christian commentator put it: "It was not decreed that they should live in toil, in sweat, in pains and in pangs [throughout eternity]. Therefore, lest Adam and Eve, after having eaten of this tree [of knowledge of good and evil], live forever and remain in eternal lives of suffering, God forbade them to eat [of the tree of life], after they were clothed with a curse." Ephrem the Syrian, "Commentary on Genesis," 2.35.1, in Oden (2001), 101.

232. See Irenaeus, "Against Heresies," 3.23.6, in Roberts and Donaldson (1994), 1:457. "Physical death merely offers us the necessary transition to eternal life." Pagels (1989), 139. See also King (1995), s. v. Moses 4:28–31; Talmage (1981), 59.

233. See Rasmussen (1993), 19.

234. Hertz (1962), 13.

235. Burton (1977), 280.

Epilogue

THE FALL IS one of the "Three Pillars of Eternity" on which the whole plan of salvation rests.[1] All three events—the Creation, the Fall, and the Atonement—were pre-planned, foreordained events. Clearly none was left to chance, nor brought about by an accident or fortunate fluke. Each was initiated and completed by one or more of God's most great and noble offspring, whom He had specifically chosen for their respective tasks. In the Grand Council before the world was, you and I witnessed calls being extended. We sustained each of these chosen leaders, and we knew of their setting apart to that very purpose. Each of these foreordained stalwarts was sent to earth to do God's will. And our wills, as well as theirs, were one with His.

As readers should be aware by now, there is an important and strong distinction to be made between the doctrine or historical event we call the Fall and the symbolic or figurative retelling of that event. The historical-doctrinal side teaches us what we *must* be if we hope to be exalted—namely men and women who willingly lay down their lives and personal desires in deference to God's will and the building up of His kingdom upon the earth. The figurative-symbolic side of the Fall, on the other hand, teaches us what we *must not* be—specifically, men and women who listen more attentively to Satan's enticements than they do to God's commandments.

Oh, the greatness of the plan, the wisdom of the Fall, and the blessing of the Atonement! As we gain a more complete understanding of these things, we cannot help but rejoice in the program of our Father in Heaven, the selfless choice of Adam and Eve, and the incomprehensible sacrifice of the Lord Jesus Christ. If we are to truly appreciate what the Savior's Atonement does for us, we must understand our need for that sacrifice. And in order to adequately comprehend that need, we must understand the Fall—not just the Fall of Adam and Eve, but more particularly, our own personal fall, as depicted in their story. Indeed, we must consider ourselves as if we were Adam and Eve.

NOTE

1. B. McConkie (1998), 190.

Brief Biographical Sketches of Ancient and Modern Non-LDS Sources Cited

ANCIENT SOURCES

2 Enoch—Circa first century AD—This work is an amplification or midrash on Genesis 5:21–32. Among other things, it teaches of multiple heavens and a pre-existence of the soul.

Ambrose—Circa AD 333–397—Bishop of Milan, and teacher of Augustine.

Augustine—AD 354–430—Bishop of Hippo and, among other things, formulator of the dogma of original sin.

Babylonian Talmud—Late fifth-century AD—A compilation of the Oral Law, and Jewish commentary on that same law, that forms the basis of Jewish religious life.

Basil the Great—AD 329–379—Bishop of Caesarea and champion of the dogma of the Trinity.

Bede the Venerable—Circa AD 673–735—British father who was responsible for the practice of dating events from the birth of Christ by using the designation AD, or *anno Domini* (in the year of the Lord).

Book of Jubilees—Second century B.C.—An account of matters revealed to Moses during his forty days on Mount Sinai.

Caesarius of Arles—Circa AD 470–543—A popular sixth-century preacher and Bishop of Arles.

Clement of Rome—Prominent circa AD 92–101—Catholics hold him to have been the third successor to Peter (i.e., the fourth pope). He was the author of one of the most important post–New Testament Christian documents, known as *I Clement* or *Clement's Epistle to the Corinthians*.

Cyril of Alexandria—AD 375–444—The Patriarch of Alexandria and the driving force behind the declaration of the Council of Ephesus (AD 431) that the Virgin Mary is the *Theotoks* or "Mother of God."

Dialogue of the Savior—Second century AD—A fragmentary Gnostic text that records a discussion between the Lord and three of His disciples.

Dorotheus of Gaza—Flourished circa AD 525–540—He was a monk who founded his own monastery and is best known for his sermons.

Ephrem the Syrian—Circa AD 306–373—A Syrian Christian commentator and composer of hymns.

Genesis Rabbah—Late fourth or early fifth-century AD—A Jewish exposition or commentary on the book of Genesis.

Jerome—Circa AD 347–420—Best known as the translator of the Latin Vulgate Bible. He was also a staunch defender of the dogma of the perpetual virginity of Mary.

John Cassian—Circa AD 360–435—Introduced monasticism in the western church and authored the first set of monastic rules and guidelines.

John Chrysostom—Circa AD 344–407—Bishop of Alexandria. He became famous for his orthodoxy and his attacks on Christian laxity.

John of Damascus—Circa AD 650–750—An Arab monastic and theologian whose writings were influential in both the Eastern and Western churches.

Lactantius—Circa AD 260–330—An early Christian writer whose works played an important part in the development of the idea, which the early and medieval church taught, that the earth was flat.

Life of Adam and Eve—Between 100 B.C. and AD 100—A Jewish elaboration on the biblical account of the Fall of Adam and Eve.

Origen—Circa AD 185–254—An influential expositor and theologian in Alexandria. He believed in the preexistence of the soul—a belief for which he was eventually condemned.

Philo of Alexandria—Circa 20 B.C.–AD 50—A Jewish expositor and contemporary of Jesus. His interpretations of the Old and New Testaments greatly influenced early Christian understandings of scripture.

Quodvultdeus—Died circa AD 453—Bishop of Carthage and friend of Augustine. Famous for his efforts to show how the New Testament is a fulfillment of the Old Testament's types and shadows.

Severian of Gabala—Flourished AD 400—A contemporary of John Chrysostom and a highly regarded preacher in Constantinople.

Symeon the New Theologian—Circa AD 949–1022—Known for his compassion and for his belief that "divine light" or revelation could be received through the practice of prayer.

Tertullian—Circa AD 160–225—Born in Carthage, he was the church's first Latin father. He wrote of his discomfort with the laxity of some Christians.

Theodoret of Cyr—Circa AD 393–466—Bishop of Cyrrhus and opponent of Cyril of Jerusalem.

Theophilus of Antioch—Circa late second century AD—Bishop of Antioch and author of the first Christian commentary on the Book of Genesis.

Victorinus—Died circa AD 304—Author of the first Christian commentary on the Book of Revelation.

MODERN SOURCES

Barre, Michael L.—Contemporary Catholic biblical scholar and theologian.

Barth, Markus—Twentieth-century Protestant biblical scholar and theologian.

Bayley, Harold—Early twentieth-century linguist, historian, and typologist.

Bloesch, Donald G.— Contemporary Evangelical theologian.

Briggs, Charles A.—Early twentieth-century biblical scholar and linguist.

Brown, David—Nineteenth-century evangelical biblical commentator.

Brown, Francis—Early twentieth-century biblical scholar and linguist.

Brown, Raymond E.—Twentieth-century Catholic biblical scholar and theologian.

Budge, E. A. Wallis—Late nineteenth-century/early twentieth-century linguist and curator of Egyptian and Assyrian antiquities at the British Museum.

Brueggermann, Walter—Twentieth-century Protestant biblical scholar.

Calvin, John—Sixteenth-century Protestant reformer.

Charlesworth, James H.—Professor of New Testament language and literature; specialist in the field of pseudepigraphical writings.

Childs, Brevard S.—Twentieth-century Protestant biblical scholar and theologian.

Cirlot, J. E.—Renowned twentieth-century author and expert in symbolism.

Clarke, Adam—Late eighteenth-century/early nineteenth-century Methodist biblical scholar and theologian.

Clifford, Richard J.—Contemporary Catholic biblical scholar and theologian.

Conner, Kevin J.—A leader and author in the charismatic movement, a branch of the Pentecostal faith.

Cooper, J. C.—Twentieth-century British typologist.

Cope, Gilbert—Twentieth-century Anglican theologian.

Cornwall, Judson—Leader and author in the charismatic movement, a branch of the Pentecostal faith.

Davidson, Richard M.— Contemporary Seventh-Day Adventist biblical scholar and theologian.

De Bona, Guerric—Contemporary Roman Catholic pastoralist.

Delitzsch, F.—Nineteenth-century German theologian and commentator.

Donaldson, James—Nineteenth-century scholar of early Christian (i.e., patristic) sources.

Douglas, J. D.—Twentieth-century Evangelical biblical scholar and theologian.

Drinkard, Joel F., Jr.— Contemporary Baptist biblical scholar and theologian.

Driver, S. R.—Early twentieth-century biblical scholar and linguist.

Dummelow, J. R.—Twentieth-century Protestant biblical commentator.

Edwards, Jonathan—Eighteenth-century Calvinist theologian and author.

Eliade, Mircea—Twentieth-century Romanian philosopher and historian of religion.

Fairbairn, Patrick—Early nineteenth-century typologist and theologian.

Faulkner, Raymond—Twentieth-century Egyptologist.

Fausset, A. R.—Nineteenth-century evangelical biblical commentator.

Fee, Gordon D.—Contemporary Evangelical biblical scholar and theologian.

Fitzmyer, Joseph A.—Contemporary Catholic biblical scholar and theologian.

Fontana, David— Contemporary British psychologist.

Ford, J. Massyngberde—Contemporary Catholic biblical scholar and theologian.

Freedman, David Noel—Contemporary biblical scholar and Hebraist.

Freyne, Sean—Contemporary Catholic biblical scholar and theologian.

Gaebelein, Frank E.—Contemporary Evangelical biblical scholar and theologian.

Ginzberg, Louis—Late nineteenth-century–early twentieth-century Jewish Talmudic scholar and author.

Goppelt, Leonhard—Contemporary Lutheran biblical scholar and theologian.

Habershon, Ada R.—Early twentieth-century typologist.

Hamilton, Victor P.—Contemporary Evangelical Pentateuch scholar.

Harrison, Everett F.—Contemporary Evangelical biblical scholar and theologian.

Henry, Matthew—Late seventeenth-century–early eighteenth-century Presbyterian biblical scholar and theologian.

Hertz, J. H.—Early twentieth-century Jewish rabbi and commentator.

Irwin, Kevin W.—Contemporary Roman Catholic professor of Liturgical Studies and Sacramental Theology.

Jamieson, Robert—Nineteenth-century evangelical biblical commentator.

Johnson, Alan F.—Contemporary Evangelical biblical scholar and theologian.

Johnson, Elizabeth—Contemporary Catholic theologian.

Johnston, Robert D.—Contemporary Evangelical author.

Julien, Nadia—Contemporary author of several texts on myths and symbols.

Keil, C. F.—Nineteenth-century German theologian and commentator.

Kidner, Derek—Contemporary Evangelical biblical scholar and theologian.

Kselman, John S.—Contemporary Catholic biblical scholar and theologian.

Kugel, James L.—Contemporary scholar of Classical and Modern Hebrew Literature.

Laffey, Alice L.—Contemporary Catholic biblical scholar and theologian.

Lewis, C. S.—Twentieth-century Anglican author and theologian.

Lewis, W. H.—Contemporary biographer and brother of C. S. Lewis.

Liefeld, Walter L.—Contemporary Evangelical biblical scholar.

Longman, Tremper, III—Contemporary Evangelical biblical scholar and theologian.

Louth, Andrew—Contemporary scholar of Patristic and Byzantine Studies.

Mann, C. S.—Contemporary Catholic biblical scholar and theologian.

McBrien, Richard P.—Contemporary Catholic theologian and ecclesiologist.

McKenzie, John L.—Contemporary Catholic theologian and commentator.

Meyers, Carol—Contemporary Catholic biblical scholar and theologian.

Meyers, Eric—Contemporary Catholic biblical scholar and theologian.

Migne, J. P.—Nineteenth-century Catholic theologian.

Morris, Leon—Contemporary Evangelical biblical scholar and theologian.

Murphy, Roland E.—Contemporary Catholic biblical scholar and theologian.

Myers, Allen C.—Contemporary Methodist biblical scholar and theologian.

Nachmanides—Thirteenth-century Jewish rabbi and Torah commentator.

Neusner, Jacob—Contemporary Jewish theologian and author.

Oden, Thomas C.—Contemporary Methodist theologian and ethicist.

Pagels, Elaine—Contemporary scholar of early Christian Gnosticism.

Peake, Arthur S.—Twentieth-century Methodist biblical commentator.

Pelikan, Jaroslave—Twentieth-century Catholic theologian.

Pellegrino, Edmund D.—Eleventh president of the Catholic University of America and a prolific author.

Pfeiffer, Charles F.—Contemporary Presbyterian biblical scholar and theologian.

Quincy, Josiah—Nineteenth-century Unitarian politician and president of Harvard College (i.e., Harvard University).

Ricoeur, Paul—Twentieth-century French philosopher.

Ries, Julien—Twentieth-century Belgian religious historian and Roman Catholic cardinal.

Roberts, Alexander—Nineteenth-century scholar of early Christian (i.e., patristic) sources.

Robinson, James M.—Contemporary theologian and former director of Claremont's Institute for Antiquity and Christianity.

Ryken, Leland—Contemporary Evangelical theologian and author.

Sailhamer, John H.—Contemporary Evangelical biblical scholar and theologian.

Schlessinger, Laura—Contemporary Jewish talk show host.

Smith, Stelman—Contemporary Evangelical author.

Speiser, E. A.—Early twentieth-century biblical scholar.

Stuart, Douglas—Contemporary Evangelical biblical scholar and theologian.

Sweet, Anne M.—Contemporary Catholic biblical scholar and theologian.

Todeschi, Kevin J.—Contemporary lecturer and author on symbolism.

Unger, Merrill F.—Twentieth-century Baptist biblical scholar and archaeologist.

Vawter, Bruce—Contemporary Catholic biblical scholar and theologian.

Virkler, Henry—Contemporary Evangelical biblical scholar and theologian.

Wallace, James A.—Contemporary Roman Catholic liturgist.

Wani, Ryoji—Contemporary geologist specializing in the Cretaceous period.

Waznak, Robert P.—Contemporary Roman Catholic scholar.

Wenham, Gordon—Contemporary Evangelical biblical scholar and theologian.

Whiston, William—Eighteenth-century translator of the works of Josephus.

Wilford, John Noble—Contemporary Pulitzer prize–winning science reporter.

Wilhoit, James C.—Contemporary Evangelical author and educator.

Williamson, Lamar, Jr.—Presbyterian biblical scholar and theologian.

Wilson, Walter L.—A twentieth-century nondenominational Christian physician who founded a theological seminary and authored a number of conservative theological texts.

Yonge, C. D.—Nineteenth-century translator of the works of Philo of Alexandria.

Bibliography

ANCIENT SOURCES

2 Enoch.

Ambrose. *Flight from the World.*

———. *Letters to Laymen.*

———. *Paradise.*

Augustine. *City of God.*

———. *On Faith and the Creed.*

———. *On Nature and Grace.*

———. *On the Literal Interpretation of Genesis.*

———. *On the Trinity.*

———. *Two Books on Genesis against Manichaeans.*

Babylonian Talmud.

Basil the Great. *On the Holy Spirit.*

Bede the Venerable. *Homilies on the Gospels.*

Book of Jubilees.

Caesarius of Arles. *Sermons.*

Clement of Rome. *The Clementine Homilies.*

Cyril of Alexandria. *Catechetical Lectures.*

————. *Stromateis.*

Dialogue of the Savior.

Dorotheus of Gaza. *Spiritual Instruction.*

Ephrem the Syrian. *Commentary on Genesis.*

————. *Hymns on Paradise.*

Genesis Rabbah.

Jerome. *Homilies.*

John Cassian. *Conference.*

John Chrysostom. *Homilies on Genesis.*

John of Damascus. *Orthodox Faith.*

Lactantius. *The Divine Institutes.*

Life of Adam and Eve.

OriGenesis *Commentary on John.*

————. *Homily on Leviticus.*

Philo of Alexandria. *Allegorical Interpretation.*

Quodvultdeus. *Book of Promises and Predictions of God.*

Severian of Gabala. *On the Creation of the World.*

Symeon the New Theologian. *Discourses.*

Tertullian. *Against Marcion.*

————. *On the Crown.*

Theodoret of Cyr. *On the Incarnation of the Lord.*

Theophilus of Antioch. *Theophilus to Autolycus.*

Victorinus. *Commentary on the Apocalypse of the Blessed John.*

ARTICLES

Adams, Vivian McConkie. 1990. "Our Glorious Mother Eve." In Joseph Fielding McConkie and Robert L. Millet, eds. *The Man Adam.* Salt Lake City, UT: Bookcraft.

Asay, Carlos E. 1997. "The Temple Garment: 'An Outward Expression of an Inward Commitment.'" In *Ensign*, August, 18–23.

Bailey, Arthur A. 1992. "Adam." In Daniel H. Ludlow, ed. *Encyclopedia of Mormonism*. New York: Macmillan. 1:15–17.

———. 1998. "What Modern Revelation Teaches about Adam." In *Ensign*, January, 20–27.

Barlow, Brent A. 1986. "They Twain Shall Be One: Thoughts on Intimacy in Marriage." In *Ensign*, September, 49–53.

Bell, Elouise. 1992. "Peace, Be Still." In Dawn Hall Anderson and Marie Cornwall, eds. *Women Steadfast in Christ: Talks Selected from the 1991 Women's Conference*. Cosponsored by Brigham Young University and the Relief Society. Salt Lake City, UT: Deseret Book.

Benson, Ezra Taft. 1980. "Prepare for the Days of Tribulation." In *Ensign*, November, 32–33.

Black, Susan Easton. 1988. "Behold, I Have Dreamed a Dream." In Monte S. Nyman and Charles D. Tate, Jr., eds. *The Book of Mormon: First Nephi, the Doctrinal Foundation*. Provo, UT: BYU Religious Studies Center.

Bradford, M. Gerald, and Larry E. Dahl. 1992. "Doctrine." In Daniel H. Ludlow, ed. *Encyclopedia of Mormonism*. New York: Macmillan. 1:393–97.

Budge, William. 1999. "Pre-Existence of Spirits." In *Collected Discourses*. N. p.: B. S. H. Publishing. 4:413–18.

Burton, Theodore M. 1986. "Love and Marriage." In *Brigham Young University 1985–1986 Devotional and Fireside Speeches*. Provo, UT: Brigham Young University.

Cannon, George Q. In *Journal of Discourses*. 26:182–93.

Clark, J. Reuben, Jr. 1997. "Our Wives and Our Mothers in the Eternal Plan." In *LDS Women's Treasury: Insights and Inspiration for Today's Woman*. Salt Lake City, UT: Deseret Book.

Clifford, Richard J., and Roland E. Murphy. 1990. "Genesis." In Raymond E. Brown, Joseph A. Fitzmyer, and Roland E. Murphy, eds. *The New Jerome Biblical Commentary*. New Jersey: Prentice Hall.

Cooper, Rex E. 1992. "Symbols, Cultural and Artistic." In Daniel H. Ludlow, ed. *Encyclopedia of Mormonism*. New York: Macmillan. 3:1430–31.

Cowdery, Oliver. 1835. In *Messenger and Advocate*, 2, no. 15 (December): 233–37.

Drinkard, Joel F., Jr. 1992. "East." In David Noel Freedman, ed. *The Anchor Bible Dictionary*. New York: Doubleday. 2:248.

Duke, James T. 1992. "Eternal Marriage." In Daniel H. Ludlow, ed. *Encyclopedia of Mormonism*. New York: Macmillian. 2:857–59.

Evans, Richard L. 1955. In *Conference Report*, April, 112–14.

Firmage, Edwin. 1992. "Zoology." In David Noel Freedman, ed. *The Anchor Bible Dictionary*. New York: Doubleday. 6:1109–67.

First Presidency and Council of the Twelve Apostles of The Church of Jesus Christ of Latter-day Saints. 1916, June 30. "The Father and the Son: A Doctrinal Exposition by The First Presidency and The Twelve." Salt Lake City, UT.

———. 1995. "The Family: A Proclamation to the World." In *Ensign*, November, 102.

Fitzmyer, Joseph A. 1990. "Pauline Theology." In Raymond E. Brown, Joseph A. Fitzmyer, and Roland E. Murphy, eds. *The New Jerome Biblical Commentary*. New Jersey: Prentice Hall.

Freyne, Sean. 1992. "The Sea of Galilee." In David Noel Freedman, ed. *The Anchor Bible Dictionary*. New York: Doubleday. 2:899–901.

Grant, Heber J., J. Reuben Clark Jr., and David O. McKay. 1965–1975. In James R. Clark, comp. *Messages of the First Presidency of The Church of Jesus Christ of Latter-day Saints*. Salt Lake City, UT: Bookcraft.

Hafen, Bruce C. 1990. "Beauty for Ashes: The Atonement of Jesus Christ." In *Ensign*, April, 7–13.

Harper, Steven C. 2004. "Endowed with Power." In *The Religious Educator: Perspectives on the Restored Gospel*, 5, no. 2:83–99.

Hunter, Howard W. "Reading the Scriptures." In *Ensign*, November 1979, 64–65.

Hunter, Milton R. 1949. In *Conference Report*, October, 69–75.

———. 1952. In *Conference Report*, April, 122–26.

———. 1952. In *Conference Report*, October, 36–39.

Hutchinson, Anthony A. 1988. "A Mormon Midrash? LDS Creation Narratives Reconsidered." In *Dialogue: A Journal of Mormon Thought* ,21, no. 4:11–74.

Hyde, Orson. In *Journal of Discourses*. 13:179–83.

Jensen, Jay E. 1992. "Spirit." In Daniel H. Ludlow, ed. *Encyclopedia of Mormonism*. New York: Macmillan. 3:1403–5.

Johnson, Alan F. 1976–1992. "Revelation." In Frank E. Gaebelein, ed. *The Expositor's Bible Commentary*. Grand Rapids, MI: Zondervan. 12:397–603.

Jones, Gerald. 1997. "Letters to the Editor." In *Dialogue: A Journal of Mormon Thought*, 30, no. 2 (summer): iv–v.

Keller, Roger R. 1990. "Adam: As Understood by Four Men Who Shaped Western Christianity." In Joseph Fielding McConkie and Robert L. Millet, eds. *The Man Adam*. Salt Lake City, UT: Bookcraft.

———. 2004. "Teaching the Fall and the Atonement: A Comparative Method." In *The Religious Educator: Perspectives on the Restored Gospel*, 5, no. 2:101–18.

Kendrick, L. Lionel. 1996. "Our Moral Agency." In *Ensign*, March, 28–33.

Kimball, Heber C. "Advancement of the Saints." In *Journal of Discourses*. 10:233–38.

———. "Living Our Religion." In *Journal of Discourses*. 9:133–36.

———. "Observance of the Commandments of God." In *Journal of Discourses*. 9:126–33.

———. "Truth to Be Received for Its Own Sake." In *Journal of Discourses*. 11:330–39.

————. "Unity—Commandments of God." In *Journal of Discourses*. 8:327–34.

Kimball, Spencer W. 1967. In *Conference Report*, October, 29–34.

————. 1976. "The Blessings and Responsibilities of Womanhood." In *Ensign*, March, 70–73.

Kselman, John S., and Michael L. Barre. 1990. "Psalms." In Raymond E. Brown, Joseph A. Fitzmyer, Roland E. Murphy, eds. *The New Jerome Biblical Commentary*. New Jersey: Prentice Hall.

Ladle, Douglas S. 2004. "Teaching the Fall of Adam and Eve." In *The Religious Educator: Perspectives on the Restored Gospel*, 5, no. 1:41–55.

Laffey, Alice L. 1995. "The Fall." In Richard P. McBrien, ed. *The HarperCollins Encyclopedia of Catholicism*. San Francisco, CA: Harper San Francisco.

Liefeld, Walter L. 1976–1992. "Luke." In Frank E. Gaebelein, ed. *The Expositor's Bible Commentary*. Grand Rapids, MI: Zondervan. 8:795–1059.

Ludlow, Daniel H. 1975. "Moral Free Agency." In *BYU Studies* 15, no. 3:309–22.

Lund, Gerald N. 1989. "The Fall of Man and His Redemption." In Monte S. Nyman and Charles D. Tate, Jr., eds. *Second Nephi: The Doctrinal Structure*. Provo, UT: BYU Religious Studies Center.

————. 1990. "The Fall of Man and His Redemption." In *Ensign*, January, 22–27.

Lundquist, Suzanne Evertsen. 1989. "The Repentance of Eve." In *As Women of Faith: Talks Selected from the BYU Women's Conferences*. Salt Lake City, UT: Deseret Book.

Matthews, Robert J. 1989. "The Pearl of Great Price Encounters the Modern World—An Appraisal." In H. Donl Peterson and Charles D. Tate Jr., eds. *The Pearl of Great Price: Revelations From God*. Provo, UT: BYU Religious Studies Center.

————. 1990. "The Fall of Man." In Joseph Fielding McConkie

and Robert L. Millet, eds. *The Man Adam*. Salt Lake City, UT: Bookcraft.

———. 1990. "The Revelation of the Gospel to Adam: The Meaning of the Atonement." In Joseph Fielding McConkie and Robert L. Millet, eds. The *Man Adam*. Salt Lake City, UT: Bookcraft.

Maxwell, Neal A. 1985. "Willing to Submit." In *Ensign*, May, 70–73.

———. 1995. In *Conference Report*, October, 27–31.

McConkie, Bruce R. 1955. In *Conference Report*, October, 12–13.

———. 1979. "Eve and the Fall". In *Woman*. Salt Lake City, UT: Deseret Book.

———. 1982. "Christ and the Creation." In *Ensign*, June, 9–15.

———. 1997. "Our Sisters from the Beginning." In *LDS Women's Treasury: Insights and Inspiration for Today's Woman*. Salt Lake City, UT: Deseret Book.

McConkie, Joseph Fielding. 1989. "The Preparation of Prophets." In H. Donl Peterson and Charles D. Tate, Jr., eds. *The Pearl of Great Price: Revelations from God*. Provo, UT: BYU Religious Studies Center.

———. 1990. "The Mystery of Eden." In Joseph Fielding McConkie and Robert L. Millet, eds. *The Man Adam*. Salt Lake City, UT: Bookcraft.

Meyers, Carol. 1992. "Apron." In David Noel Freedman, ed. *The Anchor Bible Dictionary*. New York: Doubleday. 1:318–19.

Miller, Jeanette W. 1993. "The Tree of Life, a Personification of Christ." In *FARMS Journal of Book of Mormon Studies*, 2, no. 1 (spring): 93–106.

Millet, Robert L. 1990. "Adam: A Latter-day Saint Perspective." In Joseph Fielding McConkie and Robert L. Millet, eds. *The Man Adam*. Salt Lake City, UT: Bookcraft.

———. 1992. "Jesus Christ—Overview." In Daniel H. Ludlow, ed. *Encyclopedia of Mormonism*. New York: Macmillan. 2:724–26.

———. 1995. "Alive in Christ: The Salvation of Little Children." In Monte S. Nyman and Charles D. Tate, Jr., eds. *Fourth Nephi through Moroni: From Zion to Destruction*. Provo, UT: BYU Religious Studies Center.

Mouritsen, Dale C. 1977. "The Spirit World, Our Next Home." In *Ensign*, January, 47–51.

Nelson, Russell M. 1987. "Lessons from Eve." In *Ensign*, November, 86–89.

———. 1993. "Constancy amid Change." In *Ensign*, November, 33–35.

Nibley, Hugh. 1988. "Subduing the Earth." In *Nibley on the Timely and the Timeless*. Provo, UT: BYU Religious Studies Center.

Nyman, Monte S. 1985. "The Fall of Adam and Eve." In Robert L. Millet and Kent P. Jackson, eds. *Studies in Scripture, Vol. 2: The Pearl of Great Price*. Salt Lake City, UT: Randall Book.

Oaks, Dallin H. 1993. "The Great Plan of Happiness." In *Ensign*, November, 72–75.

Ostler, Blake. 1982. "Clothed Upon: A Unique Aspect of Christian Antiquity." In *BYU Studies,* 22, no. 1 (winter): 31–45.

Packard, Sandra Bradford. 1992. "Animals." In Daniel H. Ludlow, ed. *Encyclopedia of Mormonism*. New York: Macmillan. 1:42–43.

Packer, Boyd K. 1990. "The Law and the Light." In Monte S. Nyman and Charles D. Tate Jr., eds. *Jacob through Words of Mormon: To Learn with Joy*. Provo, UT: BYU Religious Studies Center.

Pagels, Elaine. 1976. "What Became of God the Mother? Conflicting Images of God in Early Christianity." In *Signs* (winter), 293–303.

Parker, Todd B. 2003. "The Fall of Man: One of the Three Pillars of Eternity." In *The Fulness of the Gospel: Foundational Teachings from the Book of Mormon*. Salt Lake City, UT: Deseret Book.

Parry, Donald W. 1994. "Garden of Eden: Prototype Sanctuary." In Donald W. Parry, ed. *Temples of the Ancient World: Ritual and Symbolism*. Provo, UT: FARMS.

Peterson, H. Donl. 1992. "The Law of Justice and the Law of Mercy." In Monte S. Nyman and Charles D. Tate, Jr., eds. *Alma, the Testimony of the Word.* Provo, UT: BYU Religious Studies Center.

Pratt, Orson. 1880. In *Conference Report*, April, 21–29.

———. 2000. "The Pre-existence of Man." In *The Seer,* 1, no. 6 (June 1853). Salt Lake City, UT: Eborn Books.

———. In *Journal of Discourses.* 7:251–66.

———. In *Journal of Discourses.* 21:197–206.

———. In *Journal of Discourses.* 18:286–97.

———. In *Journal of Discourses.* 19:311–21.

———. In *Journal of Discourses.* 21:286–96.

Ries, Julien. "The Fall." In Mircea Eliade. *The Encyclopedia of Religion.* New York: Macmillian, 1987. 5:256–267.

Robinson, Stephen E. 1990. "The Book of Adam in Judaism and Early Christianity." In Joseph Fielding McConkie and Robert L. Millet, eds. *The Man Adam.* Salt Lake City, UT: Bookcraft.

Rockwood, Jolene Edmunds. 1992. "The Redemption of Eve." In Maureen Ursenbach Beecher and Lavina Fielding Anderson, eds. *Sisters in Spirit.* Chicago, IL: University of Illinois Press.

Romney, Marion G. 1943. In *Conference Report*, April, 26–29.

———. 1968. "Mother Eve, a Worthy Exemplar." In *Relief Society Magazine,* 55 (February): 84–89.

———. 1976. In *Conference Report*, October, 165–69.

Sailhamer, John H. 1976–1992. "Genesis." In Frank E. Gaebelein, ed. *The Expositor's Bible Commentary.* Grand Rapids, MI: Zondervan. 2:1–284.

Scott, Richard G. 1996. "The Joy of Living the Great Plan of Happiness." In *Ensign*, November, 73–75.

Skinner, Andrew C. 2000. "Savior, Satan, and Serpent: The Duality of a Symbol in the Scriptures." In Stephen D. Ricks, Donald W. Parry, and Andrew Hedges, eds. *The Disciple as Scholar—Essays on Scripture and the Ancient World in Honor of Richard Lloyd Anderson.* Provo, UT: FARMS.

Smith, Eldred G. 1958. In *Conference Report*, October, 22–24.

———. 1974. "Opposition in Order to Strengthen Us." In *Ensign*, January, 62–63.

Smith, George Albert. 1925. In *Conference Report*, October, 28–34.

Smith, Joseph Fielding. 1925. "Life Did Not Originate on the Earth." In *Conference Report*, October, 111–16.

———. 1982. "Fall—Atonement—Resurrection—Sacrament." In *Charge to Religious Educators*, 2nd ed. Salt Lake City, UT: The Church of Jesus Christ of Latter-day Saints.

———. 1990. Typescript, approved by President Smith, of an address he gave at the LDS Institute of Religion, Salt Lake City, UT, 14 January 1961. Cited in Robert J. Matthews, *A Bible! A Bible!* Salt Lake City, UT: Bookcraft.

Snow, Erastus. In *Journal of Discourses*. 19:266–79.

Sweet, Anne M. 1995. "Adam and Eve." In Richard P. McBrien, ed. *The HarperCollins Encyclopedia of Catholicism*. San Francisco, CA: Harper San Francisco.

Tanner, John S. 1992. "To Clothe a Temple." In *Ensign*, August, 44–47.

Tanner, N. Eldon. 1971. "Where Art Thou?" In *Ensign*, December, 32–35.

Taylor, John. In *Journal of Discourses*. 7:360–70.

Taylor, Joseph E. In *Journal of Discourses*. 23:242–49.

Thomas, M. Catherine. 1994. "Jacob's Allegory: The Mystery of Christ." In Stephen D. Ricks and John W. Welch, eds. *The Allegory of the Olive Tree*. Provo, UT: FARMS.

Times and Seasons. 1843. 3, no. 7 (February 1): 672.

———. 1844. 5, no. 24 (January 1): 758.

Turner, Rodney. 1990. "The Imperative and Unchanging Nature of God." In Larry E. Dahl and Charles D. Tate Jr., eds. *The Lectures on Faith in Historical Perspective*. Provo, UT: BYU Religious Studies Center.

Tvedtnes, John. 1994. "Priestly Clothing in Bible Times." In Donald W. Parry, ed. *Temples of the Ancient World: Ritual and Symbolism*. Provo, UT: FARMS.

Wani, Ryoji. 2004. "Experimental Fragmentation Patterns of Modern Nautilus Shells and the Implications for Fossil Cephalopod Taphonomy." In *Lethaia*. 37:113–23.

Warner, Terry. 1992. "Agency." In Daniel H. Ludlow, ed. *Encyclopedia of Mormonism*. New York: Macmillan. 1:26–27.

Whitney, Orson F. 1999. "Destiny of the Earth and Its Inhabitants." In *Collected Discourses*. N. p.: B. S. H. Publishing. 1:12–17.

Wilcox, Linda. 1992. "The Mormon Concept of a Mother in Heaven." In Maureen Ursenbach Beecher and Lavina Fielding Anderson, eds. *Sisters in Spirit*. Chicago, IL: University of Illinois Press.

Wilford, John Noble. 1997. "Legged Snakes? First Reliable Evidence Is In." In *The New York Times*, April 17, A16.

Woodruff, Wilford. *Journal of Discourses*. 23:124–33.

Young, Brigham. In *Journal of Discourses*. 2:298–308.

———. *Journal of Discourses*. 3:316–27.

———. *Journal of Discourses*. 9:147–50.

———. *Journal of Discourses*. 4:367–74.

———. *Journal of Discourses*. 15:121–29.

———. *Journal of Discourses*. 2:1–10.

———. *Journal of Discourses*. 7:282–91.

———. *Journal of Discourses*. 9:308–17.

———. *Journal of Discourses*. 17:139–45.

———. *Journal of Discourses*. 4:51–57.

———. *Journal of Discourses*. 8:194–200.

———. *Journal of Discourses*. 11:119–28.

———. *Journal of Discourses*. 1:46–53.

———. *Journal of Discourses*. 9:218–21.

———. *Journal of Discourses*. 4:215–21.

———. *Journal of Discourses*. 8:6–10.

———. *Journal of Discourses*. 10:308–14.

———. *Journal of Discourses*. 7:160–66.

AUDIO RECORDINGS

Adams, Vivian McConkie. 1991. *Mother Eve and Father Adam*. Lecture on two cassettes. Salt Lake City, UT: Deseret Book.

BOOKS

Andrus, Hyrum L. 1967. *Doctrinal Commentary on the Pearl of Great Price*. Salt Lake City, UT: Deseret Book.

As Women of Faith: Talks Selected from the BYU Women's Conferences. 1989. Salt Lake City, UT: Deseret Book.

Augustine, Saint. 1950. *The City of God*. Marcus Dods, trans. New York: Random House.

Ballard, M. Russell. 1997. *Counseling with Our Councils: Learning to Minister Together in the Church and in the Family*. Salt Lake City, UT: Deseret Book.

Barlow, Brent A. 1982. *What Wives Expect of Husbands*. Salt Lake City, UT: Deseret Book.

Barth, Markus. 1974. *The Anchor Bible: Ephesians 4–6*. New York: Doubleday.

Bayley, Harold. 1990. *The Lost Language of Symbolism: An Inquiry into the Origin of Certain Letters, Words, Names, Fairy-Tales, Folklore, and Mythologies*. New York: Carol Publishing Group.

Beecher, Maureen Ursenbach, and Lavina Fielding Anderson, eds. 1992. *Sisters in Spirit*. Chicago, IL: University of Illinois Press.

Bennion, Lowell L. 1959. *An Introduction to the Gospel*. Salt Lake City, UT: Deseret Sunday School Union Board.

————. 1988. *The Best of Lowell L. Bennion: Selected Writings 1928–1988.* Eugene England, ed. Salt Lake City, UT: Deseret Book.

Benson, Ezra Taft. 1998. *Teachings of Ezra Taft Benson.* Salt Lake City, UT: Bookcraft.

Bloesch, Donald G. 2001. *Essentials of Evangelical Theology.* Peabody, MA: Prince Press.

Brewster, Hoyt W., Jr. 1988. *Doctrine and Covenants Encyclopedia.* Salt Lake City, UT: Bookcraft.

Brigham Young University 1985–1986 Devotional and Fireside Speeches. 1986. Provo, UT: Brigham Young University.

Brooks, Melvin R. 1960–1965. *LDS Reference Encyclopedia.* Salt Lake City, UT: Bookcraft.

Brown, Francis, S. R. Driver, and Charles A. Briggs. 1999. *The Brown-Driver-Briggs Hebrew and English Lexicon.* Peabody, MA: Hendrickson Publishers.

Brown, Matthew. 1999. *The Gate of Heaven.* American Fork, UT: Covenant Communications.

Brown, Raymond E., Joseph A. Fitzmyer, and Roland E. Murphy, eds. 1990. *The New Jerome Biblical Commentary.* New Jersey: Prentice Hall.

Brueggermann, Walter. *Genesis: A Bible Commentary for Teaching and Preaching.* Atlanta, GA: John Knox Press, 1973.

Budge, E. A. Wallis. 1995. *The Book of the Dead.* New York: Gramercy Books.

————. 1995. *Egyptian Religions.* New York: Gramercy Books.

Burton, Alma P., comp. 1977. *Discourses of the Prophet Joseph Smith.* Salt Lake City, UT: Deseret Book.

Calvin, John. 1964. *A Commentary on Genesis.* John King, ed. Edinburgh: The Banner of Truth Trust.

Campbell, Beverly. 2003. *Eve and the Choice Made in Eden.* Salt Lake City, UT: Bookcraft.

Charge to Religious Educators. 1982. 2nd ed. Salt Lake City, UT: The

Church of Jesus Christ of Latter-day Saints.

Charles, John D. 1997. *Endowed from On High: Understanding the Symbols of the Endowment.* Bountiful, UT: Horizon Publishers.

Charlesworth, James H., ed. 1983–1985. *The Old Testament Pseudepigrapha*, New York: Doubleday.

Childs, Brevard S. 1986. *Old Testament Theology in a Canonical Context.* Philadelphia: Fortress Press.

Christensen, Joe J. 1996. *One Step at a Time: Building a Better Marriage, Family, and You.* Salt Lake City, UT: Deseret Book.

Church, Leslie F., ed. 1992. *The NIV Matthew Henry Commentary in One Volume.* Grand Rapids, MI: Zondervan.

Cirlot, J. E. 1962. *A Dictionary of Symbols.* London: Routledge & Kegan Paul.

Clark, James R., comp. 1965–1975. *Messages of the First Presidency of The Church of Jesus Christ of Latter-day Saints.* Salt Lake City, UT: Bookcraft.

Clarke, Adam. n. d. *The Holy Bible Containing the Old and New Testaments . . . with a Commentary and Critical Notes.* New York: Methodist Book Concern.

Conner, Kevin J. 1992. *Interpreting the Symbols and Types.* Portland, OR: City Bible Publishing.

Cooper, J. C. 1995. *An Illustrated Encyclopaedia of Traditional Symbols.* London: Thames and Hudson.

Cope, Gilbert. 1959. *Symbolism in the Bible and the Church.* London: SCM Press Ltd.

Cornwall, Judson, and Stelman Smith. 1998. *The Exhaustive Dictionary of Bible Names.* New Jersey: BridgeLogos Publishing.

Cowan, Richard O. 1996. *Answers to Your Questions about the Doctrine and Covenants.* Salt Lake City, UT: Deseret Book.

Davidson, Richard M. 1981. *Typology in Scripture: A Study of Hermeneutical TYPOS Structures.* Berrien Springs, MI: Andrews University Press.

Douglas, J. D., ed. 1971. *The New Bible Dictionary*. Grand Rapids, MI: Eerdmans.

Doxey, Roy W. 1973. *Walk with the Lord: Teachings of the Pearl of Great Price*. Salt Lake City, UT: Deseret Book.

Draper, Richard. 1991. *Opening the Seven Seals*. Salt Lake City, UT: Deseret Book.

Dummelow, J. R., ed. 1936. *The One-Volume Bible Commentary*. New York: Macmillan Publishing.

Durham, G. Homer, ed. 1987. *The Gospel Kingdom: Selections from the Writings and Discourses of John Taylor*. Salt Lake City, UT: Bookcraft.

Edwards, Jonathan. 1948. *Images or Shadows of Divine Things*. New Haven: Yale University Press.

Ehat, Andrew F., and Lyndon W. Cook. 1980. *The Words of Joseph Smith*. Provo, UT: BYU Religious Studies Center.

Eliade, Mircea, editor. 1987. *The Encyclopedia of Religion*. New York: Macmillian.

Fairbairn, Patrick. 1989. *The Typology of Scripture*. Grand Rapids, MI: Kregel Publications.

Faulkner, Raymond. 1994. *The Egyptian Book of the Dead: The Book of Going Forth by Day*. San Francisco, CA: Chronicle Books.

Faust, James E. 1990. *Reach Up for the Light*. Salt Lake City, UT: Deseret Book.

Fee, Gordon D., and Douglas Stuart. 1993. *How to Read the Bible for All Its Worth*. 2nd ed. Grand Rapids, MI: Zondervan.

Ferrell, James L. 2009. *The Hidden Christ: Beneath the Surface of the Old Testament*. Salt Lake City, UT: Deseret Book.

Fontana, David. 1994. *The Secret Language of Symbols*. San Francisco: Chronicle Books.

Ford, J. Massyngberde. 1975. *The Anchor Bible: Revelation*. New York: Doubleday.

Freedman, David Noel, ed. 1992. *The Anchor Bible Dictionary*. New York: Doubleday.

Gaebelein, Frank E., ed. 1976–1992. *The Expositor's Bible Commentary*. Grand Rapids, MI: Zondervan.

Gaskill, Alonzo L. 2003. *The Lost Language of Symbolism: An Essential Guide for Recognizing and Interpreting Symbols of the Gospel*. Salt Lake City, UT: Deseret Book.

Gibbons, Francis M. 1992. *Joseph Fielding Smith: Gospel Scholar, Prophet of God*. Salt Lake City, UT: Deseret Book.

———. 1993. *Harold B. Lee: Man of Vision, Prophet of God*. Salt Lake City, UT: Deseret Book.

Ginzberg, Louis. 1967–1969. *The Legends of the Jews*. Philadelphia: The Jewish Publication Society of America.

Goppelt, Leonhard. 1982. *Typos: The Typological Interpretation of the Old Testament in the New*. Grand Rapids, MI: Eerdmans.

Habershon, Ada R. 1974. *Study of the Types*. Grand Rapids, MI: Kregel Publications.

Hafen, Bruce C. 1989. *The Broken Heart*. Salt Lake City, UT: Deseret Book.

Hafen, Bruce C., and Marie K. Hafen. 1994. *The Belonging Heart: The Atonement and Relationships with God and Family*. Salt Lake City, UT: Deseret Book.

Hamilton, Victor P. 1982. *Handbook on the Pentateuch*. Grand Rapids, MI: Baker Book House.

Hertz, J. H. 1962. *The Pentateuch and Haftorahs*. 2nd ed. London: Soncino Press.

Hinckley, Gordon B. 1997. *Teachings of Gordon B. Hinckley*. Salt Lake City, UT: Deseret Book.

Holland, Jeffrey R. 1997. *Christ and the New Covenant*. Salt Lake City, UT: Deseret Book.

Holland, Jeffrey R., and Patricia T. Holland. 1989. *On Earth As It Is in Heaven*. Salt Lake City, UT: Deseret Book.

Holzapfel, Richard Neitzel, and David Rolph Seely. 1994. *My Father's House: Temple Worship and Symbolism in the New Testament*. Salt Lake City, UT: Bookcraft.

Hunter, Milton R. 1951. *Pearl of Great Price Commentary*. Salt Lake City, UT: Stevens and Wallis, Inc.

———. 1959. *Christ in Ancient America*. Salt Lake City, UT: Deseret Book.

Hutchins, Robert M., ed. 1982. *Great Books of the Western World*. Chicago, IL: Encyclopedia Britannica.

Irwin, Kevin W., and Edmund D. Pellegrino, eds. 1992. *Preserving the Creation: Environmental Theology and Ethics*. Washington, DC: Georgetown University Press.

Jackson, Kent P. 1994. *Joseph Smith's Commentary on the Bible*. Salt Lake City, UT: Deseret Book.

———. 2001. *The Restored Gospel and the Book of Genesis*. Salt Lake City, UT: Deseret Book.

Jamieson, Robert, A. R. Fausset, and David Brown. N. d. *Jamieson, Fausset and Brown One Volume Commentary*. Grand Rapids, MI: Associated Publishers and Authors.

Jensen, Nathan. 1998. *The Restored Gospel According to C. S. Lewis*. Springville, UT: Bonneville Books.

Johnson, Elizabeth. 1994. *She Who Is*. New York: The Crossroad Publishing Company.

Johnston, Robert D. 1990. *Numbers in the Bible: God's Design in Biblical Numerology*. Grand Rapids, MI: Kregel Publications.

Jones, Gerald E. 2003. *Animals and the Church*. Salt Lake City, UT: Eborn Books.

Journal of Discourses. 1854–1886. London: Latter-day Saints' Book Depot.

Julien, Nadia. 1996. *The Mammoth Dictionary of Symbols*. New York: Carroll & Graf Publishers.

Keil, C. F., and F. Delitzsch. N. d. *Biblical Commentary on the Old Testament: The Pentateuch*. Grand Rapids, MI: Eerdmans.

Kidner, Derek. 1967. *Tyndale Old Testament Commentaries: Genesis.* Dowers Grove, IL: InterVarsity Press.

Kimball, Edward L., ed. 1998. *The Teachings of Spencer W. Kimball.* Salt Lake City, UT: Bookcraft.

Kimball, Edward L., and Andrew E. Kimball Jr. 1977. *Spencer W. Kimball: Twelfth President of The Church of Jesus Christ of Latter-day Saints.* Salt Lake City, UT: Bookcraft.

Kimball, Spencer W. 1969. *The Miracle of Forgiveness.* Salt Lake City, UT: Bookcraft.

Kugel, James L. 1998. *Traditions of the Bible: A Guide to the Bible as It Was at the Start of the Common Era.* Cambridge, MA: Harvard University Press.

LDS Bible Dictionary. 1979. Salt Lake City, UT: The Church of Jesus Christ of Latter-day Saints.

LDS Women's Treasury: Insights and Inspiration for Today's Woman. 1997. Salt Lake City, UT: Deseret Book.

Lectures on Faith. N. d. Salt Lake City, UT: Bookcraft.

Lewis, C. S. 1961. *The Screwtape Letters.* New York: Collier Books.

———. 1980. *The Weight of Glory and Other Addresses.* Rev. ed. New York: Macmillan.

———. 1996. *Mere Christianity.* New York: Simon and Schuster.

Lewis, W. H. 1993. *Letters of C. S. Lewis.* New York: Harcourt Brace & Co.

Ludlow, Daniel H. 1981. *A Companion to Your Study of the Old Testament.* Salt Lake City, UT: Deseret Book.

———, ed. 1992. *Encyclopedia of Mormonism.* New York: Macmillan.

Ludlow, Victor L. 1982. *Isaiah: Prophet, Seer, and Poet.* Salt Lake City, UT: Deseret Book.

Lund, Gerald N. 1999. *Selected Writings of Gerald N. Lund: Gospel Scholars Series.* Salt Lake City, UT: Deseret Book.

Louth, Andrew, editor. 2001. *Ancient Christian Commentary on Scripture: Genesis 1–11.* Downers Grove, IL: InterVarsity Press.

Madsen, Truman G. 1989. *Joseph Smith the Prophet.* Salt Lake City, UT: Bookcraft.

Mann, C. S. 1986. *The Anchor Bible: Mark.* New York: Doubleday.

Matthews, Robert J. 1990. *A Bible! A Bible!* Salt Lake City, UT: Bookcraft.

Maxwell, Neal A. 1976. *Deposition of a Disciple.* Salt Lake City, UT: Deseret Book.

———. 1979. *All These Things Shall Give Thee Experience.* Salt Lake City, UT: Deseret Book.

———. 1982. *We Will Prove Them Herewith.* Salt Lake City, UT: Deseret Book.

———. 1999. *One More Strain of Praise.* Salt Lake City, UT: Deseret Book.

McBrien, Richard P., ed. 1995. *The HarperCollins Encyclopedia of Catholicism.* San Francisco, CA: Harper San Francisco.

McConkie, Bruce R. 1978. *The Promised Messiah: The First Coming of Christ.* Salt Lake City, UT: Deseret Book.

———. 1979. *Mormon Doctrine.* 2nd ed. Salt Lake City, UT: Bookcraft.

———. 1980–1981. *The Mortal Messiah.* Salt Lake City, UT: Deseret Book.

———. 1982. *The Millennial Messiah.* Salt Lake City, UT: Deseret Book.

———. 1985. *A New Witness for the Articles of Faith.* Salt Lake City, UT: Deseret Book.

———. 1987–1988. *Doctrinal New Testament Commentary.* Salt Lake City, UT: Bookcraft.

———. 1998. *Sermons and Writings of Bruce R. McConkie.* Salt Lake City, UT: Bookcraft.

McConkie, Joseph Fielding. 1985. *Gospel Symbolism.* Salt Lake City, UT: Bookcraft.

———. 1998. *Answers: Straightforward Answers to Tough Gospel*

Questions. Salt Lake City, UT: Deseret Book.

McConkie, Joseph Fielding, and Robert L. Millet. 1987–1992. *Doctrinal Commentary on the Book of Mormon.* Salt Lake City, UT: Bookcraft.

McConkie, Joseph Fielding, and Robert L. Millet, eds. 1990. *The Man Adam.* Salt Lake City, UT: Bookcraft.

McConkie, Joseph Fielding, and Donald W. Parry. 1990. *A Guide to Scriptural Symbols.* Salt Lake City, UT: Bookcraft.

McConkie, Mark L., ed. 1998. *Doctrines of the Restoration: The Sermons and Writings of Bruce R. McConkie.* Salt Lake City, UT: Bookcraft.

McConkie, Oscar W., Jr. 1975. *Angels.* Salt Lake City, UT: Deseret Book.

McKenzie, John L. 1965. *Dictionary of the Bible.* Milwaukee, WI: The Bruce Publishing Company.

Meyers, Carol L., and Eric M. Meyers. 1987. *The Anchor Bible: Haggai, Zechariah 1–8.* New York: Doubleday.

Migne, J. P., trans. 1856. *Troisième et Dernière Encyclopédie Théologique.* Paris: P. J. Migne.

Millet, Robert L. 1997. *Alive in Christ: The Miracle of Spiritual Rebirth.* Salt Lake City, UT: Deseret Book.

———. 2000. *Selected Writings of Robert L. Millet: Gospel Scholars Series.* Salt Lake City, UT: Deseret Book.

Millet, Robert L., and Kent P. Jackson, eds. 1985. *Studies in Scripture, Vol. 2: The Pearl of Great Price.* Salt Lake City, UT: Randall Book.

Morris, Leon. 1999. *Tyndale New Testament Commentary: Luke.* Grand Rapids, MI: Eerdmans.

———. 1999. *Tyndale New Testament Commentary: Revelation.* Rev. ed. Grand Rapids, MI: Eerdmans.

Myers, Allen C. 1987. *The Eerdmans Bible Dictionary.* Grand Rapids, MI: Eerdmans.

Nachmanides. 1971–1976. *Commentary on the Torah*. New York: Shilo Publishing House, Inc.

Neusner, Jacob, ed. 1985. *Genesis Rabbah: The Judaic Commentary to the Book of Genesis*. Atlanta, GA: Scholars Press.

———. 1991. *The Enchantments of Judaism*. Atlanta, GA: Scholars Press.

Nibley, Hugh. 1975. *The Message of the Joseph Smith Papyri: An Egyptian Endowment*. Salt Lake City, UT: Deseret Book.

———. 1986. *Enoch the Prophet*. Provo, UT: FARMS.

———. 1986. *Old Testament and Related Studies*. Provo, UT: FARMS.

———. 1988. *Nibley on the Timely and the Timeless*. Provo, UT: BYU Religious Studies Center.

———. 1988–1990. *Teachings of the Book of Mormon—Transcripts of Lectures Presented to an Honors Book of Mormon Class at Brigham Young University, 1988–1990*. Provo, UT: FARMS.

———. 1989. *Ancient Documents and the Pearl of Great Price*. Robert Smith and Robert Smythe, eds. Provo, UT: FARMS.

———. 1994. *Brother Brigham Challenges the Saints*. Provo, UT: FARMS.

Nyman, Monte S., and Charles D. Tate Jr., eds. 1988. *The Book of Mormon: First Nephi, the Doctrinal Foundation*. Provo, UT: BYU Religious Studies Center.

———. 1989. *Second Nephi: The Doctrinal Structure*. Provo, UT: BYU Religious Studies Center.

———. 1990. *Jacob through Words of Mormon: To Learn with Joy*. Provo, UT: BYU Religious Studies Center.

———. 1992. *Alma, the Testimony of the Word*. Provo, UT: BYU Religious Studies Center.

———. 1995. *Fourth Nephi through Moroni: From Zion to Destruction*. Provo, UT: BYU Religious Studies Center.

Oden, Thomas C., ed. 2001. *Ancient Christian Commentary on*

Scripture: Genesis 1–11. Downers Grove, IL: InterVarsity Press.

Packer, Boyd K. 1991. *Let Not Your Heart Be Troubled.* Salt Lake City, UT: Bookcraft.

———. 1996. *Things of the Soul.* Salt Lake City, UT: Bookcraft.

Pagels, Elaine. 1989. *Adam, Eve, and the Serpent.* New York: Vintage Books.

Parry, Donald W., ed. 1994. *Temples of the Ancient World.* Provo, UT: FARMS.

Parry, Donald W., Jay A. Parry, and Tina Peterson. 1998. *Understanding Isaiah.* Salt Lake City, UT: Deseret Book.

Parry, Jay A., and Donald W. Parry. 1998. *Understanding the Book of Revelation.* Salt Lake City, UT: Deseret Book.

Peake, Arthur S., ed. 1919. *Peake's Commentary on the Bible.* New York: Thomas Nelson and Sons.

Pelikan, Jaroslave, ed. 1958. *Luther's Works.* St. Louis, MO: Concordia Publishing House.

Petersen, Mark E. 1978. *Joshua: Man of Faith.* Salt Lake City, UT: Deseret Book.

Peterson, H. Donl. 1987. *The Pearl of Great Price: A History and Commentary.* Salt Lake City, UT: Deseret Book.

———. 1995. *The Story of the Book of Abraham: Mummies, Manuscripts, and Mormonism.* Salt Lake City, UT: Deseret Book.

Pfeiffer, Charles F., and Everett F. Harrison, eds. 1962. *The Wycliffe Bible Commentary.* Chicago, IL: Moody Press.

Pratt, Parley P. 1978. *Key to the Science of Theology; A Voice of Warning.* Classics in Mormon Literature Edition. Salt Lake City, UT: Deseret Book.

Quincy, Josiah. 1883. *Figures of the Past from the Leaves of Old Journals.* 4th ed. Boston, MA: n. p.

Random House Webster's College Dictionary. 1996. New York: Random House.

Rasmussen, Ellis T. 1993. *A Latter-day Saint Commentary on the Old*

Testament. Salt Lake City, UT: Deseret Book.

Reynolds, George, and Janne M. Sjodahl. 1955–1961. *Commentary on the Book of Mormon,* ed. and arr. by Philip C. Reynolds. Salt Lake City, UT: Deseret Book.

———. 1980. *Commentary on the Pearl of Great Price.* Salt Lake City, UT: Deseret Book.

Rich, Ben E., ed. 1913. *Scrapbook of Mormon Literature.* Chicago: Henry C. Etten and Co.

Ricks, Stephen D., Donald W. Parry, and Andrew Hedges, eds. 2000. *The Disciple as Scholar—Essays on Scripture and the Ancient World in Honor of Richard Lloyd Anderson.* Provo, UT: FARMS.

Ricks, Stephen D., and John W. Welch, eds. 1994. *The Allegory of the Olive Tree.* Provo, UT: FARMS.

Ricoeur, Paul. *The Symbolism of Evil.* Boston, MA: Beacon Press, 1967.

Roberts, Alexander, and James Donaldson, eds. 1994. *AnteNicene Fathers.* Peabody, MA: Hendrickson Publishers.

Roberts, B. H. 1907–1912. *Seventy's Course in Theology.* Salt Lake City, UT: Deseret News.

———. 1966. *The Gospel: An Exposition of Its First Principles and Man's Relationship to Deity.* 11th ed. Salt Lake City, UT: Deseret Book.

———. 1996. *The Truth, the Way, the Life.* Provo, UT: BYU Religious Studies Center.

Robinson, James M., ed. 1988. *The Nag Hammadi Library in English.* San Francisco: Harper and Row Publishers.

Ryken, Leland, James C. Wilhoit, Tremper Longman III, eds. 1998. *Dictionary of Biblical Imagery.* Downers Grove, IL: InterVarsity Press.

Sailhamer, John H. 1992. *The Pentateuch as Narrative.* Grand Rapids, MI: Zondervan.

Salisbury, Frank B. 1976. *The Creation.* Salt Lake City, UT: Deseret Book.

Schlessinger, Laura. 2004. *The Proper Care and Feeding of Husbands.* New York: HarperCollins Publishers.

Skinner, Andrew. *Temple Worship: 20 Truths that will Bless your Life.* Salt Lake City, UT: Deseret Book, 2007.

Skousen, W. Cleon. 1974. *The First 2000 Years.* Salt Lake City, UT: Bookcraft.

Smith, Joseph. 1932–1951. *History of The Church of Jesus Christ of Latter-day Saints.* B. H. Roberts, ed. Salt Lake City, UT: The Church of Jesus Christ of Latter-day Saints.

———. 1976. *Teachings of the Prophet Joseph Smith.* Salt Lake City, UT: Deseret Book.

———. 1985. *Lectures on Faith.* Salt Lake City, UT: Deseret Book.

Smith, Joseph Fielding. 1948. *Church History and Modern Revelation.* Salt Lake City, UT: Deseret Book.

———. 1949. *The Way to Perfection.* Salt Lake City, UT: Genealogical Society of Utah.

———. 1954. *Man: His Origin and Destiny.* Salt Lake City, UT: Deseret Book.

———. 1957–1966. *Answers to Gospel Questions.* Salt Lake City, UT: Deseret Book.

———. 1998. *Doctrines of Salvation.* Salt Lake City, UT: Bookcraft.

Speiser, E. A. 1962. *The Anchor Bible: Genesis.* New York: Doubleday.

Stuy, Brian H., ed. and comp. 1999. *Collected Discourses.* N. p.: B. S. H. Publishing.

Talmage, James E. 1975. *The Articles of Faith.* Salt Lake City, UT: The Church of Jesus Christ of Latter-day Saints.

———. 1981. *Jesus the Christ.* Salt Lake City, UT: Deseret Book.

Taylor, John. 1852. *The Government of God.* Liverpool, England: S. W. Richards.

———. 1882. *The Mediation and Atonement.* Salt Lake City, UT: Deseret News Company, Printers and Publishers.

Todeschi, Kevin J. 1995. *The Encyclopedia of Symbolism*. New York: The Berkley Publishing Group.

Turner, Rodney. 1972. *Woman and the Priesthood*. Salt Lake City, UT: Deseret Book.

Unger, Merrill F. 1966. *Unger's Bible Dictionary*. Chicago: Moody Press.

Vawter, Bruce. 1977. *On Genesis: A New Reading*. New York: Doubleday.

Virkler, Henry. 1981. *Hermeneutics: Principles and Processes of Biblical Interpretation*. Grand Rapids, MI: Baker Book House.

Wallace, James A., Robert P. Waznak, and Guerric DeBona. *Lift Up Your Hearts—Homilies for the "A" Cycle*. New York: Paulist Press, 2004.

Wenham, Gordon. 1987. *Word Biblical Commentary: Genesis 1–15*. Waco, TX: Word Books.

Whiston, William, trans. 1981. *The Complete Works of Josephus*. Grand Rapids, MI: Kregel Publications.

Whitney, Orson F. 1921. *Saturday Night Thoughts*. Salt Lake City, UT: Deseret News.

———. 1973. *The Life of Heber C. Kimball*. Salt Lake City, UT: Bookcraft.

Widtsoe, John A. 1937. *A Rational Theology*. Salt Lake City, UT: Deseret Book.

———. 1960. *Evidences and Reconciliations*, in 1. Salt Lake City, UT: Bookcraft.

Wilcox, S. Michael. 1995. *House of Glory: Finding Personal Meaning in the Temple*. Salt Lake City, UT: Deseret Book.

Williamson, Lamar, Jr. 1983. *Interpretation: A Bible Commentary for Teaching and Preaching: Mark*. Atlanta, GA: John Knox Press.

Wilson, Walter L. 1999. *A Dictionary of Bible Types*. Peabody, MA: Hendrickson Publishers.

Yonge, C. D., trans. 1997. *The Works of Philo.* Peabody, MA: Hendrickson Publishers.

Young, Brigham. 1998. *Discourses of Brigham Young.* John A. Widtsoe, ed. Salt Lake City, UT: Bookcraft.

Unpublished Text

King, Judd. 1995. *A Handbook to the Pearl of Great Price.* Manuscript.

Index

Armor: 86

Asay, Carlos E.: on armor, 86

Atonement: Bruce R. McConkie on Fall and, 10; meaning of term, 86, 158, 173; Fall and agency and, 117 n. 20; enmity between Jesus Christ and Satan and, 164–65; blood and, 171

Augustine: on Satan, 64; on Fall, 69; on cool of the day, 71, on nakendness, 75; on pain and habits, 79; on Adam's deep sleep, 110; on spiritual and physical death, 141; on temptation, 141; on Adam and Eve's eyes being opened, 157

B

Banishment: 85–92, 113–14, 172–76

Baptism: 32 n. 36

Basil the Great: on looking eastward, 129

Bayley, Harold: on flaming sword, 90

Beggars: 87

Beguile: 76–77

Benson, Ezra Taft: on our divine potential, 46

Birthrates: 50–51, 94 n. 23

Bitter: and sweet, 15, 50, 68, 146, 155; cup, 92

Black, Susan Easton: on tree of life and cross, 89

Blame: Eve and, 72–73, 98 n. 87; serpent and, 76–77; posterity of Adam and Eve and, 99 n. 112; Satan and, 100 n. 134

Blood: 7, 32 n. 31, 116, 117–18 n. 22, 171, 194 n. 207

Bones: 109–10, 116 n. 10, 147

Book of Mormon: 29 n. 3, 49, 165

Bread: 83–84

Breath of life: 130–31

C

Chambered nautilus: 52

Change: 79

Chaos: 137, 126 n. 20, 122–23

Cherubim: 88–91, 175–76; see also Angels

Childbirth: 79–81, 166

Children: of God, 46, 121; innocence of, 33 n. 43, 48; commandment to have, 50–51; Adam and Eve incapable

Farming: 53–54, 95 n. 36, 168–69

Fig leaves: 72–73, 162–64. *See also* Nakedness and Symbols: Fig leaves as

First flesh: 131, 180 n. 26

First Presidency: on commandment to multiply, 51; on creation of men and women, 178–79 n. 9

Flaming sword: 90–91, 175

Flesh: 109–10, 147; Adam as first, 131, 180 n. 26

Footsteps: 70–71

Four, the number: 136–37, 182 n. 59

Fruit: commandment not to eat, 16–17, 35 n. 69, 55–56, 112–13, 138–41; God will offer, 29 n. 13; commandment not to touch, 64–69, 154; forbidden, 5–6, 95 n. 44

G

Garden of Eden: *See* Eden

Garments, holy: 86, 102–3 n. 165, 172–73, 195 n. 220

Gift, Fall as, 7

Gihon River: 137

God: Adam and Eve communicate with, 11–15, 49; will offer fruit, 30 n. 13; footsteps of, 170–71; asks Adam "Where art thou?" 73–74, 162; projecting characteristics on, 72–73; curses ground, 82; banishment from presence of, 85–92, 113–14, 172–76; covenants and, 104 n. 193; as creator, 127–29; as anthropomorphic being, 128; puts man in Eden, 106; makes all that is good, 133; submitting to will of, 146–47; Satan goes against will of, 151–54; becoming like, 155–56, 174, 175–76; wisdom of, 146–47; provides for Adam and Eve, 172–73; fulfillment of will of, 176; role in man's creation, 185 n. 86; presence of, 194 n. 207. *See also* Image of God

Godhood, mortality as road to, 156, 190 n. 142

Good: and evil, 9, 13, 15, 20, 35–37, 49–50, 120, 157, 165, 174, 190 n. 147; God makes all that is, 123–24, 133

Ground, cursed, 82, 164, 168

Guilt, 70–71, 77, 91, 158, 187 n. 120

J

Jackson, Kent P.: on creation and Fall, 36 n. 74; on God's role in creation, 185 n. 86

Jackson County, Missouri: 130

Jesus Christ: Fall and, 34–35 n. 62, 38–39 n. 90; central role of, 49; will help us through trials, 82–84; coats of skins as symbols of, 85–86; as tree of life, 49–50, 134; creation of Adam and Eve as type for, 105–6; faith in, 107–8; Church as help meet for, 108–9; covenant relationship with Church of, 109–10; deep sleep and, 110; origin of, 110–111; temptation of Adam and Eve as type for, 111–113; Adam as type for, 112, 115; as protector, 113–14; Bruce R. McConkie on Adam as type for 116 n. 2; rib as symbol of Church and, 116–17 nn. 11, 14; Stephen E. Robinson on Adam as type for, 117 n. 20; serpent as type for, 150–51; Bruce R. McConkie on having will of, 153; enmity between Satan and, 22, 24, 40 n. 100; thorns as symbols of, 170; suffers in Gethsemane, 15; as mediator, 172–73

John of Damascus: on tree of knowledge, 182 n. 49

K

Keller, Roger R.: on mortality, 37 n. 74; on Fall, 31 n. 27, 38 n. 89

Kimball, Heber C.: on location of Eden, 130

Kimball, Spencer W.: on being created in God's image, 46; on Satan, 64; on sorrow in childbirth, 166; on presiding in righteousness, 167

King, Judd: on thorns, thistles, and sweat, 102 n. 157; on teaching of agency, 185 n. 76; on serpent, 188 n. 124; on good and evil, 190 n. 147; on cool of the day, 191 n. 160

Knowledge: of Adam and Eve, 11–15, 32 n. 35, 173; experiential, 14–15, 34–35 n. 62, 53, 134, 155–57, 174; and agency, 29 n. 11. *See also* Tree of knowledge of good and evil

Kolob: 55, 181 n. 33

L

Lamb: skin of, 172–73

Language, of Adam, 196 n. 90, 188 n. 123

Legs, of serpent: 163, 192 n. 172

Lewis, C. S.: 2; on our divine potential, 46; on temptation, 66–67; on Satan, 151; on importance of work, 168

Life: spirits give us mortal, 47; sacrifice as way to eternal, 11, 37, 82–84, 177, 189–90 n. 137; eternal, 196 n. 232

Light: 102 n. 164, 121–22, 124 n. 6, 151, 172

Linen: 102 n. 165

Little children: 33 n. 43, 48

Loneliness: 144–45

Lucifer: *See* Satan

Ludlow, Daniel H.: on image of God, 128; on marriage of Adam and Eve, 145

Lund, Gerald N.: on accountability, 13; on creation, 36 n. 74; on Satan and misery, 152

Luther, Martin: on Satan's fear of women, 193 n. 180

M

Man: equality and, 80–81; enmity and, 82–84; creation of, 36 n. 74, 46–47, 127–28, 130–31, 180 n. 27; God's role in creation, 185 n. 86

Marriage: of Adam and Eve, 12, 26, 57–58; rib as metaphor of, 61; equality in, 80–81; duties in, 96–97 n. 65; eternal nature and importance of, 144–47; blessings of, 187 n. 102; longing for 186 n. 99; necessity of, 186 n. 101; purpose of, 187 n. 110

Matter, organized: 121–23, 129

Matthews, Robert J.: on repentance for transgression, 20; on mortality and creation, 37 n. 74

Maxwell, Neal A.: on veil, 8; on experiential knowledge, 15; on submission of will, 60; on avoiding temptation, 154; on wisdom of God, 162

McConkie, Bruce R.: on Atonement and Fall, 10; on honoring Eve, 21; on Eve and motherhood, 85; on Adam as type for Jesus Christ, 116 n. 2; on marriage, 146; on millennial weather, 148; on having will of Jesus Christ, 153; on suffering of Jesus Christ, 171

McConkie, Joseph Fielding: on misunderstandings about Fall, 5; on Fall and agency, 30 n. 11; on placement of cherubs, 89; on Fall's effect on earth 136

O

Oaks, Dallin H.: on knowledge of Adam and Eve, 14–15; on Fall as transgression, 18–19; on honoring Eve, 21

Obedience of Adam: 91–92; to commandments, 107–8; fig leaves as symbols of, 158–60

Obey: 95 n. 39

Occupations: 53–54, 95 n. 36

One flesh: 110

One-third: 151–52

Opposition: necessity of, 30 n. 13; Satan as, 40 n. 95; agency and 49; trees in Eden represent, 141; Brigham Young on, 165

Optimism: 6–7

Ordinances: 32 n. 35, 159

Organizer: God as, 119–23

Ostler, Blake: on garment, 102–3 n. 165

P

Packer, Boyd K.: on accountability, 12; on Fall as choice, 33 n. 38

Pain, 79

Parenting, 86–87

Perfect knowledge, 30 n. 11

Philo of Alexandria: on commandment not to eat fruit, 56; on nakedness, 70; on Adam and Eve, 97 n. 77

Plan of salvation: Fall as part of, 6–11, 29 n. 8, 31–32 n. 28, 132, 175–76, 189–90 n. 137; Satan's role in, 40 n. 101; other worlds participate in, 132; experiential knowledge and, 134; marriage and, 144–47; Satan's knowledge of, 152–54, 189 n. 134; Adam and Eve understand, 190 n. 142

Planets, 131–32, 185 n. 86

Potential, man's divine, 46

Pratt, Orson: on mortality and creation, 35–36 n. 74; on commandment to multiply and replenish earth, 182 n. 51

Pratt, Parley P.; on creation of men and women, 178–79 n. 9

Pregnancy, 166

Premarital intimacy, 30 n. 13

Premortal existence, Satan lures away followers in, 151–52

Presence of God, 194 n. 207

Smith, Joseph F., on breath of life, 130

Smith, Joseph Fielding; on necessity of Fall, 9; on Adam's commandment not to eat fruit, 17, 160; on populating earth, 131–32; on contradictory commandments, 135, 140; on intelligence of Adam, 14, 143

Sorrow: 82–83, 164–65. *See also* Suffering

Soul, living, 47–48

Spirit: 122; gives mortal life, 47–48; in veins, 194 n. 206

Spiritual powers: 53

Stewardship: 54, 59, 122, 124 n. 2, 143

Submission: 146–47

Suffering: in childbirth, 79–80, 82, 166; mortality to be filled with, 82–84, 101 n. 154, 196 n. 231; of Jesus Christ, 14–15, 164, 171

Sweat of the brow: 8, 83–84, 102 n. 157

Sweet, bitter and: 15, 50, 68, 141, 155

Sword. *See* Flaming sword

Symbols: Adam and Eve as, 23–27, 43, 73, 76, 93 n. 1;

scriptures and, 40 n. 98, 44–45; fig leaves as, 69–70, 158–60; nakedness as, 73; clothing as, 85–86, 102–3 n. 165, 172–73, 195 n. 220; trees as, 49–50, 89–90, 141, 160; flaming sword as, 90; Adam's rib as, 61, 110, 116–17 n. 11, 147; the number four as, 136, 183 n. 59; water as, 126 n. 20, 183 n. 60; temple as, 40–41 n. 102, 45, 191 n. 150. *See also* Serpent: as symbol

T

Talmage, James E.: on honoring Adam and Eve, 21, 174–75; on Satan's role in plan of salvation, 153–54; on gratitude for Fall, 180; on sacrifice, 92; on covenant people, 159

Tanner, N. Eldon: on relationship with God, 73; on forbidden fruits, 95 n. 44; on withdrawing from God and Church, 100 n. 126

Teachings: Joseph Smith on, 1, 3 n. 3

Temple: as Eden, 25–27, 41 n. 113; Eden as, 49, 74, 106, 137; veil of, 85, 102 n. 165, 172–73; as place of labor,

on Fall as choice, 31 n. 25, 33 n. 42; on ignorance of Satan, 189 n. 134

Wife: duties of, 96 n. 65

Will: submission of, 60, 92, 146–47; of God, 11, 19–22, 60, 92, 156–57, 197

Woman: deception and, 21–22, 188 n. 124; role in family, 61, 79–81, 96 n. 65; enmity between serpent and, 78, 82, 163–65; equality and, 57–58, 110, 166; Eve as archetype of, 45, 72–73; Eve called, 132, 148; creation of, 116–17 n. 11, 144, 147, 178–79 n. 9, 180 n. 27

Woodruff, Wilford: on necessity of Fall, 9

Work: 54, 82–84, 130, 159–60, 168–69; as choice, 191 n. 155; for eternity, 190 n. 137; importance of, 168

Y

Young, Brigham: on necessity of Fall, 9; on Adam's relationship with God, 11; on sin, 20; on blaming Eve, 76; on endowments, 90–91; on Adam's creation, 129; on location of Eden, 130; on evil and opposition, 165; on creation of animals, 142

About the Author

Alonzo L. Gaskill is a professor of Church history and doctrine. He holds a bachelors degree in philosophy, a masters in theology, and a PhD in biblical studies. Brother Gaskill has taught at Brigham Young University since 2003. Prior to coming to BYU, he served in a variety of assignments within the Church Educational System—most recently as the director of the LDS Institute of Religion at Stanford University (1995–2003).